INSPIRATIONAL LESSONS FROM
THE WORLD'S BIGGEST SPORTS STARS

Jeff Grout & Sarah Perrin

Foreword by Sir Clive Woodward, OBE

CAPSTONE

First published 2004 by
Capstone Publishing Ltd (A Wiley Company)
The Atrium
Southern Gate
Chichester
West Sussex PO19 8SQ
http://www.wileyeurope.com

CIP catalogue records for this book are available from the British Library and the US Library of Congress

ISBN 1-84112-613-6 (PB)

Typeset in Dutch 801 11/15pt by Sparks Computer Solutions Ltd
http://www.sparks.co.uk

Printed and bound by TJ International Ltd, Padstow, Cornwall

10 9 8 7 6 5 4 3

CONTENTS

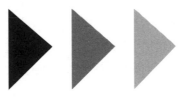

FOREWORD BY SIR CLIVE WOODWARD OBE

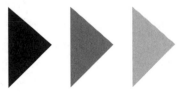

THE MENTAL SIDE OF SPORT is massive.

Before setting off to Australia for the 2003 World Cup I said that the competition would be won 'in the head'. It isn't necessarily the best team or the team with the most talented players that wins games, but the team that can 'think correctly under pressure': T-Cup for short. It's what's between the ears that counts.

This T-Cup ability separates out the true champions from the rest. Martin Johnson, Lawrence Dallaglio, Jonny Wilkinson, along with the rest of the team, don't panic under pressure. They think correctly and make the right decisions about what to do. When the England squad seized victory in the closing minutes of the World Cup final, the whole team had proved it could make the right decisions under the greatest pressure imaginable.

The great mental strength showed by the England team didn't just happen by chance. It was the result of sustained mental preparation during training.

The England team's success has also come by setting challenging goals. I have always aimed high, setting goals for myself throughout my playing career. As England's first full-time professional coach, I set one simple goal: for England to be the best team in the world.

The England team truly believed we could win the World Cup – and we did. That self-belief came as the result of a lot of hard work – repetitive training routines, meticulous preparation, attention to detail and mental rehearsal.

We also work as one team. Winning the World Cup resulted from the combined efforts of all players and all members of the coaching team. None of us could have achieved that result without the others. The England squad draws strength from a combination of leadership and 'teamship'. Leadership is about communicating an inspiring vision of the future, stimulating change, setting clear and measurable objectives and clearly communicating what is required from each individual. Teamship acknowledges the vital importance of peer pressure and peer approval, and that team decision-making encourages commitment and greater motivation to work hard.

Our shared attention to detail has proven invaluable. We use any and all information that can help us. If we can improve one hundred things by 1%, the total impact is huge. We embrace new ideas from any source in our efforts to maximize team performance.

The England rugby team's path to World Cup victory was not without its setbacks. Champions learn from their mistakes and grow stronger as a result. They don't feel inhibited by the fear of failure, but are stimulated and motivated by it. They also learn from their successes. With the England team I pay more attention to understanding the causes of our successes than our failures. It is the successes that we want to replicate.

Mind Games draws on the experiences of elite sportspeople, from many sports, focusing on the mental techniques they use to perform at their best.

Sir Clive Woodward OBE

A WORD WITH ...
RENZIE HANHAM AND
CERI EVANS

IN OUR EXPERIENCE THE MENTAL COMPONENT of sporting performance is seldom given the same level of attention as other aspects, such as physical skills. More often than not athletes only consider mental skills when they're underperforming. It's less common for an athlete to seek assistance when they're already performing well.

Yet, in the highly pressurized cauldron of international sport it is accepted that when all else is equal, it is often the individuals who seem to have the strongest mental conditioning that succeed.

The role of developing the mental skills of an athlete is often undertaken by the coach, who may or may not have had training in this area. Usually they have their own experiences to draw upon, and sometimes this is sufficient. Often coaches have a particular aspect of mental skills that they consider important. For some, it will be goal setting, for others it might be visualization, or whatever they think is relevant at the time. Generally these skills are developed in isolation with little thought given to the 'bigger picture', and there is very little connection between the core mental skills and the physical attributes they enhance.

Consequently, what would be helpful is a framework and structure that encompasses the primary mental elements that contribute to superior performance.

The same mental skills that a champion athlete uses are similar to the skills that a mother of two requires to cope with getting the children to school on time, the award-winning chef preparing his menu for the evening or a sales person pitching for a significant piece of business. The critical internal processes are essentially the same.

This is why so many businesses see relevance in how athletes prepare and cope with the pressure of performing.

This book presents real-life examples of how some of the world's premier athletes use and adapt these core skills. In each chapter you will find analysis from various experts in the field and a commentary on the theory that underpins these skills.

The book can be used as a resource or as a casual, at-a-glance read. Either way there is an abundance of useful material, which will inform, enlighten, entertain and perhaps even inspire.

Renzie Hanham and Ceri Evans,
Gazing Performance

INTRODUCTION

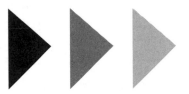

GERMANY 1:ENGLAND 5

THIS SCORELINE IN THE RUN UP to the 2002 World Cup remains a cause of joy and wonder for many an English football fan. It offered the bright promise of England regaining its long-awaited place at the top of international football.

That historic September 2001 World Cup qualifier against Germany was England's seventh match – and sixth win – under Sven-Göran Eriksson's leadership. Even more astoundingly, the England team achieved their triumphant result away from home, in Munich. The previous time England had played Germany, in October 2000, was also the last time Kevin Keegan sat in the manager's seat; on that occasion England was shamed at Wembley, defeated by one goal to nil.

So what made the difference in that one year gap? Commentators were desperate to know what magic Sven-Göran Eriksson had worked to transform Keegan's lacklustre side into this magnificent goal-scoring machine. After all, he had essentially the same set of players to select from and work with. So how had he done it? Sven's response when questioned was: 'First you must start with the head.'

That comment provided the initial inspiration for this book. Since then the England rugby team's triumphant victory in the 2003 World Cup in Australia, under the transformational leadership of Sir Clive Woodward, has stimulated further debate about what creates success in the sporting arena.

These inspirational wins fired our curiosity. We wanted to answer the question, what makes a champion? Why do some people consistently break records, cross the line first or hammer the ball into the net with pinpoint accuracy? Natural talent, regular training and fitness are obviously vital. But with two equally matched sportspeople, something else makes the difference and provides that champion factor – and that extra something is the mind.

Mind Games sets out to identify the mental characteristics that really differentiate a champion from the 'also rans'.

On our exploration we have called on the first-hand experiences of acknowledged champions from a range of sports. By talking to them about their attitudes and approaches to their sporting activities, we have tried to highlight common themes that apply to them all. We consider their beliefs, motivations and the training they do on the mental aspect of their games. We relive moments of high pressure – when a rugby match hung on one kick, when a gold medal depended on an explosive, focused race to the line. How do sports stars control their nerves, channel their adrenalin and deliver a peak performance on cue?

Sally Gunnell, one of the many champions we interviewed, had no hesitation in stating that the mental side of her performance made 'the difference between silver and gold'.

Celebrated yachtswoman Ellen MacArthur believes that mental strength, particularly determination, is an essential ingredient of any successful, competitive sailor: 'It's crucial. You can have the best boat in the world, but if you don't have the determination to finish the race, you may as well not start it. Determination counts for more than it's given credit for.'

David Platt, former England footballer and World Cup scorer, and former coach of the England Under-21 squad, acknowledges that top players have to have talent and skills. But he says: 'Mental strength is a major, major factor. They have to be ruthless; they have to be arrogant; they have to believe they are the best.'

In addition to the champions themselves, our research has also led us to sports psychologists, coaches and specialists in human behaviours. We have tapped into their expertise to identify some of the techniques that elite sportsmen and women use to strengthen their mental armoury, whether through visualization or mental rehearsal, or simply by setting ever more specific goals.

Coaches such as Frank Dick, who helped many top international athletes achieve repeated success, know how important an individual's mental outlook or attitude is to delivering winning performances. Dick says:

> *'I think 70% or 80% is about attitude. Once you've made sure that everybody's prepared for the task, it's just that – it's an attitude. The good news in life is that you can choose that. You can't always choose or change the circumstances in your arena, but you can always choose or change your attitude.'*

Our aim in writing this book is partly to offer insights into the techniques that sporting champions use to deliver their best performance when they need it. However, the insights and techniques identified here are not only valuable in the sporting sphere; they also have relevance to other areas of all our lives.

Ian Lynagh, Australian sports psychologist, and father of Australia's greatest ever fly-half – Michael Lynagh – certainly believes that sport provides a framework for personal development. Sport appeals to people because it meets a basic, instinctive need to want to take on challenges and succeed, and it encourages them to develop skills along the way.

'It's the challenge of wanting to conquer and establish control over a task. It becomes an internal challenge. Sport, at its ultimate meaning for human beings, provides us with a structure which is helpful in growing as a person. It doesn't have to be sport. If it's not sport it might be climbing a mountain or running round a country. The human race has always done this – "Let's challenge ourselves to do something that's really difficult, that requires a lot of skill development, physical and mental development and also challenges us to overcome our weaknesses as a human being." By doing it we become a better person. To me, that's the ultimate meaning of doing sport.'

Rising to the mental challenge is an essential requirement for success in all endeavours, sporting or otherwise. The techniques that proven champions use can help us all, in any situation, where peak performance is a desired goal. Controlling your nerves, developing greater belief and visualizing your success can have a positive impact on activities as diverse as making a best man's speech or improving your team leadership skills at work.

Ron Dennis, the boss of the McLaren racing team, sums up our view of the importance of mental strength perfectly. If he, and we, are right, then using any techniques we can to improve our mental strength can only be a great benefit not only to ourselves, but to those with whom we live and work. As Dennis says:

'Life is a mind game. Every relationship you have is a mind game. Where does anger, tranquillity, happiness come from? They all come from your mind. In the end everything feeds into your mind, and everything starts from your mind. If you decide to be a muscular person your mind takes the decision to do the work to be a specific athlete. If you want to be a successful athlete or a businessman, it all starts and finishes with the mind. Life is a mind game.'

Eriksson understands this supremely well.

'In football, it's difficult to do more in terms of physical, tactical or technical areas. But where you can do a lot more is in terms of mental work. In football I think we are behind other sports, such as tennis. Mental training is the future for football.'

We hope *Mind Games* inspires you to raise your game, whether in sport, your work or your personal life. The champions we met have achieved amazing feats, but they believe their success owes more to their mental strength than their natural talent. We can all learn from them and improve our own personal performances – increasing the enjoyment and satisfaction we gain from life as a result.

ACKNOWLEDGEMENTS

We could not have written this book without the help of many people. In particular we would like to thank Renzie Hanham and Ceri Evans from Gazing Performance, mental conditioning specialists. Their willingness not only to explain the Gazing approach, but also to comment on our own findings and analysis, proved invaluable. A special thank you also goes to sports psychologist Professor Graham Jones from Lane4, a specialist human performance consultancy, for sharing his research and insights. We are also indebted to sports psychologist Ian Lynagh, who helped us to develop our initial research plans and whose enthusiasm was inspiring.

We would also like to thank the following for their generous help in sharing their experiences for this book:

- Sir Clive Woodward OBE, England rugby head coach
- Sven-Göran Eriksson, England football coach
- Matthew Pinsent CBE, rower, three times Olympic gold medallist
- Nick Faldo MBE, Britain's most successful golfer
- Ellen MacArthur MBE, fastest woman to sail around the world single-handed
- Steve Backley OBE, three times European and Commonwealth gold medallist and Olympic silver medallist in the javelin

- Roger Black MBE, 4 × 400m relay World Champion and Olympic silver medallist
- Jonny Wilkinson MBE, England rugby fly-half, arguably the world's best kicker
- David Platt, former Aston Villa, Sampdoria, Arsenal and England footballer and former manager of England's Under-21 team
- Sally Gunnell OBE, former Olympic, World, Commonwealth and European 400m hurdles champion
- Dr Stephanie Cook MBE, Olympic and World modern pentathlon champion
- Lawrence Dallaglio MBE, England rugby captain
- Ron Dennis CBE, boss of the McLaren Formula One motor racing team
- Howard Wilkinson, former Sunderland and Leeds United manager and former Football Association technical director
- David Lloyd, former Davis Cup captain
- Michael Lynagh, former Australian rugby captain
- Lord Coe OBE, former double Olympic 1500m champion
- Sir Chay Blyth CBE, round-the-world yachtsman
- Jack Charlton OBE, former England footballer and Ireland manager
- Gill Clark MBE, former European badminton doubles champion
- Adrian Moorhouse MBE, former Olympic 100m breaststroke champion
- Mark Richardson, 400m Commonwealth silver medallist
- John Regis MBE, former European 200m and 4 × World 400m relay World Champion
- Richard Dunwoody MBE, record-breaking champion National Hunt jockey
- Ron Roddan, athletics coach (including coach of Linford Christie)
- Frank Dick OBE, former national athletics coach
- John Syer, sports psychologist to Tottenham Hotspur
- Graham Shaw, Neuro-Linguistic Programming (NLP) trainer
- Steve Sylvester, sports psychologist

Part I

PERSONALITY POWER

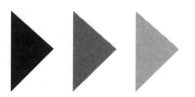

Chapter 1

TRUE GRIT

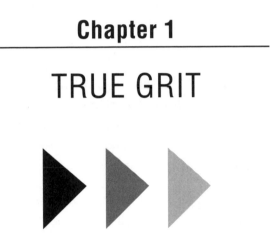

WHAT DOES IT TAKE TO BE A CHAMPION? Talent, certainly. But talent isn't enough to be a world-beater. In sport, as in other areas of life, personal characteristics and mental qualities make the difference between repeated success and failure, between taking a champion's title and finishing in the last four.

These characteristics – the desire to win, the ability to learn from failure, the willingness to try new techniques, to name a few – arise time and again in the elite sportsmen and women who have managed to maintain their form over repeated competitions. Such personal features are considered throughout this book. First up for examination is the requirement for discipline and determination, a touch of selfishness and the essential killer instinct.

EARLY DISCIPLINE

Champions generally have to start training at a young age. That means they often show a natural sense of discipline.

Ellen MacArthur surged to fame when she became the fastest woman and the youngest person ever to circumnavigate the earth in a single-handed race, completing the 2001 Vendée Globe in second place. MacArthur is dedication personified. So strong was her passion for sailing that she made sacrifices to support her activity throughout her childhood.

> *'When I was about 14 I was already thinking about trying to save up my money for a small boat that I could live on as well as sail on the coast. My first boat was a little 8-foot dinghy, but you can't really live on a boat like that and I really fancied the idea of travelling places and having something that you could live on and cruise around in. In fact, I'd been saving up since the age of 8. Saving for a boat was a massive goal, which is why for lunch at school I'd have either nothing, or soup which cost 4 pence from the soup machine, or mashed potato and baked beans which cost a total of 8 pence. I saved everything because we didn't get pocket money as kids and birthdays and Christmases were quite spaced out, so it was basically about making savings every day.'*

Jack Charlton remembers the commitment his brother Bobby – 'our kid' – showed to football from an early age. While Jack would go into the countryside looking for birds' nests and picking blackberries, Bobby would spend all day kicking a ball against a wall, or knocking it with his head. Local people who knew Bobby when he was growing up readily predicted that he would be an international player. And so he was. His early talent, combined with his great dedication, marked him out for the highest sporting success.

Adrian Moorhouse, Olympic gold medallist in the breaststroke in Seoul in1988, showed early dedication in the training regime he adopted as a youngster.

'I was pretty focused as a kid. I was training seven times a week at the age of 11. I'm a routine person, so if I know where I've got to be – the pool at a certain time – I'll get into the routine. I'm a very habitual person. I'll be there, I'll do it and I'll work hard.'

Former Olympic hurdles champion Sally Gunnell reflects with amazement on the dedication she showed in her early years. Looking back, she wonders how she did it – and she doesn't think she could do it again. Now she has had a taste of all the other things that a full life has to offer. As a youngster, while she went out to clubs with friends like any normal person, she loved her running more. It was her athletics that really mattered.

Gunnell seems to have inherited this disciplined outlook from her parents, who she describes as extremely focused and determined. Similarly, if Sally decides to do something, she just goes and does it.

Amazingly, Gunnell maintained a part-time job during much of her athletic career. From 1986, when she won the 400m at the Commonwealth Games, until she won the 1992 Olympics, she worked in the research department at accountancy firm Pannel Kerr Forster. Although many people might find this a stressful combination, Gunnell found it helpful. She says:

'It was really important to me because I could get away from athletics there. Athletes are so intense. If I got injured I could throw myself into my work. It also took some pressure off because there was always a certain amount of income coming in, but the firm gave me all the time off I needed for training.

'No one there really understood what I did. I could go and run a Grand Prix the night before and people would ask how I got on. If I was second or third, they'd say, "What a shame you didn't win." It just kept my feet on the ground.'

Sir Chay Blyth's achievements include becoming the first man to sail around the world against the prevailing winds and currents in 1971, for which he was awarded the CBE. Five years before that he broke the record for rowing across the Atlantic with British Army Captain

John Ridgeway, completing the 3000-mile test of endurance in 92 days.

Blyth describes himself as having been 'a wild young boy', but he was also one with great capacity for discipline, as his childhood experiences show. That youngster was so inspired by a chance encounter with an Olympic swimmer that he took up swimming and embarked on a demanding training schedule.

> *'Through his encouragement I took up swimming and ended up training three times a day. I was 10 or 11. We lived about two and a half miles from the swimming baths and I would get up and run down there at 7 o'clock in the morning and then train, and then go to school, then come back at lunch time, and then go back in the evenings. Training three times a day must have taken quite a lot of determination – to be able to do that at that young age.'*

It is just this kind of determination that was to support Blyth during the planning and execution of his epic voyages.

Commitment to regular training was a characteristic that champion golfer Nick Faldo showed from an early age. He relished the fact that with golf, you could spend all day out on the course practising by yourself.

> *'I played my first round on my fourteenth birthday and from about 15 I'd made the decision that I wanted to be a pro golfer. I scraped through the next year of school and left at 16. I then went to the practice ground every single day, religiously, in every weather. That was my commitment. I left the house at 8 o'clock and was on the range by 8.15. I hit balls all morning and then I played all afternoon.'*

Chris Evert, who won three Wimbledon titles and a total of 18 Grand Slams, certainly trained hard as a youngster. She was drilled by her father to practise shots over and over again, hitting forehands and backhands down every line of the court. These early years contributed hugely to her tennis success as an adult. The training approach was quite different to that used by the young Lloyd brothers, David and John, who weren't drilled to hit the same shot so repeatedly. John particularly showed huge natural talent, but perhaps didn't have the absolute discipline required to make it right to the top of the game. David says:

'John realized that practice would make him good, which he wanted to be. But sometimes he would say, "Ugh, I can't practise today; it's too hot." Or it would be too windy. Therefore he didn't follow through. Becoming a champion definitely requires a control of your mind, and it's very important to be able to learn that at a very young age.'

David Lloyd believes that aspiring tennis champions need to understand that what they do on the practice court has direct bearing on how they will do in matches. They learn their matchplay on the practice court. Therefore, coaches look for kids with the ability to practise consistently well, day after day – like Tim Henman did as a youngster. When Lloyd worked with him between the ages of 12 and 16, he never put in a bad day's practice.

Former badminton champion Gill Clark was inspired towards the end of her career by a coach called Lee Jae Bok from Korea. He demanded 100% effort in training and Clark was prepared to give it.

'I thrived on the fact that he demanded 100% all of the time, but some players started to pace themselves. If they had a four-hour practice session, they wouldn't give 100%. But what is the point in practising badly? You only reinforce bad habits. This is something that I think is the difference between contenders and champions.

'It is absolutely fundamental that you give 100%, and not only physically, but mentally. You've got to have the necessary mental concentration to practise properly, because it's that quality that you need in a match. If you play and practise with that sort of intensity, when you actually do come to the Olympics and you've got that extra adrenalin rush, your body is used to performing to that high

level that you set yourself in training, and will actually move you on to an even higher level. People who have sub-standards in training will only reach a high level in competition – but not the top.

'I've seen coaches working with players and getting them to hit 500 drop shots. What's the point? If you try to get 5 out of 50 to land within a square foot on the other side of the court, which would be a brilliant shot, to me that's fantastic. Next time you practise it you'll want to get 6 out of 50. So you start practising quality. And quality is a lot more fun than quantity.'

JUGGLING DEMANDS AND MAKING CHOICES

Dr Stephanie Cook, who took the gold medal in the modern pentathlon in the 2000 Sydney Olympics, knows all about discipline. Before becoming a full-time sportswoman she initially maintained her training regime while working as a junior doctor. This was in the days before modern pentathlon was even an Olympic event for women, so she didn't even have the inspiration of winning one of the sporting world's glittering prizes to spur her on.

'If ever I'm doing something I will always try and put 100% into it. It doesn't have to be sport. I always try to do the best I can. That was a driving factor behind me doing well in the modern pentathlon.

'I think my determination showed when it involved getting up at 5.30am to go swimming before going to work. As a junior doctor I was running around all day, so was absolutely shattered after work. But then I'd get home, put my kit on, go out for a run or sit in the car and drive for an hour to go fencing, and then come back. You're absolutely shattered. I did that because I loved it, because I got more out of my life, and I got more out of my job by doing that – but so many people thought I was completely crazy. I didn't know many other people who would actually do what I did and go to the lengths that I went to at that time. At that stage there were no guarantees that women's pentathlon was going to be in the Olympics. I wasn't looking to the Olympics at that point. I was

looking to go to a world championship. That, for me, was enough of an incentive.'

Once it seemed likely that the women's modern pentathlon would be made an Olympic event, Cook finally opted for the easier option of giving up her job to train full-time with the backing of lottery funding: 'I could sleep properly and eat properly and I wasn't rushing off to go to work. It was great,' she says.

Cook was training for between six and eight hours a day. Her motivation to keep focusing on it to such an extent came from the fact she enjoyed what she was doing so much. She just loved riding, swimming and running. The training was hard, getting injured could also cause problems, and she sometimes felt under pressure to achieve certain results. But despite all that, she still thought of her sport as fun. Having the opportunity to train full-time was, she says, 'brilliant'.

However, success at the Olympics brought fresh challenges.

'I was being pulled in all sorts of directions, with invitations to be here, there and everywhere. You have to find a balance in terms of what you want to do. I remember a conversation with my performance director. He said to me, "I know that if you decide to carry on taking pentathlon seriously, the only way you're going to be happy is if you actually train hard and concentrate on your performance, so that you will do well. Therefore you need to be able to say no to certain things in order to be able to focus."

I'm the kind of person who loves doing everything, and I wanted to accept all the invitations as well as do all my training. But I needed to find a balance.'

Cook learnt to be more selective in terms of how she spent her time and, as a result, won gold in both the European and World Championships in 2001.

Even when champions are established stars in their field, there are no shortcuts in terms of the hours of training required – hours that are often unsociable. Three times Olympic champion Matthew

Pinsent starts rowing on the Thames at 7.30 in the morning. Does he ever ask himself why he's doing it? Yes, he certainly does – most mornings. Training for four years just to win one race – Olympic gold – isn't easy. He knows it is inevitable that there will be some bad days, as well as the good ones.

His training routine puts him out of step with most people's daily lives. He may get some time to himself that other people would be spending at work, but the strange hours aren't easy.

'Today we finished around 1 o'clock – that's a lot earlier than anyone else. So I get this afternoon and evening to do whatever I want and then come back tomorrow and do some more. It is a different routine to everyone else in life, which is kind of tough. You lose your weekends too.'

Nevertheless, Pinsent has sufficient reserves of discipline and dedication to keep turning up at the river for more training.

'Part of it is simply knowing that there are going to be bad days. You just have to accept that there is no one in life who gets out of bed every morning thinking "Yeah, great, hooray", whatever job they do, however much they love it. But compared to 99% of the population … I love my job more than most.'

Former badminton champion Gill Clark accepted the commitment she made to her sport because she alone had decided this was what she wanted to do with her life. She doesn't think it appropriate for people to talk about having to make 'sacrifices'. What top performers do is make 'choices'. Clark stresses that she chose to concentrate her efforts on developing her sporting career – it was a conscious decision to put other things to the side and make badminton her priority.

This choice wasn't necessarily an easy one. In Clark's experience her commitment to competitive badminton at the highest level made it hard to maintain personal relationships.

'I was forever on the road. It's not as bad as for tennis players, but you're on the road. Whilst it's getting better, it's still not really accepted that the woman travels and leaves the man at home, and he's got to do the laundry and cook for himself and all those sort of things. It's quite all right for a man to do that, to travel on business, but it's still not really acceptable for a woman. The other thing is, if you're deeply in love, and I'm flying off to Taipei and Japan and Korea, and I'm going to be away for three and a half weeks, you start missing him. So then, because you have all these negative emotions, it impacts your performance. Therefore, I made the choice that that was all going to have to be put on hold.'

Former 1500m Olympic gold medallist Sebastian Coe loved running. The pleasure made the effort worthwhile. Like Gill Clark, he doesn't think of himself as having made sacrifices. He enjoyed what he did and wanted to do it. Maybe this enjoyment was due to the fact he was successful at running. He admits that if he had bombed out in the county championship heats, maybe he wouldn't have continued training three times a day. Nevertheless, he genuinely enjoyed trying to go just that little bit quicker and finding out what he could do to improve further. He was intrigued by what he could do to improve.

RESOLVE, PIG-HEADEDNESS AND COMMITMENT

Ron Dennis, boss of the McLaren racing team, has had plenty of experience in assessing what it is that makes a top quality Formula One racing driver. The vital ingredient for him is 'steely resolve'.

'You can often see if someone has got what it takes. It's not when discussing with someone whether they should join your team, but when they are under stress and being pushed to succeed that you see their resolve. In our sport there are many drivers who are capable of winning races and world championships in the best car, but you rarely have a situation where the car is the best all the time. It's how the driver finds it in himself to make up for the performance

deficiencies of the car. It comes from their resolve and if they want to succeed.'

Just this quality attracted sports psychologist Steve Sylvester to Peter Ebdon, former World snooker champion, with whom he has been working. Sylvester recognized the 'steely reserve' that Peter has. He's the kind of guy who can come up with a strong performance when the chips are down.

David Lloyd certainly has great belief in the power of determination, which he applies in his business life. He likens the challenges you meet in sport and general life to an enormous wall. If there isn't an easy way through, you have to continue to find a way to get past the wall – even if it means making a compromise.

'Walls will come down all the time in everything you do – bloody high walls. When one does, you've got to get over it. If you can climb it, terrific; if you can't climb it, walk around it. You might have to compromise to get around the other side, but if you don't get around the side, you're dead anyway. You may have to compromise in tennis in the way you're hitting the ball; in business you may have to compromise on giving away a little bit more of the deal. But you've got to get around the other side of that wall.'

Michael Lynagh, the former Australian rugby captain, is one of Rugby Union's modern greats and Australia's greatest ever fly-half. He scored 911 points in 72 appearances for his country: until recently, the highest number of points scored in international rugby. Although a naturally gifted sportsman, Lynagh also acknowledges a somewhat determined streak in his own character. If he decides he wants to do something – such as winning a World Cup – he is almost pig-headed about trying to achieve it.

Lynagh's disciplined approach to the game actually increased over the duration of his career.

'When I first started playing amateur rugby at school and after school, I didn't do a huge amount of goal kicking practice because

I was very lucky – it was a natural thing for me. Though I used to get very uptight and nervous about it and think, "My god, I hope my goal kicking's all right today". With the advent of professional rugby I started to practise a lot more because it was getting pretty important – people's livelihoods depended on how well I kicked. My percentages went up enormously. I also found I was feeling less nervous beforehand because I knew that I had put in the time to practise and I couldn't do much more; secondly, I felt much more confident – "I know how this is going to come out today because I have kicked all week".'

Sebastian Coe's talent and dedication took him to the top of the athletic world, twice winning the Olympic 1500 metres. He also once held the 800 metres, 1000 metres, 1500 metres and one-mile records simultaneously. Coe's success depended in part on his amazing natural talent, but he couldn't have achieved such sporting heights without a lot of hard work and commitment.

'Without getting boring and scientific about it, I do have a very low heart rate; I have a very large oxygen ability for oxygen uptake … I have a light frame and I always ran in balance. That was the luck of the draw. I don't think that in itself would have been enough to get me beyond being a useful national standard competitor. The difference between that and getting onto a rostrum for major championships is 80 miles a week, ten to twelve hours in the gym and all the other things that go with it.

'There are plenty of athletes I have worked with – and you can see them from relatively young ages – who have precocious talent but fall through the net. Sometimes that's because they just are not prepared mentally to commit to it. If they are not prepared to do that then they will be much happier going off to do something else. There is nothing worse than seeing people in sport at 14, 15 and 16 being pushed into something that really doesn't interest them and they don't want to commit to it.'

England fly-half Jonny Wilkinson derives confidence and belief from the work he puts in practising kicks. The training gives him greater confidence when preparing for a difficult kick, or one with the potential to win the game. He believes he 'deserves' success because of all the hard work he has put in when training; his dedication gives him the right to succeed. He knows that natural talent can count for a great deal of a player's achievements, but the harder an individual works, the better he will get. Certainly, the ability to put in a consistently good performance, rather than just a one-off stunt, relies on dedicated practice. Top athletes have to make a personal investment in time and effort if they want to improve their chances of being successful when the pressure is on.

Wilkinson had this realization that training hard is the best route to consistency when he was 16.

'Some days I was great and some days I was terrible. I went to see the team coach and I realized that it wasn't about having a gift, about having good and bad days that you weren't in control of. There was something you could do to improve your chances of getting the ball over. If you practised hard and did the right things, you could have good days every day. Now I won't ever go into a situation where I'm not prepared. Any kick I miss, I can explain everything about why I missed.'

Former England Under-21 coach David Platt doesn't think about giving up when things have not gone well on the pitch. He knows he's just got to get back on the training ground.

'If we've won I enjoy days off, but if we have lost I just want to get back on the training pitch. Even as a player I knew that if we had had a bad result, come Monday morning I would have to put my boots back on and go on and do my job. If you have a bad day at the office you know you have to put your suit back on and go back and do it again. You are not going to run away from it.

'Days off when you have lost can be hard because you want to get back on the training pitch. You want to put that result behind you, get back to training and start focusing on the next game.'

Platt knows that the best response to a poor result is to start winning.

'What takes away pressure is results, and what gets you results is working on the training ground, putting the right team out and using the right tactics. If you get the result then the pressure disappears. It disappears very quickly – one win and it is gone. So you just have to live to the next day.'

Determination to win against an aggressive opposition is the mark of a top quality rugby team. England captain Lawrence Dallaglio recalls the battle between England and France in 2000, when the England squad were playing away from home in Paris.

'We had a number of opportunities in that game to give ourselves a comfortable lead, but we didn't take them. As a result, there was always going to come a time when the French were going to come back at us – and they did. It ended up being real "backs-to-the-wall" stuff, but the character of the England players came through.

'The match ended with the French peppering the English line, but it was a line that was firm. There's a great photo which shows it – a line of Englishmen repelling a French attack and they are all glowering at the French.'

England held on to win 15–9.

Swimming gold medallist Adrian Moorhouse would refuse to lie down and accept defeat. Even after he'd had a bad run with illness when he was trying to break the world record, he still picked himself up again. This bloody mindedness was there in his character as a teenager. If he didn't win a race, he'd be determined to win the next one. When he was 15 he raced future Moscow Olympic gold medallist Duncan Goodhew as a junior. Goodhew beat Moorhouse, though Moorhouse himself broke the British Junior record. That wasn't enough though. The record didn't matter. He just wanted to beat Goodhew.

For round-the-world yachtswoman Ellen MacArthur, determination is essential if she is to survive the extreme demands she makes of herself. For example, sleep deprivation is the norm. Before competing in the Vendée Globe for the first time, MacArthur sailed her then newly built boat *Kingfisher* back from New Zealand to the UK. During the trip she analysed her sleep patterns.

> *'We studied when I slept naturally when I was at sea 24 hours a day. The weather has an impact, but generally speaking you can sleep when you want to. I learnt when I had the most tendency to sleep and therefore when I benefited most from it. Of course, at the end of the day a lot of your sleep is controlled by the weather and you have to sleep when you can. But the study showed me how much I slept in 24 hours. It's easy to lose track of that when you're on the boat. In the single-handed transatlantic race I slept for 4.2 hours in every 24 on average over two weeks.'*

For MacArthur, this kind of knowledge was invaluable when trying to pace herself in long, solo races. She believes that being mentally aware of what state you are in is one of the biggest factors in determining success at sea. You simply can't give 100% for three days and then be exhausted if you are competing in a race lasting seven days. Pacing yourself, forcing yourself to control your energy expenditure, is essential.

Avoiding exhaustion is a real challenge when sailing single-handedly.

> *'You cannot get in your bunk and think that for the next two hours or even half an hour nothing's going to happen. Who knows what's going to happen next? You don't. It could be a squall at the equator. Squalls hitting you at night can be disastrous. I lost a sail once on the way down to the equator because I was hit by a small squall*

when I was asleep outside. So you can't ever really relax and that's the biggest thing that wears you down – it doesn't stop. It never stops. Day and night, you just can't switch off.'

Sports psychologist Steve Sylvester understand that champions have an unquestionable desire to persist, regardless of what's happening around them. They are the kinds of people who never give up. They will face their opponent squarely, look them straight in the eye, and keep going. Alongside these mental characteristics, if they also have the physical ability and technical skill required, that's when they become truly great.

SELFISH STREAKS

If you're dedicated to winning, that may mean you need a degree of selfishness to get you onto the winner's podium. Former champion jockey Richard Dunwoody admits that a lot of champions or high achievers in sport are very, very selfish. He believes they have to be, because they have to dedicate a great deal of their time to get where they want to get to.

Dunwoody found that for him, being tough was also required – particularly when horses got injured or were even killed accidentally during a race.

'Racing is a hard sport and even when cantering down to the start, horses can injure themselves. I did have horses that were killed. If that happens you've got to get out there and go through it all again in the next race. You've got to get your mind straight. You've just got to do your job.'

Adrian Moorhouse, who fulfilled his dream of winning an Olympic gold medal in the breaststroke in 1988 in Seoul, certainly thinks so. Moorhouse admits that champions have to be so focused on what they are trying to achieve that 'you're not necessarily the nicest person to be around'.

'Being nice didn't matter when you wanted to win. You would be nice if you knew it would get you to where you wanted to get to, if it would contribute to your performance. They are not things I am proud of in hindsight, but I wasn't a nasty person. I know I was quite selfish. I mean, my mum has called me selfish. I think it's different in real life, particularly in business.'

Moorhouse acknowledges, however, that being a member of a sports team requires a slightly different attitude. In a team, individuals are relying on each other. They cannot, therefore, have the same kind of totally selfish attitude they might have when competing in individual races.

When racing solo Moorhouse didn't worry about being nice; he made good use of legal gamesmanship. If Moorhouse was ahead of one of his close rivals in a race, he would move over to swim at the side of his lane that was nearest to that rival. It was a move he knew might just give him the edge to win.

Long-standing athletics coach Ron Roddan says that aiming for an Olympic gold is a high target, one that requires significant effort. Not only does the sports person have to 'put themselves out' to make it to the top, so the people around them have to make any necessary sacrifices too. Friends and family have to be generous enough to accept that they can't expect to come first in the athlete's priorities.

It may be that top champions need such dedication and focus on achieving their goals that they simply appear selfish. According to sports psychologist Professor Graham Jones, research shows that motivation, relating to mental toughness, falls into two dimensions. There is the determination to come back after failure, because the individual believes in themselves, but there are also internalized motives to succeed.

Jones says that lots of performers will talk about doing what they do in order to 'show' somebody, perhaps an ex-teacher who told them they would never amount to much; but underpinning that desire are really strong, internalized motives – the individual is really doing it for themselves. As Jones says, people don't train at 5 o'clock in the morning seven days a week just for the recognition they get for winning a gold medal. Something else has to drive the person on – their personal sense of pride and satisfaction. This is why many elite performers can come across as selfish – because they know what they want to do, why they are doing it and they are not going to deviate or be distracted from that.

For some athletes, hurting those they are close to is part of the preparation for competition. Former national athletics coach Frank Dick recalls Daley Thompson's approach to the build-up:

'His preparation, eventually, was nothing to do with anyone other than himself. He took it upon himself in the run-in to a major championship to almost exercise his aggression on the people who were closest to him. He really was not easy to live with at those times. He'd worked out that if he could hurt the people who were closest to him, everybody else would be easy to handle in the arena.'

KILLER INSTINCT

Winners seize their opportunities to win. They have an attitude that says 'take no prisoners'. David Platt, former coach of the England Under-21 squad and former England player, doesn't think players should have any feeling for the opposition. He can't understand why someone on a winning team might fccl sorry for the losing side. He believes the better players don't really care. If his team is winning 3–0 at half time, Platt will challenge them to go out and win 6–0. They shouldn't think the game is over. Nor should they feel sorry for their opponents, but accept that it is the other side's fault they are losing so badly. Above all, they mustn't let them off the hook.

Howard Wilkinson, former Football Association technical director, believes that players can learn to be winners, even if they don't have the most natural talent. He recalls a boy he came across as a teenager who was intellectually very bright, though technically not in the top league.

'By the time he was 27 or 28 he was earning a very good living out of the game. Whilst technically he undoubtedly got better, the biggest improvement occurred elsewhere: he learnt to be a winner.

'He recognized certain moral messages, that you should always try your hardest, that you should be unselfish, you should respect and recognize an opponent who's been better than you and so on. He understood those things, but he also twigged that if he was to succeed, he had to become a winner. Winning had to be important to him. He had to realize that each game and each performance was important. Doing the best he could was important. In football that often means that you are against someone else – your winning is his losing, and you've got to deal with that. That's no more true than in the boxing ring.

'This player learned that, and consequently became a much more reliable and efficient player than some people who as young-sters were much better than him, but who didn't have this potential to develop mentally.'

In general, mental development takes longer for footballers than the development of their physical and technical prowess. Wilkinson says:

'Physical development occurs much more quickly than mental development. Somebody can be very gifted physically, yet not be so good in terms of their football sense or their sense of life. But by the time they are 24 or 25, both come together. The cake's gone in the oven with all the ingredients and it comes out fully developed. The best cake you get in football terms is around the ages of 25, 26, 27, 28.'

When football players don't give their all or let that killer instinct slip, there is a danger they will underperform. Take the England football team's apparent ability to raise their game when playing real threats – such as Germany or Argentina – but the tendency to crum-ble against lesser sides. England coach Sven-Göran Eriksson says:

'It relates to the mental approach to the game. If you meet Argentina or Germany, you know that the match will be difficult and you must perform at your absolute best. When you meet Macedonia at home, you think it will be okay. So the mental approach to the games is different. But it's not only England where that happens. I think it happens in football in general.'

Theoretically, a side should have a better record at home than away, emboldened by the familiarity of the ground and the home support. However, as 2002 drew to a close, Eriksson noticed this didn't seem to be the case with England. Contrary to expectation, England were doing better away than at home. As he said, 'It's very strange'.

'Maybe we think it's easy at home. When you think things are easy, you are not prepared to kill your opponent, and so you will never have a good result. You must have that killer instinct. The ball is a 50:50 ball and you think, "That's my ball".'

For some sporting champions, competitions become almost like real battles. Javelin champion Steve Backley likens champions to 'warriors' and the experience of entering a competition to going into battle. Backley doesn't feel that he is playing a game; he feels that he is 'fighting for my life'. In major championships he convinces himself that it is a case of 'live or die'. The event is, in a sense, blown out of all proportion in his emotions.

Backley likens the contest between top javelin throwers to a fight, with each throw a punch landed on the other. This was how he saw his battle for silver in the 2000 Olympics, when Backley was facing stiff competition from Sergei Makarov of Russia.

'I think he thought he'd beaten me and went to sleep. But I had a response, and went ahead of him. Then he had a chance to respond. In the fight analogy, it was as if I'd just squared him on the chin. It shook him a bit. He threw a reasonable 86m, which made me think he was capable of doing it, but he overcooked it. I caught him on the hop.'

In the end Backley threw 89.85m, a longer distance than Makarov's best effort, so taking the silver and pushing the Russian into the bronze medal position.

Having considered the discipline, determination and sometimes downright selfish pigheadedness shown by sporting champions, we move on to consider some of the influences that helped to make them what they are.

Chapter 2

FAMILY AND FATE

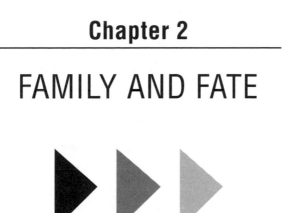

SPORTING CHAMPIONS DON'T EMERGE out of the blue as fully-formed elite athletes. They all had fathers and mothers, coaches and sometimes other individuals who influenced their ambitions and activities. They were all encouraged along the way to pursue their sporting ambitions. They also took the opportunities that presented themselves.

According to Ian Lynagh's sports psychology model (see Appendix I), early influences help to determine an athlete's future success. The first part of Lynagh's model considers the personal characteristics of champions, which can be shaped by the people around them at an early age. When growing up, champions receive messages about themselves and their ability to do things, as well as about sport and the value of discipline. According to Lynagh, the messages can come from parents, school or coaches. For example, mothers and fathers who play sport give their children a sports model to learn from. These children may pick up messages about what good sport is all about, messages about discipline and striving. These messages can have a positive impact on their sporting – and other achievements – through their lives.

FAMILY EXAMPLES

Adrian Moorhouse, Olympic breaststroke gold medallist in Seoul, was inspired by the example of his father, who played Sunday league cricket in Yorkshire.

> *'The fact that we used to go and watch my dad play cricket on a Sunday was quite significant. We watched him score 50 and we all felt good about it! Then, also, when I was 14, I moved my training to Leeds. At the time, my dad had been a director of a wool company and he left that to set up his own business at the age of 49. He still got up every morning to drive me to the pool. He was goal-focused and I saw the application of hard work. He was a self-driven kind of person. So I've got that in my genes and I also got a model from it.'*

Golf champion Nick Faldo feels he inherited his ability to commit himself to a task from his parents.

> *'My father was an accountant and my mother was a dressmaker, trades they started from a young age. They learned their professions. My mother is probably the stronger one for commitment. If she's going to do something, that's it. She's very disciplined. I'm sure I got that from her.'*

Round-the-world yachtsman Sir Chay Blyth's mother was also an inspiring influence. He describes her as a very hard worker and a great assertive force. She had three jobs and brought up a family of seven. Blyth recalls that she made sure she did whatever she said she would do. Her example had a positive impact on Blyth in influencing the determination with which he approaches every project he undertakes.

Mark Richardson, 400m Commonwealth silver medallist, says he received considerable encouragement from his parents, although they stressed the importance of gaining a good education and that his training should not affect his exam results. His parents came to the UK from the Caribbean, bringing very little with them. His father had no formal qualifications, but set up his own business, and his mother trained as a nurse. They worked very hard to make a success of their lives.

Richardson believes that his parents instilled self-discipline in him, something he has drawn on during the years of training.

'In winter in particular the objective is to go out to try to hurt yourself – putting money in the bank so you can withdraw from it during the competitive season.'

POSITIVE SUPPORT

Olympic swimmer Adrian Moorhouse enjoyed the support of his parents during his early training years. He describes them as kind, encouraging, supportive and 'just pushy enough'. They were challenging enough to ask Moorhouse, if he missed a training session, why he had done so and whether he was feeling alright. But they would never actually wake him up and tell him to go to training. They left that to his own self-discipline.

Moorhouse recalls how his father would take him to the pool and sometimes record his times with a stopwatch. But his coach persuaded his parents that they could be more help by just being normal parents, not extra coaches.

'When I got to 14 or 15 and started to show real promise my coach had a big conversation with my parents. He told them, "You be the dad and the mum, because when he's here, I'm the coach. If you're the coach at home, he's never going to get away from it. When he

gets home he wants you to love him. When he gets home he doesn't need you to talk to him about what times he did, or how much training he did. He wants you to talk to him about other stuff."

'So my coach had a fundamental conversation with my parents which helped, and they were very supportive.'

Nick Faldo first became inspired to try his hand at golf when he was 14, after watching Jack Nicklaus play on television.

'I went to my parents and told them I wanted to try golf. They knew nothing about it, but they booked me in for six lessons. That was the start.'

Although naturally talented at other sports, it was golf that captured his imagination. He was a good bowler, with a good throwing arm, and he also played tennis, though was told he was too tall for the game. He was also told he was too tall for golf, but he wasn't put off. He found the practising too interesting, because every single shot, every single day, was different. He was gripped by the challenge of trying to recreate good shots day after day.

When Faldo told his parents he wanted to leave school to concentrate on his golf, they remained supportive.

'They obviously had an awful lot of trust in me, because I was never checked up on. I went to the range for two years and virtually lived and breathed there until I played tournaments. I played a lot more tournaments from 1975 and they had to take me to all of those, so that was their commitment.'

Lawrence Dallaglio, England rugby captain, appreciated the help of his parents, who he says were always incredibly supportive and helpful, though not pushy. They had a very positive approach to life, and told the young Dallaglio that he could achieve anything he wanted to achieve in his life – and they would do what they could to help him.

Dallaglio found that commitment extremely helpful; it gave him a great starting point and encouraged him to aim high. He says:

'I've always been taught that you shoot for the highest level. Don't be happy with shooting for the middle ground. If your expectations are high in life, then you're going to get to the top. If you are happy to get to middle management, that's what happens. It's how some people approach rugby. They are happy just to play for their club. But when you are younger and you are shown that anything is possible and it's there for you, I think you're already in a bigger place.'

Sebastian Coe, twice Olympic 1500m gold medallist, was supported in his training by his father – who was also his coach. But his mother played a vital role in maintaining balance in the family.

'When you are coached by a relative there are pressures on the rest of the family too. I have four other brothers and sisters. So having balance in the family so there wasn't a focus just on one kid was important. My mother was very instrumental in making sure there was equilibrium for the family, which could have tilted too far in one direction.'

Former Olympic hurdles champion Sally Gunnell's parents supported her when she decided to take up athletics. They would drive her to the clubs and watch her perform. They paid for her kit and always appeared willing to support her, whatever she wanted to do. When she left school she decided to go for a part-time job while she tried to make a successful career from her athletics. Her parents supported her decision and told her to 'Go for it'.

As an adult, Gunnell also benefited from the support of her husband, Jon Bigg.

'He was my backbone. I probably couldn't have done what I have done without him. He gave me stability and a relationship where you didn't have to go out to clubs or wherever. He'd train with me.

He understood everything. He was the one making me eat properly and making me feel guilty if I didn't. I was very lucky to have him and it was very much a partnership.'

Champion National Hunt jockey Richard Dunwoody appreciated the support of his father, a horse trainer, who he describes as a big influence on his life. He would watch the jockey in the making when he was riding as a toddler and later, when Dunwoody's career was underway, he would offer advice. Dunwoody says:

'In racing, you don't tend to have coaches. The trainers are almost supposed to be coaches, but apart from giving you a right bollocking now and then, they don't coach you as such. So I was very lucky to have my father there.'

Yachtswoman Ellen MacArthur was introduced to sailing as a child by her aunt and was thrilled by the experience.

'I first sailed when I was four years old and I absolutely loved it. Initially it was the adventure I loved, the feeling that if you get on a boat you can go anywhere in the world. We sailed overnight when I was quite young. It was an amazing experience to be out in the ocean and then arrive somewhere else, yet your home was with you.'

She sailed regularly, achieving a significant milestone at the age of 14 when she navigated her aunt's boat, *Cabaret*, around the east coast of England.

'There were three of us on board – my auntie, one of my school friends and myself. I was in charge of navigation and making the decisions. I was nervous because I was responsible for the boat, but it was a big confidence booster.'

The parents of former badminton champion Gill Clark supported her sporting ambitions, although neither of them was sporty. Her father wasn't particularly interested in badminton and only watched her play about three times, but Clark didn't need his physical support. It was the emotional support that both he and her mother gave that she valued.

Clark was the youngest of four children, all of whom went to university, and this was what her parents initially expected her to do. However, they listened to her and accepted her sporting ambitions. If Clark became injured and her sporting career looked in jeopardy, her parents never criticized her decision to follow her badminton dreams. They never turned round and told her she should have gone to university instead.

> 'My father had scraped together the money to educate us all. But I didn't want to go to university. The way I persuaded him was by explaining that I had to have a go at badminton because I had a need to find out how good I could be. I couldn't bear the thought of sitting here 22 years on from when I should have gone to university, and saying, "I could have been a good badminton player. If I hadn't gone to university I could have been very good." How many times do you hear people saying that? Saying "if only", or "maybe if". Those are some of the saddest words in the English language.
>
> 'I know what I was capable of because I've done it, and I have my medals from World Championships and World Cups. I've ten medals from those two competitions, not one of them is gold, but that's not a big deal to me. That doesn't matter because I know that I did everything possible.'

David Lloyd describes his parents as 'Mr and Mrs Tennis', playing every day. His father was besotted with the game. His mother didn't initially play, but was taught by Lloyd senior and picked up his enthusiasm, becoming a good club player. Both parents' love of the sport had a great influence on the young Lloyd children. David says:

> 'It was predetermined that all three boys would play tennis. There was pressure, but I think as parents they judged the right amount of pressure. If Dad hadn't made us come down to the club and play,

we wouldn't have done what we have done. I think Dad would have encouraged me to play any sport – I had trials for Southend United – but tennis is what he wanted me to play. He allowed me to leave school without any qualifications. In those days that's a pretty brave step. He knew I had a talent and therefore I should use it early. So I left school at fifteen and a half and he helped me play.'

Michael Lynagh, former Australian rugby captain and renowned fly-half, tried his hand at different sports as a youngster, with plenty of parental encouragement. Whether it was cricket or rugby league, surfing or swimming, young Lynagh loved having a go. If he wanted to try something new, his parents supported him. They didn't push him towards any activity, however, but let him discover sport for himself. The same went for his sister. Whatever they wanted to do, they were encouraged to go on and do it.

Lynagh's father, Ian, played rugby and cricket and Michael used to go and watch him play. Sometimes he would join in and field.

'There was one occasion when I was about 13 and Dad was sick. He phoned the team captain and told them he couldn't play that day, but that I would play instead and field for the team. I went along and the captain asked what I did. I said I was a wicket keeper. So the captain told me to pad up. Then in the second over I took a catch – a really good catch – and the opposition captain came over and said, "Look, we don't mind seeing a kid fielding, but putting him in a prime position is a bit much." In the end our captain said he'd move me, so I went and fielded off at gully and then took another catch. There was another protest and I was moved again. Eventually I was down at fine leg or somewhere like that and I took another catch there. I took about five catches during the day. The captain phoned my dad up during the week to check he wasn't feeling sick again …

'But I just used to play for fun. I remember wanting to play for Australia, but I never thought I would.'

Although Lynagh clearly had natural talent, he didn't really appreciate how much.

> *'I remember when I was 16 or 17 Dad sat me down. He said, "You have got something special." I said, "No I haven't." He said, "Go and use it. Go and be confident." I remember little talks like that.'*

COACHING AND OTHER INFLUENCES

In addition to benefiting from his parents' encouragement, as a boy Michael Lynagh was also influenced by his school headmaster. Lynagh recalls an occasion when the headmaster had come to watch the first eleven cricket team, which Lynagh was captaining. Lynagh won the toss and chose to bat, but suddenly doubted whether he had made the right choice.

> *'My headmaster said, "The decision has been made. All you can do now is make it work. You will do your best to make it work." It's such a simple point and I've remembered it all the way through my life. You make the decision, and then you just do your best to make it work. If it doesn't work, well, you did you best. You had the guts to make a decision and you have done your best to try and make it the right decision. Once you have made the decision, worrying about it is irrelevant. All you can do is make it work.'*

Elite rower Matthew Pinsent didn't realize he might have what it takes to win medals at the Olympics until he was 18 or 19 – when coaches where he trained at Leander Club in Henley started telling him so.

> *'I was in the British team from the age of 17, but even then didn't realize I could go to the Olympics. It was still a dream for me. But when I finished school I decided to take a year out from education and came here to Henley. I started training with the guys who were*

coming back from the 1988 Games. It was then, at the end of 1988, that some of the coaches said, "You're really good".'

Soon after Pinsent was invited by the coach of the men's team to go and train with them and he seized the chance. Pinsent never looked back.

Sir Chay Blyth's encounter with an Olympic swimmer gave him early encouragement to achieve. Blyth, who couldn't swim, was thrown in the deep end of a swimming pool by a gang of boys.

'The guy who pulled me out was in the Olympic team. He spent a bit of time with me, to tell me about swimming. But it was his charisma and encouragement that made me go back to the swimming pool. He encouraged all the youngsters, but through his encouragement I took up swimming and ended up training three times a day. He was a mentor in terms of training. I saw him train, so I had to train.'

When Blyth joined the paratroopers he found inspiration in one of his fellow soldiers – someone he met on his very first day.

'He was very fit, a very good football player, very athletic, charismatic and a great leader. I modelled myself on him. He had done a lot of running before joining the paras, and I hadn't. There were lots of rumours about how we would have to do a ten mile run carrying lots of kit. I decided I needed to do some running, so we ran down a road and I was knackered. I didn't think I'd be able to do it. He encouraged me and it wasn't so bad because the barracks teach you how to run and there was a build-up. But this guy was a great mentor – inspirational.'

THE HAND OF FATE

For some champions, fate plays a hand in shaping the course of their lives – though the champions have to go on and seize the opportunities that present themselves. Renowned round-the-world yachtswoman Ellen MacArthur appreciates that fate took a hand in determining her sailing future.

'If ever there was a moment that determined I was going to sail for a living, it was probably when I was 17 and had glandular fever. I wanted to get into veterinary school and was working stupid hours, trying to get the grades. While I was working like that I got glandular fever. When I was ill I thought "Life's for living" and I've not looked back since.'

Athlete Roger Black had a similar experience. When he left school he had no expectation of athletic success. His school didn't pay much attention to athletics. It was just an option for boys who didn't play cricket.

'None of my school teachers really realized what ability I had. When I was 17 or 18 I ran the 400m in about 48.4 seconds. If you told me now about a kid who ran that time in school sports and didn't train, I'd say, "There stands the next British champion". But nobody at my school had that sort of knowledge or understanding. It didn't mean anything to them.

'When I left school after we had finished our A levels, I went to the pub with about six other friends. I said, "I wonder what we'll be doing in five years' time?" I didn't know.'

Black had decided he wanted to study medicine at university. But fate took a hand. He 'messed up' his A level exams, with the result that he wasn't able to go to his first choice, Newcastle University, to study medicine. He decided to take a year off to retake his exams. That was when a friend told him that Kriss Akabusi was training down the road at Southampton Athletic Club and suggested Black go and join him. Two months later he was running indoors for Great Britain.

Black realized he really had a talent for running. Akabusi had just come back from the 1984 Olympics. Black recalls the dawning of his ambition: 'When Kriss Akabusi, who has trained all his life to run

45.5 seconds, tells you you'll be the best 400m runner the country's ever seen …'

Black then became serious about training.

'Athletics suddenly became fun. It was never fun at school. Suddenly you're training five times a week with a group of guys who were great fun, total idiots but top runners. You would train hard and it was hard physically, but it was a great life.'

After retaking his exams and getting the grades he needed to study medicine, Black did head off to university.

'I still wanted to be a doctor. But at the end of the first term I realized I had to make a decision between becoming a doctor and becoming an athlete. It was the biggest decision of my life. It was a difficult one, but it was made easier by one of my professors. He came up to me and said, "Black, there are two ways to get a degree from Southampton University. The first way is to spend the next five years here reading medicine. You can cut up dead bodies, you can do microbiology and whatever. At the end of those five years you will be totally stressed out as all doctors are, but you get your degree and you will become a doctor."

'He continued: "Of course, there is another way. You could leave now and become a full-time athlete. You could train for three hours a day, spend three months of every year in sunny California, go to the Olympic Games, get paid to run, get paid to wear running shoes, become famous, but more importantly, lad, you can have ten thousand women screaming at you." I chose athletics, obviously. He was right and five years later I got an honorary degree from Southampton University.'

Former Australian rugby captain Michael Lynagh's first love was actually cricket. He made his school's first eleven cricket team when he was thirteen, but rugby began to become an interest not long after. Lynagh was initially placed in the B rugby team, the result of being made to play a position he hated. However, he decided to try for the first fifteen.

'I was only 14 at the time and it was rare for a kid to play for the first fifteen when he was only 14. The reason I wanted to try out was because the first fifteen squad were going on a tour to New Zealand that year. I thought that sounded pretty good. I made the team and was then fortunate enough to have a really good schoolboy coach who helped me enormously. I played in the first fifteen at school for three years.

'Then in my last game for the school I broke my collarbone. There was an Australian schoolboy's team going to the UK, Ireland and America in the summer and I had my heart set on that. Everybody was saying I would make it because I had been in the Australian team the year before, but I broke my collarbone six weeks before the trial. You had to play in the trials to get on the tour.

'I managed to get better just in time, stood up in the trial and got selected. That was my first summer out of school. When I came back from that at the end of January I got selected for the Queensland Senior rugby team. And that was it. The selectors made the choice between rugby and cricket for me. I haven't played cricket since, except for charity matches. I often wonder, if I had followed a cricket path, where it would have led me. But I have no regrets with rugby. It's been fantastic for me.'

So fate stepped in and shaped Lynagh's future, setting him on the path to becoming a famous rugby player – captain of the Australian team. But did he, early on, ever believe he would achieve such sporting heights? In the next chapter we look at one common ingredient amongst elite sportspeople – their great sense of self-belief.

Chapter 3

I BELIEVE!

ONE OF THE CHARACTERISTICS THAT LEAPS OUT from most champion sportspeople is the depth and strength of their self-belief. That belief not only encourages them to keep training year after year, but helps them come back to form after injury and hold their nerve in the heat of competition.

BELIEF MATTERS

Professor Graham Jones has been researching the qualities of mental toughness that distinguish the truly elite performers from the rest. (See Appendix II). His studies of athletes have generated a ranking of qualities required for mental toughness. Self-belief has emerged as the top requirement, the most important characteristic of all.

Elite sportspeople from a range of disciplines, including swimming, sprinting, triathlon, golf and rugby, determined that this was the most important characteristic of mental toughness: 'Having an unshakable self-belief in your ability to achieve your competition goals.'

Belief also appeared in another form, ranked third in importance: 'Having an unshakable self-belief that you possess unique qualities and abilities that make you better than your opponents.' Champion athletes need to believe that they are better than the competition.

Whatever sport you look at, belief is essential. Ron Dennis, boss of the McLaren racing team, says: 'Ego is an essential ingredient in winners.'

In her competitive days, Olympic hurdler Sally Gunnell had a strong bond with top sprinter Linford Christie and hurdler Kriss Akabusi. What common characteristics did they all share?

'I guess it's believing in yourself. If you don't believe in yourself when you stand on the line, then you're not going to go anywhere. We believed in what we'd done, who we were and what we're made up of. We were all quite selfish people. When people know me I'm not a bitchy character. A lot of people used to say I'm like the girl next door, but I was someone very different as soon as I stepped onto that track.'

Athletics coach Ron Roddan, who worked with Linford Christie, believes in the power of belief and convincing yourself of your own ability to triumph. He says there are some people who are very talented but haven't got the mental ability to convince themselves that they can be successful. If they can't do that, they get stuck. Someone with the right attitude – strong belief – can outperform the rest. Time and again, Roddan says, someone with the talent to be a world-beater has lost to someone with theoretically lesser ability.

Before Linford Christie won his Olympic gold in Barcelona, Roddan recalls that he was very positive about his chances of success.

'He promised himself and the people around him that he would win that gold medal. He always said he would. He felt huge satisfaction when he won that Olympics.'

Daley Thompson, Olympic gold medallist in the decathlon in 1980 and 1984, had huge self-belief, as former national athletics coach Frank Dick recalls:

'Just after a hard day's work, when we were sitting back and feeling the sun on our faces, Daley said to me, "Frankie, who's the greatest athlete you ever saw?" I asked if he meant even in videos, and he said yes. I named someone who had made four world records in one day. Daley said, "Forget it, buddy, you're looking at him".'

Former Davis Cup tennis captain David Lloyd says the great sportspeople he has met really do have something different. They have an in-built belief in themselves – total belief – even though they might not show it in an arrogant way. Lloyd was inspired by the great Australian tennis player Ken Rosewall, who he says had a 'mind of iron'. People wouldn't know it just by watching him, because he was never unpleasant or arrogant, but when he talked, his stubbornness and belief in his own ability came through.

When preparing the England Under-21 football squad for the European championship, team manager David Platt emphasized the importance of belief in the team's ability to win. What mattered was whether the players in the squad believed it themselves. It didn't matter what they said to Platt or anyone else; what mattered was what they really thought on the inside. That inner belief was essential.

DEVELOPING BELIEF

There clearly is no doubt that belief is an essential ingredient of champions, top athletes who can rise to major occasions and pull out medal-winning performances. The question is, where does that belief come from? Is it inherent or can it be developed?

According to sports psychologist, Steve Sylvester, the factors that enable champions to have rock-solid belief, and that therefore enable them to win consistently, are unique to each individual. This unique formula for strong belief is based on the individual's past experiences and how the person feels about the people around them. Sylvester notes that there are common ingredients that world champions exhibit, and the first one is the 'never say die' approach – the ability to work and persist in what they are doing, no matter what. The question he asks is, where does that come from? Is it innate? A lot of the people Sylvester works with persist for a combination of two reasons: because they *want* to achieve something (their dream), and because they *need* to achieve it.

For many top athletes, belief develops over time, as the individual meets and surpasses graduated goals. No one can give someone else belief in themselves, it has to be generated by each individual for themselves.

Frank Dick, former national athletics coach, says it is essential to give people the opportunity to build self-belief for themselves. He says:

'I cannot give you self-belief. This is a bridge that only you have to build and only you can cross. The self-belief comes from believing that you can explore, that you can challenge, that you can win. It's a growing thing, all the time. You've got to have "a guid conceit o' yersel".'

Hurdling gold medallist Sally Gunnell built up her confidence and belief little by little.

'I was OK as a junior, but I wasn't brilliant. I wasn't one of these people who went and won junior championships. But I was a confident athlete. If one year I got into a senior international, I gained a lot of confidence from it. Then I would set myself the next goal. I would just build up gradually like that. A lot of people talk about being Olympic champion one day. I was never really like that. I guess the first time I realized I could win the Olympics was about

four years before it actually happened – when I was 15 in Seoul in 1988.'

Round-the-world yachtsman Sir Chay Blyth has needed great depths of belief not only to complete his epic voyages, but also to get them off the drawing board. Blyth developed his great sense of self-belief during his time in the army with the paras.

'They make you develop self-belief. They convince you that whatever you're about to take on, you will achieve it. There were 67 of us at the start of my training and we ended up with 12 or 14 passing. They start building your confidence through doing things you've never done before, such as an assault course – a miniature one to begin with and then it gets more sophisticated. They also injected you with confidence when someone failed the course. If someone failed they would come down on that guy really heavy, tell them they're useless and the scum of the earth. It was all designed to make you feel better about yourself. They would throw the guy's kit out of the window and he'd be given all the worst jobs in the dining hall.

'When they give you your wings, it's a great moment in time. They make you feel you could conquer the world.'

For David Platt, former England player, belief in how high he could rise in the game of football developed gradually. Platt started out with Manchester United.

'I have always been a realist and I didn't actually think I was good enough to go to Manchester United. I signed a Youth Training Scheme [YTS] contract with them. I never trained with the first team, but every now and again we would have a practice match against them. You didn't believe you should be in the same building as them. To be awarded a pro contract at the end of that twelve months' YTS was fantastic. I was on cloud nine. But six months in I had the chance to go to Crewe Alexandra on loan. I knew I couldn't replace the likes of Norman Whiteside, Mark Hughes or Frank

Stapleton at Manchester, so I went to Crewe. Even though it was a massive step down club-wise, it was a big step up in terms of the level of football I was going to be playing. I had been playing third team football at Manchester United and the odd reserve game. So to go and play league football was daunting. Even then you think you are not good enough to play in this and it takes a while to come to terms with it. Then you realize you are good enough to play, but you think maybe this is the highest you are going to go.'

Even when Aston Villa paid £200,000 – a huge fee at the time – to buy Platt from Crewe, he still doubted himself. Platt says:

'I had gone from being the big fish at Crewe to being with players who were top of the old second division. I began thinking maybe that was too much for me.'

For Platt, absolute confidence in his own ability came some time after he first began playing first-class and international football. It was scoring a match-winning goal against Belgium in the 1990 World Cup in Italy that made the difference. The goal, right at the end of extra time, put England through to the quarter-finals.

'Scoring that goal in the World Cup put an expectancy level on me from everybody else. Scoring that goal in the last minute changed my life completely. I had already played ten or eleven times for England, but scoring that goal in the World Cup finals was something else. Afterwards I went to Hong Kong with Aston Villa. I got off the plane and there were thousands of people waiting to see me.

'So then I had to keep delivering, and keep delivering, and keep delivering, and I did. After the World Cup I started to score at Aston Villa on a regular basis. I kept scoring goals at international level against good teams. And once you keep doing that you start thinking, "I can do this". And then you go week in, week out, and there is no fear inside you whatsoever. In fact, there's just an excitement level. It sounds horrible, but it's almost an arrogance. But as

*long as that arrogance is channelled in the right way, I don't think
there's anything wrong with it. In fact, it's total confidence.'*

Platt's confidence fuelled itself as he kept scoring goals at international level, but he actively worked to reinforce it too:

*'I had a video of all my goals that I would watch before I went out
to play a game, because it made me feel good. They were good
goals I had scored against good players.'*

For Jack Charlton too, belief in his ability came slowly. He was compared to his brother Bobby and always seen as less talented. Jack worked briefly in the mines before leaving home for Leeds United at the age of 16, where he was a member of the ground staff. At that time he describes himself as a five foot ten beanpole; thin with long legs – 'a gawky bugger'.

At the age of 17 the club decided whether it wanted to sign its youngsters. When Jack was 17, Leeds signed him up on the standard one-year contract, giving him a £10 signing fee and first team pay – about three and a half times what he had been earning on the ground staff.

*'I walked out of the office and across to John's, a shop on the
corner. John asked me if I had signed and I said "yes". John said,
"Thank god for that." I asked why and he replied, "I have had half
the Football League in here this morning to see if they had signed
you. Scouts from all the clubs in the area and from all over the
place have been in here asking about you. They all knew it was your
birthday and they wanted to know if you had signed." I suddenly
thought that I must be able to play.'*

Charlton enjoyed the feeling and began to absorb the fact that he really was a professional football player.

While 400m runner Roger Black knew that he had natural running ability from a young age, he didn't have particular desire to become a top athlete. He just happened to be good at sport, and he knew it.

'I realized I was good at sport from the moment I could run, from the moment I could kick a football, from the moment I could catch a ball. I knew I was fast, because you can always tell who the fastest kid in the school is, and that was me. So I knew I was good; the thing is, I didn't know how good. I played rugby. I sat out on the wing and they chucked the ball to me and I ran past everyone. I was seriously quick.'

At first, athletics didn't inspire him as much as rugby and he didn't take his running very seriously.

'I ran for the school and then ran for Hampshire in the school championships, but I never ran for a club; I never trained. I'd rather be in team sports than winning individually. I was a bit embarrassed as well, to be honest; it was so easy.

'I didn't enjoy beating people by 20 metres over 100 metres. I would turn up in my plimsolls, with no tracksuit. I would go on the track and comfortably beat kids who were training six days a week.

'I'd always win in school sports and I'd always win the Hampshire championships. I went to the English school championships two or three times and scraped into the final and came fourth or fifth or sixth. That's when I should have known. To come fourth or fifth or sixth against all the best kids in the country when you don't train ...'

THAT 'KNOWING' FEELING

Some top sportsmen and women develop such a strong sense of belief that they feel they 'know' they will do well. This sense of knowing what the outcome will be results from absolute and unshakeable confidence in their abilities.

Multiple gold medal-winning rower Matthew Pinsent talks about 'knowing' how his boat should do in a race.

'I've been lucky enough in the Olympics to know that if the boat I was in rowed its best, we would win. That was the bedrock of it: "we are the best crew in the event and if we row well, we will win".'

Olympic gold medal hurdler Sally Gunnell had an overwhelming sense of self-belief when standing on the start line before the Barcelona Olympic final.

'I remember standing on the line thinking, "I know I'm going to win this". I suppose I knew I was capable of winning it beforehand, but then I just knew. Something said to me, "You're going to win this".

'I don't remember much of the race. I don't remember going over the first hurdle, second, third … Then I was at the eighth. A key thing I had done in visualizing the race was to say, "If I can be ahead at eight, I know I can win it," because I was stronger than the others. And then that was it – I was crossing the line.'

Belief is generated in large part from knowing that everything has been done as well as it could be in preparation for the competition. Effective training builds up confidence, which leads to belief.

For Gunnell, having belief that she would win at the start of a race depended on her having trained well and knowing that she was in good shape.

'Confidence is everything. Thinking that I'd eaten no chocolate or whatever for six months just made me ooze confidence. Knowing that I hadn't had an injury gave me confidence. The mental side of it played the biggest part; that was the difference between silver and gold.'

When Gunnell was injured in 1996 and missed training, she lost her sense of belief.

'I think of myself as mentally a very strong character, but I didn't do very well when I was injured. I had to be able to stand on the line knowing I was at my best.'

Sebastian Coe believes that the mental aspect of success is huge, but he also sees a link with the physical.

'I always found I was mentally at my best when I was physically in good shape. If I knew I had run and trained and done everything I could possibly have done; if I knew I had left no stone unturned in training and had been uninjured and had a good, clear run through to a championship, then I was always mentally bouncy about it.

'If you are not in good shape, that is where good poker players take over. I have gone out onto the line before a race knowing that in reality the training had gone badly and that I was not in good shape. Maybe I had been injured. In poker terms you have a handful of crap, but you have got through it because you have maintained a mask. People think you're as good as you were six months ago. If you don't let them know you have been injured or out of form for a bit, then you can normally wing it a bit.'

England rugby head coach, Clive Woodward, believes really top sportsmen strive for every marginal advantage they can get. They build up their belief by knowing they are the fittest, the strongest, the sharpest – whatever it takes.

'Everybody is looking for the edge. It's getting smaller and smaller the more competitive the world of sport becomes. Take Tiger Woods. If someone asks him why he's better than the rest of the world, he talks about his fitness; he doesn't talk about his golf swing. He talks about feeling mentally stronger and that comes down to believing he's the fittest. He's an athlete. He's as fit as the 100m champion. He thinks he's fitter than any athlete in the world. He has massive mental strength.'

Athlete Mark Richardson knows that strong self-belief and confidence in one's ability are essential ingredients of the champion's psyche. He acknowledges that first you need to be fit and to have prepared well for competition through training. Those factors then combine to give the athlete confidence – 'so much armoury' – that you arrive at the start line in the optimal mental state.

One of Richardson's most memorable races was when he beat the Olympic champion Michael Johnson in a Grand Prix race in Oslo – at a time when Johnson seemed virtually unbeatable. To make the achievement even more impressive, Richardson was drawn in lane one – the lane that everyone hates.

'It's a difficult lane because it has very tight bends. But I ran my own race, and as a result, I was able to finish extremely strongly.'

Thorough practice and training forms the bedrock of strong self-belief for champions in all sports. Former badminton champion Gill Clark drew on her belief when competing in the Olympic Games, where she and her partner, Julie Bradbury, qualified as the number sixth ranked pair in the world. In the first round of the Olympics they had to play the fifth ranked pair.

'In the third game we were 14–7 up and then they caught back up to 14–all. Then the Indonesian smashed at me and I played a deceptive block across court. I was asked afterwards about it – that surely it took a lot of courage to play that shot and go for an outright winner at 14–all. But I knew it wasn't a risky shot. I'd practised it thousands of times. I knew I could make that shot. I didn't hope I could make that shot, I knew I could make it. It was more than belief – it was knowing.'

EXPECTATIONS SET BELIEF SETS REALITY

What an athlete believes can determine the outcome. There is no doubt that in sport as in many other areas of life, there is such a thing as the self-fulfilling prophecy. If you limit your beliefs, you limit your potential to achieve.

Steve Sylvester, sports psychologist, works with sportspeople and people in business to try to help them improve their self-belief. By talking to them and asking questions he brings to light what it is that is stopping someone achieving their goals. Nine times out of ten, people are blocking their own performance, Sylvester says. They stop themselves believing that they can achieve. He has found that when it comes to the critical match situations or key moments in games, what people choose to say to themselves really matters. That's what makes the difference between success or failure, winning or losing.

Nick Faldo had huge belief in himself and his ability to succeed in golf, even from a young age. He recalls going to his youth employment office when he was leaving school and being asked whether he was good with his hands and so on, in an attempt to identify suitable work.

'I said, "Excuse me, I'm going to be a pro golfer." They said, "No, no, only one in two thousand or ten thousand makes it." So I said, "Fine. I'm the one." I had that level of self-commitment.'

Faldo's belief in himself developed gradually after he began going on tour. In the first four years he won roughly one tournament a year and he began wondering how he could win more. He realized that back on his first tour in South Africa, an influential person had told him he was good enough to win one tournament a year. And that's what he had done. Armed with that insight, and assisted by a psychologist, Faldo developed the belief that he could win multiple tournaments, which is precisely what he then started to do.

Athlete John Regis also knows that what you believe tends to come true. He recalls a Grand Prix race in Nice fairly early in his career. Also in the race were Frankie Fredericks, Michael Johnson and Linford Christie.

'I thought, "Michael's in the race, so I'm second." Then there was Frankie so I thought, "I haven't beaten him yet, so I'm third," and

so on. I crossed the line fourth. It was a self-fulfilling prophecy because I told myself I was going to finish fourth. It was as if my body gauged it to finish fourth. It was a strange feeling. When the gun went bang I took off really well. I came off the straight and felt strong. Then Michael kicked and ran away a bit and Frankie kicked and ran away a bit, and then Linford kicked and ran away a bit. I thought it was my turn, but then all of a sudden it seemed my mind was saying, "No, leave it alone John, they're too good."

'Afterwards I sat down with my coach and he said it looked as though I was going to go, but I didn't. I told myself I would finish fourth, and I did.'

After that race Regis trained hard and his times improved. He realized he was good enough to be at least as good as the three who had beaten him. He began to feel he could win.

'From that race onwards I've never been intimidated by anybody. I didn't care who was in the race, or what lane I was in – apart from lane one. No athlete in history has won a major championship from lane one. I'm not saying somebody can't, but the chances are you're not going to.'

As Regis says:

'If you believe you can, you have a chance. If you don't believe, you have no chance. Your mind can manipulate you from a no-win situation to a win-win situation.'

Regis recalls how he ran badly in a race in France, running a time of 20.9 seconds – what he calls a 'pedestrian, ugly' performance. Regis' coach then changed his training over the next week, making him focus on one area – really attacking the turn so hard that Regis worried it would use up too much energy. Despite Regis' concerns, they kept practising it all week. Eight days after his disastrous race, Regis competed in Lausanne. He ran the turn hard, as he had practised and finished in 20.1 seconds; he had knocked eight tenths of a second off his time in eight days.

'I'd improved eight and a half yards in seven days. It was huge. If you tell yourself you can, you can. All these little instances where I have overturned a negative and turned it into a positive helped me to perform at major championships and be more relaxed and just believe. You get yourself into shape no matter what anyone else is doing. Get yourself into shape and believe that you can. When it's your time to perform, it's your time to perform.'

One of the tennis matches that gave David Lloyd greatest pleasure was when he was playing Davis Cup doubles with his brother John against Italy. The Italians looked like they were going to take the match, but John kept saving match point after match point. In the end, the UK turned the tables and triumphed. David's huge sense of belief that they could win helped to pull off the victory. He recalls how he kept telling John they couldn't lose.

'I didn't think we could lose and I bullied John into thinking we couldn't lose either. He was my younger brother. John used to hang his head when I was always thinking that no one could ever beat me, although I actually couldn't really play. But John didn't think he could win, when I didn't think we could lose.

'We're talking about the semi-final of the Davis Cup. We're two sets to love down and if we lose that match we're out of the Davis Cup. It was the biggest arena I've ever played in. It meant so much to win for your country in a situation where you're playing at home – and you made it happen. Suddenly the Italians stopped waving and we started.

'We weren't supposed to win and we won. Obviously that gives enormous pleasure.'

With the Lloyd brothers, there is no doubt that John had more natural racquet talent than David, while David perhaps had more mental strength.

'John got to number 17 in the world. If it had been possible to combine the two of us, I think we would have been a pretty good player.

'John's racquet talent was enormous. He has physical talent because he can run, jump and he was quick. But in terms of mind talent, he was weak. He's strong today, funnily enough. I think being married to Chris Evert and living in America, where being number two doesn't count, had a big influence. I think if you'd trained his mental talent at 12, 13 and 14 he definitely would have been better.'

BOUNCING BACK

Steve Backley, four times European gold medallist and twice Olympic silver medallist in the javelin, believes there are three key requirements for success: belief, motivation and talent. Backley first started believing he had something special when he was 16 and competing for the England Schoolboys.

As Backley knows, belief is essential not only when things are going well, but also when trying to recover from a setback. Backley suffered from many injuries during his career, the first real one occurring in 1991.

'All of a sudden I'm down. But underlying all the fear, pain and inability to perform in the short term there is an underlying belief in the medium to long term – you know it's a minor setback.

'Then there are more major setbacks, which might knock you out for a year or two, when you lose the grounding of work and your performances are impaired. But if you believe that you are as good as you were, you can get it back.'

Golfer Nick Faldo's belief was put to the test when he was already successful at the sport and European number one. Despite this, Faldo began to have doubts about his swing and decided to take some time out to improve his technique.

'I led the British Open in 1983 with nine holes to play at Birkdale and couldn't finish it off. The little voice began saying, "You ain't got it mate; you ain't got the next level." I was tinkering with my swing for a couple of years on my own and then I met David Leadbetter [a leading golf instructor] in Sun City at the end of 1984. I asked him what he thought of my swing and he gave me his view. I thought it made sense. I really struggled at the beginning of 1985 and started work with David in May 1985.'

Playing tournaments while trying to work on the swing proved extremely stressful for Faldo.

'The media's on you. You've gone from European number one and now your game's gone, so you're under pressure. It was brutal. I lost corporate deals. Just two companies stuck with me. Everybody else disappeared. My manager would come to the house bringing doom and gloom that someone else had gone. Your income's not happening.

'But I just kept going. I guess it was self-belief; every week saying, "Yes, I believe it's a little better this week." I'd go to the next tournament and believe I was doing the right thing. I remember seeing even the guys on the range mimicking me and thinking I'd lost the plot.'

Faldo carried on regardless and finally, in the spring of 1987, his swing clicked. He played at a B class tournament in Hattiesburg, Mississippi, and came second. Then he went to the Spanish Open and won. He finally began to believe he could win the British Open – The Open – and went to compete at Muirfield, in Scotland.

'I had all the right feelings that week. I knew something was going to happen. I actually had a premonition way back. In 1978 I played in The Open and finished four shots back in seventh. I said to myself, "I will win The Open one day".'

Winning in 1987 required Faldo to contend with dreadful weather, as the Scottish fog closed in.

'I was nervous. I was trying to make birdies and I couldn't hole the putts. Then the East Lothian pea soup set in. Everything beyond a step and a half around me was out of focus. But I just kept plugging it out.'

Faldo describes himself as 'cocooned' that week.

'I could see myself walking down the fairway. All I knew was that one great shot would win me that Open, and one bad shot would lose it.'

As history shows, Faldo won.

Olympic swimmer Adrian Moorhouse's worst disappointment came at the Los Angeles Olympics in 1984, when he was 20. In the run-up, things were looking good.

'I'd won the Commonwealth Games when I was 18, in 1982. I won the European Championship in Rome in 1983. The year before the Olympics I was ranked fourth in the world. Then I went to the US Open in January of the Olympic year and won it. My time ranking was number one in the world and I was heading the world ranking all the way through the year.'

As a result, expectations began to mount that Moorhouse would take Olympic gold. At the Games things didn't go well, however. Moorhouse believes that he had become too intense – the outcome of winning had become too important. He and his coaches didn't place enough emphasis on relaxation.

In the 1984 Olympic final Moorhouse finished fourth. There was plenty of press comment suggesting he give up the sport. He considered quitting, but he didn't. He carried on training mechanically in the months afterwards.

'In July to September I swam just because I knew where the swimming pool was. It was a routine and I followed routine. My performances slipped dramatically though. My whole goal framework had collapsed and the motivation had collapsed because I didn't believe I could win the Olympics. I'd just been in the Olympics and not won it.

'I thought that I'd got to fix this myself. So on New Year's Eve I stayed up all night and wrote and reset my goals. I thought to myself, "If I'm going to quit, why don't I give myself a little bit more time, because I've got nothing to lose? So how about the British Nationals in four months' time?" I set some times for that and I remember sitting there all night thinking about it. I was thinking, "Okay, the best I can do is win the British Nationals. I'll try and win that. Now what's the time going to be?"'

Moorhouse then thought about what he needed to do in training to try and realize his goals. He discussed his ideas with his coach, and then got down to work.

'It went really well. I really started getting back in form within a week, because I was more focused on what I was doing. I believed in the steps and I got to the British Championship – I not only won the race, but broke the world record.'

There is no doubt that belief is a powerful element in the mixture of qualities that makes up a sporting champion. So is the ability to think positively about life and whatever happens to you, even if it doesn't initially seem that good. We examine this characteristic, one displayed by many elite sportspeople, in the next chapter.

Chapter 4

POSITIVE POWER

When talking to top athletes, one characteristic that stands out is their ability to think positively – even when injured or during other tough times. The ability to see a silver lining in every cloud and turn what appears to be a negative experience into a positive helps them to succeed, time and again.

POSITIVITY COUNTS

When Sven-Göran Eriksson is selecting players for the England football team, their mental characteristics are taken into account alongside their physical skill. Whether a player has a positive outlook or not is a key issue.

'To join the team, you must have a positive attitude and you must believe that you can go to Germany and win. If they don't believe we can do it, then it's impossible; we will never win. You must have that positive attitude for everything you do in the team.

'Some mornings you wake and life is difficult; it's raining and windy, but you must have a positive attitude anyhow. If you have one or two negative players, the next morning there will be four of them. Negativity spreads like cancer.'

David Beckham is one of the England players who impresses Eriksson because of his mental strength and attitude.

'Beckham is very positive. He's still young, but he's a leader. He doesn't talk very much, but that's positive about him. He works very hard and always tries to find solutions for difficult tasks. That's important.'

In Italy, Eriksson was impressed by Roberto Mancini when he was a player, describing him as a leader too. Mancini, who went on to become manager of Lazio, has a wonderfully positive attitude and believes everything is possible. As Eriksson says, it's wonderful to work with people like that.

Jack Charlton always had a positive outlook before games, including the 1966 World Cup competition.

'I never expected us to lose. When you go onto the field, you don't go on expecting to lose. I can't remember ever going out for a game where I felt we hadn't got a chance because the other side was so good. That's truly negative thinking. I wasn't brought up that way.

'The one player that did worry me in the World Cup was Eusebio [Portugal's striker], because I had seen him play many times and he was very gifted, a very strong player. The thing that worried me was that he had a small backlift with his foot before he hit the ball. I remember thinking that meant I had to get a yard closer to him. You couldn't let him have space if you were going to block the ball

or stop the shot. I didn't always get close to Eusebio, but I made sure somebody else did by yelling at them to get there.'

Former indoor 200m champion sprinter John Regis remained positive even when running against Michael Johnson.

'A lot of athletes would go into a race thinking, "Michael's here, I'm coming out second". I used to go into the race thinking, "Right, you put your head together and take him out of his comfort zone – make him focus on you, and then you've got a chance to beat him." That was the game plan I had.'

Former 400m champion Roger Black chooses to see the positive side of whatever happens to him. He has noted that some people who are perfectionists get very upset if they don't achieve, but Black has never been like that. He has always had a belief that there is a reason for everything. He says:

'You achieve what you can and most of the time things fall into place. They always have done for me. I've had major failures in my life that other people would have been destroyed by, and I've turned them around very quickly. And I'm not just talking about athletics.

'I choose to see the positive. You've got to be clear about your beliefs in life; then you're going to be OK.'

Black's world view was heavily influenced by the tragic death of one of his closest friends, a talented sportsman who was murdered when travelling in South America.

'I've always made the most of things. I don't live as if it's my last day, but I know that it could be. I travel a lot and accidents happen. You don't know what's around the corner. I don't expect much and I also make the most of what I have got.'

BANNING NEGATIVE THINKING

Olympic gold medal-winning hurdler Sally Gunnell is a great believer in the power of the mind to influence performance. She believes that for any athlete who stands on the starting line, as much as 70% of the race outcome is shaped by mental aspects. She says that this is based on her own experiences.

'In two key races – the 1992 Olympics and 1993 World Champion-ships – I don't think I was stronger than anybody else; I just think I was mentally prepared. I taught myself not to let any negative thoughts come in, because that's what the brain wants to do all the time. I just used to stop myself and then turn it around to say, "I can do this, I've eaten well, I've done everything I can." I fed myself loads of quality thoughts until, I guess, the brain took it all in.'

Even though there was increasing speculation about some athletes taking drugs, Gunnell refused to get her attention diverted by this. She just didn't want to know about any speculation. She didn't want to find herself standing on the starting line thinking that someone else had an unfair advantage through taking banned substances. That was a negative thought, as far as she was concerned. Gunnell felt it would be like telling herself she was inevitably going to come second and therefore spoiling her chances before the race even started.

Having won the Olympic title in Barcelona in 1992, Gunnell's next major challenge was the world championships the following year. She had prepared herself mentally and was feeling good. Then a week beforehand she came down with a cold. When she arrived at the athletes' village the doctor put her on antibiotics. Suddenly something negative had entered the equation and Gunnell felt anxious about her ability to perform at her best.

'I ran the heat and felt okay. Time-wise it wasn't too bad. Then I ran the semis and felt good again. I was running a pretty reason-able time. I said to myself, "Well, if I'm going to do this, I'm going

to do it properly. I can't go into the race saying to myself that I've got a cold and I've got a good excuse. I'm just going to have to go for it."

'Every single moment I would not allow this cold to get into my head. I was stopping myself coughing and feeding myself good thoughts. I told myself, "I'm feeling fantastic. I can do this. I'm in the best shape ever."

'Every time a negative thought started I wouldn't let it finish in my mind. I would stop it and turn it around into something positive: "I feel really good, I've eaten fantastically well."'

Right up to the start of the race Gunnell concentrated on not letting her rivals realize she was slightly under the weather. She says: 'I remember standing in the call room beforehand and not letting everybody else know that I'd just coughed and that I had a cold.'

When Gunnell then won the world title, and set a new world record in the process, she was amazed:

'I couldn't believe I'd done it. There was relief, but I was in shock that I'd done it. I was freaked out to think that I'd actually talked myself into doing that – into winning.'

POSITIVE DEVELOPMENT

While some top athletes may naturally have a positive outlook on life and on their sporting challenges, positive thinking can be deliberately encouraged by coaches.

Former badminton champion Gill Clark's coach used subtle techniques to encourage her to build a positive outlook when she was a teenager.

'When I was in the Under-15 age group I was playing in the All England Under-16 age group. I got to the quarter final and I had to play against the number one seed. I lost 11–0, 11–0. I came off court and had a big smile on my face, because it was a great experience.

'My coach said, "Let's sit down and talk about the game. What did you do right?" I said, "Well, I can't have done anything right – I didn't score a point." He said, "No, no, you made three winners with that cross-court slice we've been practising. That was absolutely tremendous." Then he asked me what I'd done wrong and we sat there for another half an hour. Then he went back to the cross-court slice – "That slice is super. We'll keep on working on that and we've got some other things to work on when we get home." So he taught me positive thinking without me realizing it.'

When former Davis Cup captain David Lloyd ran the Slater Scheme for talented young tennis players, he worked hard to encourage a positive attitude amongst them. His actions were influenced by Australian tennis champion Ken Rosewall, with whom Lloyd had lived and travelled for a period of time.

'Ken used to say that 90% is in the mind. When I had the Slater Scheme with kids who were 9 or 10 I tried very hard when I did anything with them to subliminally bring up the mind. We used to play tunes like "When the Tough Get Going". If the kids were in the car and had had a bad day, we'd play a tune like "One Moment in Time". I'd ask them what they'd hear out of this song. It was all to get them gently aware of the fact that the mind is the most important thing. Your heart and mind win matches. In my opinion, your forehand down the line, just because it's got a certain grip, doesn't win matches. The mind does.'

HARD TIMES

Few sporting careers run without a hitch. However, bad experiences can bring unexpected benefits. Professor Graham Jones believes that the elite performers who have encountered some adversity along the way can emerge even stronger champions than people who have sailed through to the top. He believes that failure can do people good as long as they can cope with it and come back from it. He has noted that many of the people who become the world's best have not had complete success along the way. On the other hand, those who have always been successful don't necessarily last for long at the top. For some reason they appear less able to handle the number one spot.

Mark Richardson the 400m runner has certainly faced adversity – and he believes he has emerged the stronger for it. Richardson suffered one of the worst things that can happen to a top athlete – being excluded from competition for using the banned substance nandralone in February 2000. He spent much of the two years following the ban arguing his innocence and trying to prove he was a victim of circumstance. Even so, he sees a positive side to the whole drama.

'I believe you are shaped by your experiences, and this whole situation has only made me mentally stronger. I believe I'm now much stronger on the track.

'It was a very difficult situation. It felt like staring down the barrel of a gun – it was completely out of my control. But during that time I continued to train and refused to give up. I drew on my own inner strength, driven by the fact I knew I hadn't done anything wrong. And part of it was just pure bloody-mindedness.'

Sir Chay Blyth also has an impressively positive outlook. He doesn't let a negative situation put him off. Instead, he always tries to turn it into a positive one.

'If I hear really bad news … Say I'm waiting for a yacht sponsor to say "yes" and I get the message "no". I still go and open my bottle of champagne. It's not going to stop me. One door closes, another one opens.'

Injuries provide some of the toughest yet most common challenges for athletes and top sportspeople. At such times the true champions draw deeply on their positive attitudes to enable themselves to return to competition quickly.

Former badminton champion Gill Clark suffered from injury problems at certain key points in her career. She recalls how she remained positive when recovering from injury in the run up to the European Championships.

> *'I can remember lying in my hospital bed the day after my first knee operation. I was stuck in plaster the physio came along and said, "I can't let you out of bed, not for any reason, until you can do ten straight leg raises." She said it would take me two or three days to do that. I held on to the bar of the bed that stopped me falling out and did ten straight leg raises.*
>
> *'From that moment, the day after the operation, it never occurred to me that I wouldn't get back into competition. I lay in the hospital bed and I imagined standing on the top of the rostrum at the European Championships, with that gold medal around my neck again. I'd get all excited about it. And therefore my training watch would go off every hour on the hour and I'd do ten more straight leg raises, ten minutes of exercise every hour on the hour.'*

Champion 400m runner Roger Black's career was dogged by injury, not counting a congenital heart valve problem, for which he is monitored every year. That was less of a problem than the other physical setbacks he faced. Black says:

> *'I broke my foot in 1988 after winning the European Championships, the Commonwealth Games and two gold medals in the relay. I was British record holder … It was so easy, and then I broke my foot.*
>
> *'That was when I started to learn about myself because up until then I had done everything off talent. It's not very difficult if you are blessed with a lot of talent. Up until this point I thought it was so easy and then I broke my foot and it wasn't quite so easy.*
>
> *'I was out of the sport for two years and had a metal screw put in my foot. I found you get forgotten very quickly and lose money very quickly if you are not performing. My motivation was never obvious to me. But then I realized my desire was to reach my full potential. My motivation to come back from injury was simply that I recognized the talent I had been given and I didn't want to look*

back and say, "If only I'd done that". I wanted to be able to end my career, move on and say I had done the best I could. That is why I had to win my Olympic medal. If I hadn't, I would have known I never really got it right.'

In addition to various physical injuries, Black also suffered from viral infections.

'When you have a broken foot everyone sympathizes with you because they can see you have a problem. The illnesses were worse because when you have a virus but you haven't been diagnosed yet, no one knows. You feel tired and your training partners think you have lost it, and that you are mentally weak. But I was proud of my mental toughness.

'When you get diagnosed and realize you have a virus, it's awful. You feel pathetic, your confidence goes, your physical strength goes. That's when you find out whether you're prepared to wait and to go right back to the start again. Fortunately, I was.'

Black doesn't think he would have won an Olympic silver in 1996 if he hadn't suffered all the setbacks he did in the preceding years, and if he had won the World Championship in 1991. 'I'm not sure I would have been around five years later,' he says.

Black feels that without the illnesses and injuries he might have run faster, but he wouldn't have won his Olympic medal. He says:

'The only reason I won Olympic silver in 1996 was because of all the things that had happened to me in the eight years prior to that. The injuries give you a burning desire, because you appreciate health so much more when you have been injured. And in 1996 I was healthy. When you have full health going into the Olympics you appreciate it so much more. I don't think I would have lasted in the sport until I was 32 if I had been healthy all the time. Your successes in life are what people see, but it's your failures and dis-appointments that shape you, and how you deal with those. The

*strength I have is not from having gold medals around my neck,
but from being out of the sport for two years.'*

England rugby captain Lawrence Dallaglio is a naturally confident
sportsman. On match day he becomes excited at the prospect of
showing what he can do, believing he's a great player. Although this
isn't quite so easy when nursing an injury, Dallaglio keeps himself
thinking positively.

*'In an ideal world you should be 100% fit and you shouldn't really
play if you are carrying an injury, but there are inevitably going to be
knocks and bumps. Say you haven't had the benefit of two or three
days' practice, but still get picked because it's felt you can perform.
That's when you lean back on the experience of previous successes,
where you haven't had an injury. You say: "I'm going to focus and
concentrate on doing certain things well, that I know I'm going to
do well." That helps to overcome the injury aspect.'*

Positive thinking also sees the pain that comes with supreme effort
as a positive and welcome thing. Professor Graham Jones has been
studying the differences between the top sporting performers in the
world – people who win medals in the Olympics – and international
athletes who might make it to the top ten in the Olympics. He has
found there are differences between even these groups. One concerns the reaction to pain. Professor Jones says that international
performers who are extremely good at what they do – but not the best
in the world – talk about pain and tolerating pain – coming through
it. In contrast, the world's best performers also talk about pain, but
they talk about loving it. They know the pain is going to happen and
when it does, it's fantastic. They think: 'This is what I live for, this
is what I train for, and it's great; it's here and I'm going to beat it.'
As Professor Jones says, the world's top performers live for these
moments; those who don't quite make it are the ones who, when they
feel the pain, realize they don't really want it.

Former 400m champion Roger Black agrees that training for the 400m was not fun. It never could be because you have to push yourself so hard. Those who do well at the distance have incredible ability to thrive on the pain.

> *'Most people will not try the 400m because it hurts. Certainly with the training, you know you will suffer. Lactic acid is created more in the 400m than any other event. Psychologically, to do something five or six times a week knowing that you can't walk at the end and it will take you two hours to recover and you are going to be sick – that frightens quite a few people off. You have to have a warped sense of perspective.'*

COURAGE TO FAIL

A champion's positive outlook also demonstrates itself in the form of courage – having the courage to fail. Sportspeople who think positively accept that whenever you aim high you risk falling short, but that doesn't stop them trying or inhibit their attempt.

Having the courage to fail is essential if anyone is to make it to the top in sport; every time a champion competes there are new rivals making a challenge. Like love and hate, success and failure are extremely close bedfellows. Ron Dennis of McLaren believes that having the courage to fail isn't only essential for sports stars and racing drivers; it's vital for anyone in any activity if they are really to get the most out of life.

> *'How often do you go through life avoiding decisions because you can't contemplate the potential of failure? Lots of people don't get married because of it. Lots of people carry lots of insecurities. It holds them back in their lives.'*

Former national athletics coach Frank Dick believes there are four fears that can seriously impede a sportsperson. These are fear of losing, fear of making a mistake, fear of rejection and fear of embarrassment. Fear of losing is like thinking about drowning when you should be thinking about swimming. Worrying about making mistakes means you don't take risks, and that means no progress. Fear of rejection, in terms of not being selected, again leads to playing safe, as does fear of embarrassment or being concerned about what other people think. Dick calls these 'fatal fears' because they take people back off the edge. Champions have to want to live on the edge; they have got to be comfortable being there.

Gill Clark didn't let fear of failure hold her back when as a teenager she decided not to go to university, as her three siblings had done, but to focus instead on her badminton. She accepted that she might not succeed in fulfilling her sporting aspirations, but she was willing to face that outcome if need be.

> *'Logic says to you, this is one heck of a risk. But I guess one of the differences between contenders and champions is that champions have the courage to fail. If you want to succeed you've got to have the courage to fail. For me it was saying, Okay, throw caution to the wind, I'm going for it, I'm going to try and be a full-time badminton player. I'm going to try and see how far I can go and explore my own personal boundaries.'*

In 1993 Roger Black's running career was looking extremely uncertain and he went to Australia in order, he says, 'to escape'. He was crippled by the fear of failure.

> *'My career seemed to be nearly over, and as a person I was all over the place. Everything was a struggle. I picked up a simple book and it had a graph in it showing need for achievement and fear of failure. I looked at it and thought, "That's me. I'm scared of failure."'*

Black's fear of failure was starting to limit his performances and he decided to address this fear. He thought about what was the worst that could happen. He thought about what 'failure' meant. He realized that there was no such thing.

'I could lose all my money. I could lose my house. But I can't fail, because there's no such thing as failure. If you're an athlete or whatever you do, the worst thing is to be afraid of failure.'

Black believes that you either have the ability to perform under pressure, or you don't. He suggests that Michael Jordan the basketball player lives for the moments when there are two seconds left in a game and he gets the ball. However, many players don't want that, because pressure is about the fear of failure. Black says he spent much of his career thinking about what would happen if he didn't succeed. He finally worked out that there was no such thing as failure, and when he knew that, he really had the ability to perform under pressure.

'When I went to the Olympic Games, I knew I couldn't fail, I knew I couldn't run a bad race. For me it was a pressure situation. There were 85,000 people in the stadium, millions of people back in Britain and a billion people round the world. It was pressure, but you don't think about those things.'

David Platt, former England football captain and England Under-21 coach, is convinced that what makes a great player is the fact that they have the mental ability to win. Some people, however, are simply frightened of winning. On an amateur level Platt plays golf with people who get into closing situations. But can they see that through? Too often they become too frightened to win and throw their advantage away.

Platt also believes that true champions have the courage to examine their own performances before allocating blame for poor results.

'A winner, because he's a leader, if his team loses, he will look at himself first and wonder whether he could have done anything else. If you haven't got that edge you may turn around and blame somebody else.'

A positive approach to life – the ability to consider experiences in a positive way – helps champions to keep going through the hard times they inevitably face when pursuing their dreams. This is the final personal characteristic we examine in Part I. In the next few pages, we draw together our key findings and suggests how we can all learn from these champions in our own lives.

Analysis I

PERSONALITY POWER

In Part I we focused on personality traits of proven sporting champions, looking for common threads and sources of inspiration that helped to make them successful over and over again when competing at the highest level.

CHAPTER 1

In Chapter 1: True Grit, we found that champions often show a natural sense of discipline, being able to train regularly and effectively, often from an early age.

They recognize that if they are to achieve their best possible performance in the heat of competition, then they have to make choices – sometimes tough choices – about how they spend their time. They can't live a 'normal' life like the rest of us, but must be prepared to train when others are asleep; or to put their social and personal lives second to their sporting activities.

Champions show great determination – what Ron Dennis, boss of the McLaren racing team, calls 'steely resolve'. The need for discipline and determination may mean that champions have to be selfish if they are to achieve their ambitions. They have to focus their time and energies on themselves.

Renzie Hanham from mental conditioning specialists Gazing Performance notes that elite performers have the ability to *accept* conditions of extreme discomfort, both physical and psychological, and to carry on functioning. Hanham explains that acceptance doesn't mean you have to like what's happening or that you agree or acquiesce. What it does mean is that you accept the present moment for what it is. This is important because when you accept, you cease resisting and thus free up your attention to seek solutions to the challenges you face.

Hanham notes that elite performers develop this ability over time by repeatedly putting themselves 'at risk' and developing coping mechanisms for dealing with high-pressure situations. In addition to their physical training and skills development, they undertake deliberate mental conditioning – training their minds to be able to remain focused on the processes they need to complete in order to be successful. In this way they develop the resilience they will need to win gold medals and claim world championships.

Repeated winners also have a strong 'killer instinct'. They won't feel sympathy for the opponent they are about to defeat; they won't quaver at the thought that they just need one more point to win Wimbledon. They seize their chances with relish. As far as javelin champion Steve Backley is concerned, he is a warrior doing battle and fighting for his life.

Not everyone has this killer instinct to the same degree. If you don't really mind whether you come in the top three or not, let alone come first, then you probably won't be a champion. The same goes in other areas of life too. If you don't mind whether you are an accounts clerk or a financial director, then you are more likely to remain as a clerk, because becoming a financial director requires years of training, hard work and pressure.

None of the personal characteristics we found in the champions we interviewed can compensate for a lack of physical talent and training. Similarly, there is no doubt that you can't expect to be a consistent winner in any area of life outside sport without having the fundamental talent and competence required for that activity. If you have the essential ability required for what you want to do, you then need to build up the skill levels required bit by bit. That also means that, unless you are uniquely gifted, you will need a high degree of determination and discipline to succeed. As the saying goes, Rome wasn't built in a day.

Applications

- Recall times in your life when you showed some discipline or determination. These may be in any area – completing a difficult school project, working late to prepare a presentation or training to complete a long-distance charity walk. Understand that you have the ability to display these characteristics when you are motivated to do so.
- What are you trying to achieve now? Confirm to yourself that you have the commitment required. If you have doubts, consider whether you are sufficiently motivated: do you really want to train for a new job?

CHAPTER 2

In Chapter 2: Family and Fate, we focused on the early influences on our sporting champions, looking to see whether they all had some key figure who fired their imaginations and sparked their ambitions.

All of us need some inspirational trigger if we are to be motivated in our lives. Those who are lucky will find sources of encouragement and support in their families. This is often the case in our childhood, when we are trying new things and attempting to learn new skills.

For many of our interviewees, mothers and fathers were important role models. Some displayed discipline in their own lives that their children sought to emulate. Some parents became highly involved in their talented child's sporting development, offering practical and emotional support during the years of early training.

Some parents inspired the burgeoning champions to set high goals and aim for the top level in their sport. They believed in their youngster's potential and encouraged its full realization. For some young champions, seeing the pleasure that their parents derived from sport gave them positive feelings about wanting to compete and be successful.

Note that, as Ceri Evans from Gazing Performance says, there does not appear to be one particular personality type that is most associated with becoming a sporting champion. Consistent top performers can have very different personalities. For example, some may be naturally shy, others extroverted. Whatever an individual's personality, one of the keys to success will be the ability to maintain focus on the processes required to achieve goals.

Parents aside, other family members can also play an inspirational part. Thus Ellen MacArthur's aunt sowed the first seed that inspired her niece to become a top international yachtswoman.

Individuals outside the family group can also have an inspirational impact on our lives. For the champions we interviewed, schoolteachers, coaches and even fellow soldiers provided sources of inspiration and encouragement.

Ceri Evans from mental conditioning specialists Gazing Performance notes there is evidence that when young children form secure attachments with their caregivers, there are likely to be positive flow on effects in terms of their psychological adjustment and how they relate to other people in later life. Even if a child grows up in a difficult environment, it is sometimes enough to have just one person providing a positive influence. It doesn't matter whether this is a grandmother or a schoolteacher, for example. What this means for later sports performance is hard to predict and is likely to be variable. For some individuals, a sense of stability and security in their early lives appears to have assisted in their capacity to deal with pressure situations. Alternatively, overcoming early adversity seems to have been significant for others in developing resilience. However, for others again, early instability and insecurity appear to undermine an ability to tolerate extreme pressure and to maintain concentration in stressful conditions.

Of course, we can't change our childhoods or our history, but we can change our perceptions. In fact, two people can perceive and react to the same situation in different ways.

Clearly chance influenced the path that some of the young champions followed, as when athlete Roger Black initially failed to get the grades he needed to be able to study medicine at university. However, the champions responded to the opportunities that presented themselves and went on to create their own success. When life takes an unexpected turn, champions and other successful people have the flexibility of outlook to be able to respond. Anyone who can do the same and seize an opportunity that arises can look forward to a rewarding life.

Applications

- Review the people who have inspired you in your life – whoever they may be and whenever you met them. Think about family members, friends, colleagues and chance acquaintances.
- Ask yourself what is it about these people that has inspired or impressed you. Are there lessons you can learn from them? Are there things these people do that you could do yourself and so achieve the same results?
- Get into the habit of trying to learn from other people, whoever they are. If you meet someone who is particularly effective in some action, think about why they are successful and see if you can emulate what they do.

CHAPTER 3

In Chapter 3: I Believe!, we focused on the depth and strength of the champions' self-belief. Time and again, champions demonstrate a virtually unshakeable self-belief in their abilities.

The key question is, can that degree of self-belief be developed or is it innate? For many of our champions, their self-belief developed over time as they began winning competitions. As they moved up through to the higher levels of their sports and kept on winning, that self-belief became stronger. It certainly didn't appear overnight. David Platt, former England football captain, only began to think 'I can do this' when he had scored goals repeatedly in international matches.

Ceri Evans from mental conditioning specialists Gazing Performance explains that, for sustained sporting success to occur, self-belief has to be underpinned by competence, which means that developing self-belief is an incremental process. Self-belief is likely to have stronger foundations if confidence is gained in tandem with competence. It is vulnerable unless those skills have been tested in situations of increasing pressure.

Some top champions describe the self-belief they have as a sense of 'knowing' they will do well. However, that belief often results from a period of consistent training and peak performances, when the individual is in top shape and injury free. It also comes from knowing that they have trained hard and are perfectly prepared. For Sally Gunnell, for example, self-belief came from knowing she had done all she could in the run-up to the competition, from training well to eating a healthy diet.

Champions don't limit themselves by limiting their beliefs or expectations. The self-fulfilling prophecy applies to sporting champions as it does to anyone else. They learn that how they perceive a competitor can influence their own performance. As sprinter John Regis found out, if you put someone on a pedestal, it becomes impossible to knock them off. If he allowed himself to be intimidated by the reputations of Frankie Fredericks, Michael Johnson and Linford Christie, he pushed himself into a losing position before a race even started.

The ability to bounce back is a trait that many of our champions display. When they are injured and prevented from training or competing, they still somehow hold onto the belief that they will come back and win again. Even if they have suffered an unexpected loss or a period of disappointing performances, they still have the ability to raise their game once more and become a winner again.

Applications

- Think back to times in your life when you felt confident about something you were doing or were about to do, and that went well. Try to identify why you were feeling confident. Had you prepared for it in some way? Had you done a similar activity before? Had someone advised you about or encouraged you in the activity?
- Think about something you want to do or will have to do in future, that you don't currently feel confident about. Can you apply anything from the exercise above to this activity? Is there anything you could do to prepare, that would develop your skills and so improve your self-confidence? Is there anyone with experience in this area who could advise you?
- Try to identify any areas of your life where the self-limiting prophecy applies. This could be at home, at work or in any area of your life. If you are a golfer, do you tell yourself you're no good at bunker shots and so always make a tough situation even harder when you find yourself in the sand? Make a promise to yourself that you will challenge these self-limiting beliefs wherever you spot them. Try asking yourself how you could improve your performance in the area, rather than just judging yourself poorly.

CHAPTER 4

The ability to focus on the positive aspects of an experience, rather than the negative ones, is a trait that many champions show, and one we considered in Chapter 4: Positive Power. Sven-Göran Eriksson considers whether a player has a positive outlook, as well as his football talent, when selecting members of the England squad.

Former 400m champion Roger Black displays this ability himself, by looking for the positive side of whatever happens to him. Being able to feel positive and avoid negative thoughts was important to hurdler Sally Gunnell when she was competing for her Olympic and world championship medals.

Developing this kind of outlook can be helped over time, by coaches encouraging young sportspeople to learn from their experiences – whether good or bad.

In fact, facing setbacks early in a sporting career can make the emerging champions stronger and tougher later on. If they have overcome a challenging situation before, or come back from injury in the past, that experience gives them added belief that they can do so again.

Top champions can even see pain in a positive light. They are able to tolerate pain and extreme discomfort, in training and in competition, because they see it as bringing them the sporting success they desire. The same approach can be applied in ordinary, non-sporting life. You may not be looking forward to completing a certain piece of work, but once you have done it and done it well, maybe you will be one step nearer promotion.

For some champions, their success results from not being afraid to fail. They accept that if they aim high, they increase the risk of failure, but that doesn't stop them from trying.

Clearly our sporting champions have high levels of skill and competence underpinning their positive outlooks. Renzie Hanham from mental conditioning specialists Gazing Performance notes the importance of positive thinking being supported by reality in the form of competence. He says that too often, in many areas of life, people mistake confidence for competence. If you just think you can do something but never initiate an action plan of how to develop the necessary skills, you will never be able to function optimally at the highest level.

Applying a positive outlook to life is a skill that can be developed. We can be moody, negative and depressed if we choose to be so, but by focusing on processes rather than our emotions we can learn to create positive outcomes from the situations and experiences we encounter.

However, it is not enough to simply tell someone to think positively. As Ceri Evans from Gazing Performance explains, if you do that, you may just add to the busy and conflicted dialogue going on in that person's head. It is usually more effective to encourage people to focus attention on the processes that lead to their desired outcomes, rather than the outcomes themselves. In other words, if you are feeling negative about a piece of work, trying to convince yourself that things will work out positively may be counter-productive. It is often more useful to return your focus of attention to what you need to do to complete the work effectively. Once you start focusing on these processes, emotional responses can move into the background and become less distracting.

Applications

- Try to get in the habit of thinking about the processes involved in the things you do, rather than your emotional responses to them. For example, rather than fuming about the fact that you have five more tasks to complete before you can go home for the weekend, focus on what you need to do to complete them quickly and effectively.
- What is it that you are feeling negative about? Look for anything positive that is associated with it. For example, if you are feeling negative about having to study for a professional exam, remind yourself that you are aiming to gain a qualification that will better your career in the long term.

Part II

MOTIVATIONAL MATTERS

Chapter 5

THE SUCCESS MAGNET

STRONG MOTIVATION IS AN ABSOLUTELY ESSENTIAL requirement for any sporting champion. The dedication required to train constantly, push the body to the limits and cope with competitive pressure can only be sustained where there are strong drivers to succeed.

Steve Sylvester, sports psychologist, says that world champions have an ability to sacrifice to the extreme, but where does that come from? Is it because it's a dream planted in them over the years? Or is it because there's a deep-seated need that they have to satisfy?

In both the sports psychology model developed by Ian Lynagh (see Appendix I) and the research of Professor Graham Jones (see Appendix II), motivation emerges as a key requirement. The champion sportspeople Professor Jones involved in his research determined that the fourth most important characteristic of mental toughness was: 'Having an insatiable desire and internalized motives to succeed'.

Former double Olympic 1500m champion Sebastian Coe has read widely on the topic of what it is that makes a champion sportsperson, but he has developed his own view of what really makes the difference between a champion's drive and the rest.

> *'Everybody is different; we're all motivated by very different things, for extrinsic reasons and intrinsic reasons. Some people want to be successful because they like the idea of having a big house and a Porsche on the drive; others want to do it to explore how hard and how mentally tough they are.*
>
> *'For most of us it's probably a mixture of all those things. If you ask me, the one continuum that runs through all those different models is just, actually, the bloody-minded self-determination to be better than the next person.'*

NEEDING TO WIN

For many champions, the need to be first – to win – exceeds everything else. Coming second just isn't good enough.

Former national athletics coach Frank Dick certainly believes that champions don't accept second best. He says that people like Daley Thompson are completely uncompromising. Anything short of first doesn't count. Dick and Linford Christie have had many fights, but Dick says he respects him completely for his sense of purpose and his attitude. Christie, he says, would leave no stone unturned in his quest for success. He would go for it all the way.

Former 400m medallist Roger Black has no doubt about champions' obsession with winning. For champions, whatever the sport, he believes that winning is essential. Whether it's Michael Jordan or Michael Johnson, Andre Agassi or Daley Thompson, they all have an absolute desire to be the best they can. That desire keeps them going in the bad times. Similarly, Black says, all champions set goals. They don't think about them, they write them down. They are proactive about them. Champions don't just *want* to win. Most people want to win, but the champions in the world of sport *need* to win – and they know why they need to win, which is different for different people. Black says:

> *'In the end they love the pressure. They absolutely welcome the pressure moments – that's what they live for. I was not a very good runner on the circuit – I could count on one hand the number of Grand Prix meetings I won throughout my whole career. I only lived for the championships because when you go to a championship you've got four races in four days or five days; you've got pressure every day and I loved all that. The champions in sport want the pressure. They want the pressure to come because they know most people will fall by the wayside and they embrace it.'*

In Black's opinion, champions not only need to win, they need to win when it really counts – at Olympic Games rather than ordinary Grand Prix races.

Similarly, 1500m champion Sebastian Coe relished the big occasions. He learnt early on that what mattered was winning major titles, and that was what he set his heart on. Coe says he loved running and he enjoyed training, but the real thing that excited him was competing in major championships. He says he always knew the difference between going into a year where there were big races but no major championships, and going into a year where he knew that in August he was going to defend an Olympic title or hope to win a European title. Coe says:

> *'When I was 18 I was racing up at Gateshead. The night before one of the races I had supper with Brendan Foster, who was a big influence on me. Brendan always said to me that at the end of your career, if you put your cards down on the table to declare, people would ask what medals you had won. They wouldn't ask whether you had won Zurich in 1978. It would be, how many Olympic titles did you win? How many world records did you break? Brendan made me realize that major championships were important and*

the other races, as important as they were, were only building
blocks along the way. They weren't the be-all and end-all.'

When choosing between world records and championships, Coe
sees the championships as more important.

'There are more variables in a championship than in a world
record. With an attempted world record you have so much more
under your control. You can pick the race that you want to do it in,
you can pick the time of year you want to do it in, you can even pick
the way the meeting is structured. If you know you are in a stadium
where you know the wind drops at 8.30 or 9 o'clock at night, you
want your race on the programme at the end of the evening, not the
beginning. You cannot do those things in a major championship.
You don't have control over the timing of the race, or the field or
the way the race is run. You can't stick pacemakers in. So winning
a major championship is a much tougher process. You have to go
through rounds. When I won in 1984 I had seven races in nine
days. A world record is just a one-off. I'm not downgrading world
records – I was pretty pleased when they came along. But it's not
the same as going through the mental and physical bruising of an
Olympic campaign.'

For round-the-world yachtswoman Ellen MacArthur, winning is
key when she's sailing competitively. That doesn't mean it's the only
thing she thinks about when she's out at sea, because the lengths
of races vary so much. Sometimes just completing the race is an
achievement. As she says, in a round-the-world race it's a miracle
just to get round without stopping. What makes sailing in a race so
hard is that you are pushing so hard. Then MacArthur says, there's
never a second of any day when you're not thinking about whether
you're sailing the boat to its full potential.

When MacArthur was preparing to compete in *Kingfisher* in the
Vendée Globe, her goals were high.

'My objective was to get across that line first. I knew in reality that some of the other guys had a lot more experience and stood a good chance of winning the race. There were several boats that I believed at the start could have won the Vendée Globe. But your objective is to do well and never give up. If you think, "Oh well, I'm just going to finish third anyway," you may as well stop. You'd probably end up being fifth or sixth. You have to keep driving; it's not over until you get to that finish line.'

England 1966 World Cup footballer Jack Charlton admits that he was never a particularly good player – but he had a winning attitude.

'I had a good head into the ball, and I was pretty hard to run away from. I was never quick off the mark, but I had a little mean streak in me – and that's the need to win. You want to win. You've got to have that need to win.'

Former England football captain David Platt always had a strong desire to win, even from an early age. He has a brother, four years older, who he used to hang out with as a boy. Though David had more talent, his older brother was inevitably stronger and so would always win in physical games. David was annoyed by losing – he liked to win. As he says: 'Losing doesn't exist for me.'

When Platt moved into football management he still got a buzz from match days. However, he still finds that nothing beats the excitement of being a player – particularly the high that comes from winning a match.

'I miss the adrenalin surge week in, week out. I miss that knot in your stomach when you go out and you don't know which way it's going to go. It's not nerves, it's just the tension, the excitement. Then there's the low you get when it's not gone right, when you haven't scored a goal, when you haven't performed well.

'There's the low and the high – it's extreme.'

England rugby captain Lawrence Dallaglio was highly motivated to do well in sport – and beat the opposition – from his childhood.

> *'I always went out on a sports field believing that I was the best player on the pitch, regardless of my position. I wanted to come off knowing that everyone else on the pitch respected me as a player. Whenever I go out to perform I want to leave people with an impression. Rugby is a game where you can talk about 31 people, including the referee, and you want to be the one player people are happy with.*
>
> *'You have to respect your opposition, no matter who they are, but you only take that to a certain level. You have to have the desire to want to beat them one on one; because if everyone does that, then you are going to win.'*

EARLY TASTE OF SUCCESS

Adrian Moorhouse, Olympic swimming champion, found that his ability in the pool gave him an early liking for the sweet taste of success. Doing well at sport became linked with his sense of self-esteem. Winning felt good.

Moorhouse describes himself as having been quite a small, shy child. However, he was a good swimmer, competing in local competitions as a member of Bradford Swimming Club, and success in the pool was important for his sense of self-esteem.

> *'When I was 12, in 1976, David Wilkie won the Olympics. As a kid I didn't have much going for me. I didn't have many mates. I was pretty small and very shy, so I latched onto something that made me feel good about myself. I was the sort of kid who would run back from school down the road imagining I was a great athlete, winning the Olympics. I was always imagining myself being good and being applauded. A lot of it is to do with self-esteem.'*

Moorhouse vividly remembers winning his first swimming medal, and it's a moment he still treasures.

'I still have the little medal. I keep it in the same box as my Olympic gold medal. I won this first gold when I was nine, for the nine-and-under backstroke in the Airdale Championships at Harrogate. I remember the pool and everything about it. My arms were going round like windmills to get there first and I hit my hand on the end of the pool. I remember walking back down the side – it was only one length – to collect my tracksuit. I remember feeling really proud – inflated with pride – and looking at my mum and dad. It was a big night.'

OVERWHELMING EMOTIONS

The winning feeling can take many forms – elation, disbelief and even relief.

Former national athletics coach Frank Dick recalls watching Martin Johnson walk up for the presentation after winning the second British Lions test in South Africa. Johnson had become only the second man to lead the Lions to a series win in South Africa, and he was clearly moved by the achievement. Dick says:

'They'd won the test series with a team of players that nobody believed could do it. Johnson pulled his hat right down over his eyes so you couldn't see he was crying. But there's nothing wrong with that. It was a genuine response to the situation, nothing contrived.

'You've got to want it, you've got to want it enough. There's got to be a need. You've got to believe you can do it. You've got to persist until you get there.'

Dick also recalls Daley Thompson whistling along to the national anthem while standing on the podium after winning his Olympic gold medal for the decathlon in 1984.

'People were saying he was being disrespectful, but nothing's further from the truth. It was the relief, the enjoyment – "This is what I came here for – I've got the gold medal in front of the Americans."

*It was just him. The real achievers, the champions, the gold medal-
lists, the record breakers will be nothing short of 100% who they
are.'*

Adrian Moorhouse recalls what it felt like to win swimming gold at
the Seoul Olympics in 1988 – a feeling that brought him to tears.

*'In a close race over 100m you've got to look at the scoreboard
to see where you finished. You look for your name – Moorhouse
– and then you look at the numbers at the end – your time and your
position. I remember looking at my time and seeing that I was only
one hundredth of a second ahead of the second guy. I knew it was
close. I was thinking, "Shit, that was close, but I've won it."*

*'I remember being elated and hypersensitive to everything. In
Seoul you had to go from the pool along an underground corridor
to a room where you brushed your hair and put your tracksuit
on. I'm soaking wet, with my goggles in my hand, and everybody
else around me is dressed. Everyone's running around. There are
people going for the next race, and people from the previous race
walking with medals. You're walking with about 20 people around
you, herding you down this corridor and you're soaking wet. You're
not shivering, but you're tingling. You've won the Olympics and
you're tingling. It was such a sensation. All these people were pushing against me, shouting at me. I saw my coach and he runs over
to congratulate me briefly. Then they pushed me in this room and
it goes really silent. The door opens and they push the guys who
came second and third in; the three of us are sitting in this room
without a tracksuit, looking at each other. There's the Hungar-
ian, the Russian and me and the other two don't speak English.
I thought, "Alright then. That's it." You put your tracksuit on but
you're sweating so much it's hard to get it on. And because it's a
quiet moment, the realization starts to sink in.*

*'They opened the door and asked if we were ready for the medal
presentation. There was the fanfare and I burst into tears, just
when I walked through the door. I thought, "Shit, I can't cry all the
way round." But I did pretty much cry all the way to the podium.*

When I got on the podium I stopped myself. And that was it. I don't really remember the rest.'

Former badminton champion Gill Clark found winning a fantastic feeling. The sheer joy she has experienced through her sport, and all the emotions that have come from it, have surpassed anything else on a happy level. The highs of winning are higher, but the lows are nowhere near as low, she says. The disappointment that comes from failing to achieve a desired result in a major championship is nothing in comparison to the hurt that people can feel in their private lives – for example, the pain she felt when her father became ill.

Throughout the sporting highs and lows, Clark simply loved her badminton.

'I won the Under-14 nationals in badminton and at Under-16 I was triple national champion in singles, doubles and mixed. At the Under-18 stage, there was a girl from Guernsey who I'd beaten at Under-14 and Under-16, and by the time we came to Under-18 she was beating me. But we had won the European Junior Ladies Doubles Championships together, so I must have realized that I had talent. But it never occurred to me that I was somehow very gifted. I just thought badminton was so much fun. It was just what I loved doing.'

When Clark became an international player and began to realize her talent, winning was a personal affair. She was proud to represent her nation, but that wasn't her main motivation for doing well.

'I was hugely honoured to play for my country. When you are at the Commonwealth Games and competing for England, or in the Olympics for Great Britain, that gives you an extra pride. But you don't go out and perform for your country – you go out and perform for you, solely for you.'

Former Davis Cup tennis captain, David Lloyd, loved winning. He says:

'It meant a lot. If you're going to be successful in life, winning is your food. Winning is your payment. I played Davis Cup for nine or ten years. I didn't lose at home. You can't take that away. And we beat guys who were Wimbledon champions.'

For champion hurdler Sally Gunnell, the realization that she had won Olympic gold in Barcelona took a while to sink in. Those first moments after winning were moments of disbelief rather than exhilaration.

'I had gone through this race so much in my mind that I felt I could well have been lying on a bed visualizing it. So I didn't know whether this was actually the real race. I was thinking, "Is this for real?" It feels like you're in a cocoon. It's like it's all in slow motion. Then you start to realize what's happened.

'One of my friends came running onto the track and you start jogging around. I did my lap of honour and started spotting people in the crowd. I saw Linford Christie up there shouting his head off at me. I remember hearing my dad's voice in the crowd and seeing his face – amidst all the thousands of people there. That's when I first thought this was going to make a big difference to my life. Then I saw my husband Jon and it started to sink in. But it was still so weird and I had a sense of disbelief that I'd done it.'

The feeling of achievement, once there, was powerful. Gunnell says:

'You are just floating. You are on a cloud. I've never taken drugs, but you just don't feel as though you're there. I used to say I wanted to find a little box and be able to put it all inside and just go away. Then six months later I'd open it up and see it all again. I just couldn't take it all in at the time.'

In the aftermath of winning her Olympic gold, Gunnell found herself wondering, 'Why me?'

'I felt I was such a normal sort of person, a good old Essex girl brought up on a farm. I wondered why I was so lucky. It took a few weeks for me to say, "Why not me? I train hard." I had the natural talent and the dedication and the motivation. I was prepared to work hard.

'When I saw the effect at home, on family, I really started to realize what I'd achieved. People told me about where they were on that night when I won the gold in Barcelona, how they were reduced to tears. It made me want to go out over the next few years and create that feeling for people again.'

Former European 200m champion sprinter John Regis just wanted to be the best in the world. Making it to a final and knowing he was among the top eight in the world wasn't enough. He didn't want to be top eight; he wanted to be the top person in the world.

In 1990 Regis won a bronze in the 100m in the European Championships in Split in a time of 10.07 seconds – 0.07 seconds behind gold medallist Linford Christie – even though that wasn't his ideal distance. As a 200m runner, the 100m was just too short. Regis was looking for gold in the 200m.

'There was pressure, because everybody said, "You're a winner". I didn't want to listen to that, because then you get complacent. If I got second I had failed. Second is a good medal, but it would be failure. There was also a bit of needle between me and Linford – the sprinter (Linford) against the endurance runner (me), power against speed – all the clichés.'

Regis handled the pressure and came through to take gold in a time of 20.11 seconds.

'When I won I thought, "Yeah, this is why I train hard, this is why it's all worthwhile." Athletics is hard. In winter it's cold and nasty. You vomit for three and a half months of the year. Your legs are full of lactic acid. But I'll take twenty minutes of pain a day in return for standing on that rostrum. No problem at all.

'It's like having a dream, going to heaven and waking up and you're sitting on top of the world. You go to the rostrum and the announcer is saying, "In first place, John Regis". You stand up there and look at the crowd cheering. You think "Wow!" All the work I had done, all the pain I had gone through flashed through my mind in the blink of an eye. It's like climbing Everest. Everyone is congratulating you.

'But the funny thing is that the drug lasted for ten minutes. Then I was thinking about the next championship. I never used to dwell on it. It's a great feeling but it's like adrenalin. Adrenalin lasts for a certain period and then it's gone.

'I loved winning. I got the medal, felt the acclaim of the crowd and then had the national anthem. Lovely. But then I'd be thinking about getting ready for the world championship next year. That's how my mind worked. I've climbed this mountain. Great. Now I've got to get ready for the next mountain because it's going to be at least as tough.'

Champion National Hunt jockey Richard Dunwoody managed to win the Grand National twice, first with West Tip in 1986. He tried to savour the feeling second time round when he won in 1994.

'For my second Grand National win I rode Freddie Starr's horse, Miinnehoma. I didn't expect to get round. It rained very heavily and we knew that probably only five or six horses would complete the course. I'd only ridden Miinnehoma once before in a race and schooled him once at home. He wasn't big. I thought he'd end up on the floor and I was quite expecting to be getting an ambulance rather than having Martin Pipe, the trainer, run up to me at the end of the race. So that was by far the most memorable race. The first time you win the National it's a complete blur – you don't come down out of cloud nine for three or four days afterwards. With the second win, I spent a lot of time taking it in and actually enjoying the success.'

When Dunwoody began to experience success, he just wanted more. He was driven to win.

> 'Success brings success. Success drove you on to more success. You got on that wagon and you just couldn't get off it. It became totally all consuming. There were about three seasons where I finished second in the championship. The one aim then was to become champion jockey.'

BEATING YOURSELF

For some top sportspeople, the motivation isn't just to beat others but also to amaze themselves by their own achievements.

England rugby fly-half Jonny Wilkinson derives immense satisfaction from kicking a goal that wins the game or provides enough of a buffer to really put pressure on the opposition. He says he sometimes amazes himself when he pulls off a difficult kick.

> 'For me personally it comes down to constantly trying to impress myself. I may be kicking the ball from right out on the touchline and there's a breeze across the posts. The margin for error is very small. I have to aim exactly just inside the left-hand post, because the wind should push it across slightly so that it goes through the middle.
>
> 'You do all your preparation and hit the ball. Everything feels right and you look up and see that it's exactly just inside the left-hand post. The wind does move it that little bit and it does go through the middle. Most of the time you find yourself thinking, "Crikey" rather than "That's just what I do". You need a balance of setting high standards and trying to achieve them, and then also being able to pat yourself on the back when there was a real need to get it perfect and you got it right.'

Wilkinson has had many occasions where he delivered the goods when needed.

'When I was around 19 in 1999, we had about three games before Christmas where I had a kick in the last three minutes that won the game. Although you say you shut everything out, you shut out all the noise, you never can. You can never forget that you are being watched by so many people, that you are on TV. You never forget that if you miss the kick your team can lose. You never forget that, but you accept it rather than let it bother you.'

One kick that provided Wilkinson with huge satisfaction didn't actually determine who won or lost the match. He recalls:

'The first time I played against Australia at Twickenham Dan Luger scored a try literally on the final whistle. We had a big wait to see if the referee gave it or not, but he did, so that meant we had won the game. So I then had the last kick of the game. It was right on the touchline. I knew we had won, but from a personal standpoint I was absolutely desperate to kick this goal, because I had been under a huge amount of pressure that week and in the months leading up to this game. I felt things had worked out all right, but I still had the opportunity to make things perfect. I wanted to make that kick almost more than if we needed it to win the game. It mattered because there was a chance for me to enjoy it more, because the pressure was off. The crowd was in great spirits and singing away because we had gone into the lead in the last minutes.

'For once I decided not to think about the kick in a mechanical way. I said to myself, "Look at all the work you have done. I really want this one for me. It doesn't matter for the team, it matters for me."

'That kick went straight over. I hit it, looked up and it went straight between the posts. It was a really great feeling. I rewarded myself, rather than seeing it as doing something for the team. This one was for me.'

A year later, Wilkinson found himself in a similar situation.

'Dan Luger scored again on the final whistle and put us 29–9 ahead. I had the same scenario kick from wide out on the touch-

line. I asked myself to do it for me again. This time I hit the post and missed. That one I regret. It was going over and then the wind caught it and pushed it onto the posts. I was absolutely distraught by that. The pressure was off, the game was over, and you think you've an opportunity to enjoy this kick without worrying about the outcome. That missed kick really took the shine off the day for me.'

When middle distance runner Sebastian Coe felt there was nothing more he could try in his search for improvement, he realized the time to retire was approaching. He used to live by the Thames in Twickenham and would run along the towpath in the mornings.

'I was running on a November morning and I suddenly came to the conclusion that I would never probably be able to run any quicker. At the start of every season, which is roughly October or November, I was always able to sit back and think that I could probably lift a few more weights or do something different in the gym, or I could do more speed work or perhaps more mileage or less mileage. There was always something I could picture myself doing differently. But that morning – for the first time in my career – I thought there was nothing I hadn't already tried. I knew I could probably run pretty quick for two or three years, but the realization that I wouldn't really improve on any of my times gave me the clearest signs of the door closing on my athletics career.'

Coe's motivation rings true to round-the-world yachtswoman Ellen MacArthur, who is also motivated by the desire to keep challenging herself. She set herself tough challenges from an early age. She believes one of her greatest challenges was to sail a 20-foot boat single-handed round the coast of Great Britain when she was 18.

'That still fills me with amazement. You could say it was the toughest race ever to date, but every race you do pushes you to your limits and that's how you learn. When I sailed round Britain in a little 20-footer, I was pushing myself to my absolute limits to make it. It

was a tiny boat and a really hard trip to do. It took me four and a half months.

*　'Then the next thing I did was a single-handed transatlantic race. Alright, I sailed twice across the Atlantic in bigger boats first as a test, but then I crossed the Atlantic on my own in a race and that again was a massive test. It was the hardest thing I'd ever done.'*

After that, completing the Vendée Globe became the next hardest challenge for MacArthur.

'I pushed myself further in the Vendée than in any race before, but I know that in future I'm going to take myself to those same limits. Life's about pushing yourself further and learning and that's what I intend to do.'

Ron Roddan, who worked with Linford Christie throughout his competitive career and who has coached many athletes over the years, certainly believes that champions are always striving for improvement.

'After any major race, athletes would come back and ask, "What did you think?" Well, you should never have a perfect race. If you have a perfect race, where do you go? You may as well finish. For a champion, perfection is always around the next corner. You are never satisfied.'

Similarly, former England football Under-21 manager David Platt believes really great players are always striving to be better than they are. He says:

'When Michael Owen was earning £10,000 a week he didn't want £20,000 a week – he wanted to be a better player. I don't know what Michael is earning now, but whatever it is, he doesn't want more money – he wants to be a better player. And if he gets more money his edge doesn't go down, his performance level doesn't go down. Michael just wants to do better.'

Platt recalls Owen's determination to be the best when he was at the School of Excellence as an early teenager.

'There was a speed test. You set off and ran through to the other end, turned round and came back. It was a speed and power test, because you had to turn. We sat them all down afterwards and told them their times. Michael wasn't the fastest, but he said there was no way he hadn't got the quickest time in. He made us let him do it again. He just wouldn't accept that he wasn't fastest. He's unbelievable. That's being a winner.'

Platt himself, when a player, always wanted to keep improving. When he reached an age where he felt he could no longer do so, he retired – just before his thirty-second birthday. At the time he was playing for Arsenal, but didn't have a regular place in the team.

'If everybody was fit I wouldn't play. But Arsene Wenger didn't want me to play in the reserves in case I got injured and he might need me for the next game. When that happens your fitness starts to leave you. I had always been somebody who wanted to improve, but with my age and the condition of my knee going against me, I couldn't see myself improving. I thought I had to set myself a new goal, which was to go into management – because I knew I could improve in that. I could have played for another twelve months or maybe two years, but I would have been on a downward spiral. I wouldn't have had a goal to aim for, which is what gives me my drive and desire.'

For Dr Stephanie Cook, feeling she had done everything she could in a competition and performed at her best was almost more important than winning. This was where her drive to keep training and competing came from.

'For me, it's never been so much about winning; it's much more about my own personal performance and achieving my potential – being the best that I could be on the day. I've always tried in compe-

*titions to put 100% into everything I've done. As long as I had done
that and felt there was nothing more I could do, I'd be happy with
whatever the outcome was, be it winning or not. There were times
when you might do well but not really feel you deserved it, because
you weren't happy with certain aspects of your performance.*

*'The great thing about pentathlon is that it involves such a diverse
range of disciplines that over the course of a day of competition you
might have one event that didn't go so well, and others that exceeded
expectations. There are always positive things to draw out of a
competition. You learn from the mistakes that you made. But it's
incredibly difficult to get five events all going perfectly on the same
day. That's why pentathlon really is the ultimate challenge. That's
what attracted me to it; that's why I got such a buzz out of doing it.
There's always something you can be working on and improving.'*

In the Sydney Olympics, even though she won the gold medal, Cook
didn't feel she had performed at her peak. It was in the following
year, in 2001, when she won the European and World Championships that she really felt she had delivered.

*'My performance in Sydney was far from perfect from my point
of view; I felt in Sydney I hadn't really achieved my potential in
the sport. It took an extra season for all the hard work I had done
in training to come to fulfilment. I was also having to deal with
various injuries. So in some ways my performance in the World
Championship was more satisfying than my performance in
Sydney. Obviously Sydney was the pinnacle, in that winning the
modern pentathlon World Championships doesn't get the same
recognition as winning a gold medal at the Olympic Games. But
from a personal fulfilment point of view, I was much happier with
my performance in the World Championships.'*

The need to win, and the thrill that comes from achieving goals, is
clearly a powerful motivator for many top sportspeople. In the next
chapter we consider how the desire not to fail also drives many champions forward.

Chapter 6

FLEEING FAILURE

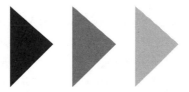

THE FACTORS THAT MOTIVATE PEOPLE – whether sportspeople or anyone else – can usually be divided into two camps. Firstly, there are motivating factors that attract people – the thrill of winning, the elation that can come with achievement, as considered in the previous chapter.

On the other hand, there are also powerful 'away from' motivators. Some people may hate to lose so badly that they push themselves harder than anyone else. Some people are frightened of letting other people down, a fear that drives them to even greater efforts to win.

HATING TO LOSE

Ron Dennis, boss of the McLaren racing team, doesn't just 'need' to win. He hates the pain of failure.

'The gratification of success is easily matched by the pain of failure. Whilst you would initially think that the biggest driver is the search for the rush of success, it doesn't drive you as much as the pain of failure. I feel psychological pain in failure, and it's a great motivator.'

That said, for Dennis it's important to feel you have won well. He says the worst feeling for him, even if he is winning, is to think that he didn't give something his best shot. In contrast he can get satisfaction from coming second if he knows he gave it everything. The frustration of not winning is there, but it is softened by the sense that there was nothing more that could have been done.

England rugby head coach Clive Woodward believes that fear of losing helps to motivate the England team.

'The biggest thing, especially with the Six Nations, is that you've got to create a fear factor – a respect factor. In some games it's not difficult; if we are playing a team we can clearly lose to, the fear factor is there. The difficult games are against teams we know we can lose to, but we know we really should beat – so you've got to create this fear factor. This England team certainly plays far better when there's this real fear factor. That's why we tend to play better against the bigger teams – we tend to play better when there's something at stake. We knew that if we wanted to do something special in the World Cup, we would have to beat these big teams week in, week out. You've got to be meticulous in the detail and the easier the opposition, the more meticulous you've got to be.'

Champion 400m runner Roger Black isn't clear where his motivation to succeed in athletics came from, but he feels he was driven strongly by the desire to move away from the pain of failure. That had a greater motivating force on him than the pleasure of success.

'If you work on the pain and pleasure principle, you have to go away from pain or towards pleasure. The great pain to me in life is to look back and know that I didn't do something properly – what-

ever it is. For me it's about being able to say I did as well as I wanted to, or as well as I could.'

Round-the-world yachtswoman Ellen MacArthur's sense of all the people who have worked behind the scenes to get her racing across the ocean helps her to give her all when the going gets really tough. For example, when competing in the Vendeé Globe she had to climb up a mast to make emergency repairs.

'With a project like the Vendeé I'm not just doing it for me. A huge amount of energy and commitment goes into preparing for a race like that. There are so many people who prepared the boat and then who are working every day, communicating with you. There's all that energy behind you and it's not up to you to give in. You're damn well going to hang on in there and not let anyone down. Probably fear of failure is one of the biggest motivators – not wanting to let people down.'

England rugby fly-half Jonny Wilkinson hates the feeling of making a mistake. He believes he is in control of his performance, and when things go wrong, he accepts responsibility.

'In every aspect of the game, whether it be tackling, or running with the ball and passing, whether it be kicking the ball off, everything is under my control to a certain extent. Of course you could kick the ball and the wind changes direction and ruins it. I am learning to have the composure to step back and accept that's not my fault, so I won't beat myself up about it. But when I do get things wrong, mostly often it is my fault and that doesn't tend to make me feel good about myself. I will do my best to not let that happen again.'

PROVING OTHERS WRONG

A different form of 'away from' motivator is the desire not to give others the satisfaction of being right when they have told you that you can't do something. For some champions, this desire to prove others wrong has provided a major spur to achievement.

Olympic hurdle gold medallist Sally Gunnell recalls how many people said she would never win because she was not 'hard enough'. Comments like that spurred her on to try harder. Gunnell recalls one such spur.

> *'There was a guy at the top of athletics organizing Grand Prix and so on. He actually said to me that I would never make it, because I was the wrong colour, the wrong size. He said I wasn't in the glory events – I wasn't a sprinter. He stood there as a 45-year-old man telling me, a 17-year-old, that I may as well forget it, that I would never be good enough. He wouldn't give me the break that I wanted – he wouldn't give me the races that I wanted to try and progress.*
>
> *'Part of me thought that maybe he was right and I should try and find another career and give up on athletics. But luckily, deep down I thought, "No. So what if I'm not black and I'm not six foot tall and I haven't got the longest legs in the business?" I decided I was going to prove him wrong. It was one of the first setbacks that really made me think, "Yes, I can do this." This was the first time I started setting myself goals, including that dream goal of being Olympic champion.'*

Like Gunnell, middle distance runner Sebastian Coe recalls being told that he didn't have what it would take to excel at his chosen sport. He also proved his detractors wrong. Coe says:

> *'I was told when I was 18 that I was too small, not tall enough, to be a good 800m runner. I rather enjoyed proving them wrong there. I was also told I would never make a 1500m runner and I rather enjoyed proving them wrong too.'*

Former badminton Gill Clark was also motivated to succeed when injury threatened her sporting future. She won her second European Championship just six months after completely rupturing the cruciate ligament in her left knee. The orthopaedic surgeon who treated her told her mother he didn't think Clark would ever play international badminton again. Nevertheless, six months later, Clark and her doubles partner, Karen Chapman, won the European Championship final. She recalls the sense of elation, the pure euphoria she felt having proved the medics wrong. Clark says nobody was going to tell her when she had to quit.

Former Davis Cup tennis captain David Lloyd, now a successful businessman, still enjoys proving others wrong.

'I've had more success in business in sport, and I think one of the reasons I get a real kick out of it is because I was told so many times that I was a dumb idiot: "You're a tennis player – you can't do it". A lot of people do things because other people say they can't. I'm sure Steve Redgrave won another gold medal because people said it was impossible to do. Anything that's impossible is worth going for. When people say "you can't", I think, "Right, I'm going to do it".'

THE RELIEF OF SUCCESS

The fact that champions are driven by not wanting to experience the pain of failure is indicated by the sense of relief many feel when they succeed. For them the winning sensation isn't all euphoria and high emotions.

For javelin champion Steve Backley, winning becomes a matter of survival. When he is competing, he sees it as if he is fighting for his life. But that kind of pressure means that winning doesn't tend to result in a sense of elation. In part, if he and other people have expected him to win, he feels a sense of relief. He also feels a huge sense of achievement and satisfaction – real contentment.

'It's satisfaction for all the work you have put in for the 12 months before, all the focus, and the last minute calls you have made. It's not an outward euphoria, but very much a quiet, content feeling. It's much stronger and deeper than feelings generated outside sport, because it comes after such a big time span and such a high

level of commitment. When it's a matter of survival, which it has to be to create the kind of motivation that's needed, the result is a quiet contentment and satisfaction with everything.'

Michael Lynagh, former Australian rugby captain and renowned fly-half, had a strong competitive streak regardless of what sport he was playing. His desire to achieve and do as well as he could was very strong. At one stage he couldn't play any sport, whether golf, tennis or anything else, without treating it extremely competitively – to an extent that was almost embarrassing. He has mellowed with time, however. He says he can now play sport and be pretty relaxed about it. He realizes that the result doesn't really matter and so he can just go out and enjoy it a bit more. That sense of perspective developed towards the end of his career in rugby. He began to see sports other than rugby as providing a form of stress release.

Winning didn't necessarily deliver a great buzz, however. Lynagh's greatest win was perhaps the World Cup in 1991 at Twickenham.

'I knew it was a huge occasion, but I can't remember much of the game. You go into a daze where you are just doing what you do. When we won, I felt triumph, satisfaction and relief. Fantastic though it was, my overwhelming feeling was a sense of relief that the opportunity had come and I had taken it. I find it difficult to get too excited about it. I guess I would get more emotional about it if we had lost.'

Lynagh also found it difficult to talk about his successes.

'I thought modesty was very important. Accept what you have got, and be thankful for it. If you are successful at things – that's very nice, thank you, but I don't want to talk about it.'

Professor Graham Jones has confirmed through his research that achieving major success doesn't always generate as euphoric a feeling as might be expected. For one thing, there is often a substantial amount of relief mixed in with the euphoria. That can come from the realization that other people have high expectations of your performance. Professor Jones gives the example of Steve Redgrave when gearing up for the Sydney Olympics. Everyone expected him to do well and would have been disappointed if he hadn't. Winning in such circumstances must inevitably be associated with feelings of relief as much as jubilation.

Secondly, some people feel a sense of anticlimax, because of the extent of all the build-up and preparation beforehand. When they achieve their goal they sometimes expect to feel more than they do, particularly if the achievement is one that the individual has been striving towards over a long period of time. Finally, given the packed sporting timetables that many champions face, they may not have much time to celebrate their successes before gearing up for the next competition. That means they simply have to control their euphoria and quickly get back to the business of training and preparation.

Winning – whether it brings euphoria or relief – always marks the achievement of a sporting goal. We look at the importance of goals and goal-setting for champions in the next chapter.

Chapter 7

GOALS GALORE

EVERY CHAMPION ATHLETE, FOOTBALLER AND SWIMMER – every top sportsperson – sets goals. Without goals, no one fulfils a dream to be the best, to win Olympic gold or to set a new world record.

Champion 400m runner Roger Black believes that it is absolutely essential for champions to set goals. He says that if you set a goal, then your subconscious will attract things that will support that goal. If you don't set a goal, you'll drift. Black has no doubt about this. He also points out that goal-setting is an important activity, because if you make your goals too hard, you'll destroy yourself; if you make them too easy you're going to underperform.

Sir Chay Blyth has always been goal-oriented and derives huge satisfaction from fulfilling his goals.

'With any project I take a blank sheet of paper and I write down the aim of the exercise – the goal – and take it from there. It's very fulfilling when you've written down an aim, planned everything and then you bring it to a successful conclusion. It's tremendous. I use the same process for business that I used for my sailing adventures. I set down the goals, I set down all the relevant factors involved and carry on from there.'

Olympic hurdle gold medallist Sally Gunnell also believes that goal-setting is invaluable, as long as the targets are reasonable.

'Even from a young age it's great to set your goals. But it's important to have your dream goal and realistic ones. Too many athletes have a dream goal and haven't worked out how they are going to get there. Then they just get disappointment after disappointment and never build up confidence.

'You need realistic goals that are achievable – whether it's getting into the club team or jumping a certain distance. Make them achievable.'

Goals also need to be fired with passion, linked to the individual's emotions to inspire them. Sports psychologist Ian Lynagh says that goals provide direction, while desire gives energy and passion. If coaches can help athletes develop an emotional attachment to their goals, then they are energizing and empowering the athlete to achieve them. He says a goal that is just cerebral, without any energy or emotional empowerment, is usually not achieved. It is, however, if someone feels strongly about it.

Effective goal-setting requires real commitment, which can be demonstrated by writing the goals down – committing them to paper. Former Davis Cup captain David Lloyd did this in his competitive playing days.

'I would write my goals down. If I had Wimbledon coming up a goal might be to get to the last 16, and I would write down what I wanted to do. Next year I want to be number 7, then the year after

something else. I had achievement goals and improvement goals – such as to work on my backhand.'

Roger Black didn't fully admit to himself the importance he attached to winning an Olympic medal until late on in his competitive career. At the start of 1996, the year of the Atlanta Olympics, Black was already a successful athlete, with Commonwealth and European gold medals to his name for the 400m. His only Olympic medal though was a bronze in the 4×400m relay in the 1992 games in Barcelona. If 1996 was to be his year, he realized it was time for another change of gear in terms of his approach to his running.

'I became the chief executive of Roger Black Ltd and ultimately took responsibility for my performance. When you do that, things fall into place. When you're clear about your goals … All it was really was the growing up process. It was standing up, not being complacent, and actually admitting for the first time in your life that what you do matters. All I do is run around the track. No, it's far more than that.'

GOAL TYPES

The goals that athletes use aren't simply related to winning a title. There are different types of goal that all play an important part in the competitive athlete's training.

As Professor Graham Jones explains, there are three types of goals that sports psychologists talk about and sportsmen and women typically use. Firstly, there is the outcome goal – the aim being simply to win. That, however, is dependent on how people perform, so they also need to have performance goals, such as swimming the race in 60 seconds. Thirdly there are process goals, which mean that the swimmer will swim the race in a particular style – perhaps focusing on particular aspects of technique.

Athletes will use different combinations of these goals, depending on where they are in their training programme. For example, Professor Jones says, at a certain time some athletes may not be so bothered about actually winning a race; what they are focusing on is the particular performance (such as the time) and the process (the push off from the starting blocks). Professor Jones says:

> 'Adrian Moorhouse talks about how he apparently failed in Los Angeles in 1984 because he came fourth in the world. He was expected to come first. He focused on outcome goals – winning – and he realized that he needed people to help him build other goals. His goals in 1988 were different. Sure, they were to win – that's what kept him motivated for four years – but the other goals were about swimming a time and swimming in a particular style. One process goal he had for the 1988 Olympics was to stay strong and hold his stroke in the last five or ten metres. In the race, he won it in the last five metres. He won it by a fingernail. So that process goal won him his Olympic gold medal.'

Sports psychologist Ian Lynagh confirms the importance of making use of the different types of goals. He says it is important for an athlete to be able to separate goals into outcome and performance goals. The outcome goals keep the athlete motivated and give them a sense of direction, but they have to focus on performance goals. Lynagh says:

> 'Going out to play a game of rugby and saying your goal is to win is a bullshit goal. Of course you want to win, but what are your goals today? Maybe you want to make more tackles in the opposition's half. Good athletes always have performance goals and if they achieve them, they maximize their chances of getting an outcome goal.'

England rugby head coach, Clive Woodward, encourages every member of the squad to set goals. He says:

> 'We have individual goals in terms of certain aspects of the game. All our goals are performance related, things that are measurable

even if they are subjective. We try to set the standards higher than any other team in world rugby.'

As for himself, Woodward now has one overarching goal.

'My only goal is for England to be the best team in the world. I make no apologies for that. The only reason I wake up in the morning is for England to be the number one team in the world – not just Europe.'

In addition to outcome and performance goals, process goals focus on the manner in which the sportsperson wants to perform. Dr Stephanie Cook used all types of goals when training to compete in modern pentathlon.

'I used to have a sports psychology session once a week. We covered lots of aspects, including setting your goals. Those might be in terms of results, or performance related, but also process related. For example, instead of focusing on a particular time that you wanted to achieve, you might focus on the fact that you wanted to stay relaxed during the race.'

Former badminton champion Gill Clark set herself process goals that related to her daily training regime. While she had outcome goals to win championships, she found these daily goals were more important because competitions were so spread out. Her daily training diary might include a five mile run and each day she would try to beat her previous time. Daily goals like that were her main motivating drivers.

Clark had a new goal when badminton became an Olympic sport. The goal of competing in the Olympics gave her renewed motivation to push herself harder.

'The challenge of seeing how good I could be was very important to me, so one of the best sporting experiences I have ever had was

badminton's first ever Olympics, in Barcelona. I lost in the quarter final and didn't get a medal.

'But the point was that the Olympic Games wasn't a possibility when I was a child, because badminton wasn't an Olympic sport. Then all of a sudden, I was part of it.

'By the time I competed in Barcelona I was 30, so I was probably a little bit past my best. But when I knew that I could be a part of the Olympics I would leap up every day, thinking, "This is such an opportunity for me – I can go to the Olympic Games!" Each day on the morning run I thought about the Olympics and what it might be like to be on the podium. You don't even notice that you're hurting. You don't notice that you're out of breath. You just fly.'

Just to achieve her goal of attending the Olympics was an incredible experience for Clark.

'I surprised myself. It was wonderful. At one stage I didn't think I'd qualified. I'd had five knee operations and another knee problem. The surgeon spoke to me before he put me under and asked about my plans. I said I needed to qualify for the Olympics, so I couldn't have major surgery.

'The obstacles and problems I faced actually added to the enjoyment.'

EARLY GOALS

Top sporting performers are habitual goal-setters. Michael Lynagh, former Australian rugby captain and renowned fly-half, began setting goals for himself in his childhood. He recalls how when he was in an Under-12 school cricket team he wanted to play for the Under-13s. The Under-13s played in long white trousers on grass pitches, whereas the Under-12s played in shorts on concrete. It was a simple, but powerful, early goal.

As a professional rugby player, Lynagh's goals were, not surprisingly, more sophisticated than those he set himself as a child.

'I would think about my percentage, and how I could improve it. I would think where I was missing goals from, or whether I wasn't kicking as well from my left as my right. I had specific performance skills goals that needed to be achieved. I never set out saying, "I am going to win the World Cup", though if you'd have asked me I'd have said it would be nice.'

David Lloyd, former Davis Cup tennis captain, says he used to dream a lot as a child – and he still does.

'Those dreams really were goals. I made those dreams goals. I would see something – like a new bike in the shop – and I had to have that new bike. It was a dream that I had to make come true. The only way I made that come true was by passing the eleven-plus so Dad gave me the bike, because that was the deal.'

Javelin champion Steve Backley set his first goal soon after taking up the javelin. He tried throwing it at school and enjoyed it, even though he wasn't particularly good at first. However, he decided he wanted to throw further than one particular boy, which meant he would need to throw about 30m. So, Backley went to a local field, put a marker down and kept throwing. In this way he proved himself a natural goal-setter. He set his outcome goal (beating the boy) and broke it down into a performance target (the required distance) and then practised the throw. Only later did he discover that was the correct model for goal-setting.

The process of continually setting new goals came easily to Backley.

'It's something I did naturally. If you create a goal and achieve it, the first thing you do is create a higher goal. And when you achieve that, you create another higher goal. If you do that six times on the trot you develop a real sense of achievement. I never really saw anything beyond my immediate goal. I wasn't even confident enough to say I could be British Champion.'

Backley is still setting goals – including winning gold at the 2004 Olympics. This, he says, would be the icing on the cake. Though happy with his achievements so far, Backley says he is as keen as ever to win gold. As competitions approach, he can still develop the necessary levels of desire and the need to win. However, Backley prefers to focus on process rather than outcome goals. For example, he would rather focus on optimizing his running at the throw, rather than thinking about gold.

> *'I am very uncomfortable broadcasting medals. OK, it's an outcome goal, and you need that if you're lacking desire. But if you're full of desire, all you need is direction. I want to win. That's what I set my life up to do.'*

Champion National Hunt jockey, Richard Dunwoody, dreamt of riding in the Grand National from an early age. Brought up near Belfast in Northern Ireland, his father trained horses and horses were in his blood from the start.

> *'The Grand National really captured my imagination from the age of four or five. My dream wasn't so much about being a champion jockey, but about riding in the Grand National. When I became a teenager we moved to Newmarket and I wanted to be a flat jockey, but unfortunately my weight was never going to allow that.*
>
> *'From the day I left school my goal was to get a ride, first in a point-to-point, then on the course, then to ride a winner, then to ride more winners. In the first season I had 4 winners; the next year I had 24. From that time on it was always to ride more winners the next year, and for about 11 or 12 seasons I did ride more winners every year. Then my final goal was to be champion jockey.'*

Former badminton champion Gill Clark had a competitive, goal-setting streak from an early age – even when playing with her three brothers and sisters.

'I can remember as a small child when the four of us were playing in the garden. My father made us a high jump stand and each day I had to jump higher. We put canes on the grass for long jump; if you missed you hurt yourself because we ran in bare feet. We'd go running along and leap over these canes, whether it was high jump or long jump. We always wanted to do better. Being four children all very close in age, we were very competitive. As I was the little one I always had to try that much harder to keep up with the big ones.'

GOAL DEVELOPMENT

Adrian Moorhouse began setting his first goals early on, as a young swimmer inspired by the success of David Wilkie in the 1976 Olympics. At the age of 14, he transferred from Bradford Swimming Club to Leeds, where he found himself an Olympic coach.

'Terry Denison was one of the Olympic team coaches in 1980 and he was the head coach at Leeds. He asked me what I wanted to do, and why I was there. That's when I said, 'I want to win the Olympics because I've seen David Wilkie do it.' Terry started talking about how it might be possible. He made me look at what I was doing, and what I needed to do. The first question he asked me was: "If you're going to win the Olympics, what time are you going to win it in?" I had no idea.'

Denison effectively broke the big dream – winning Olympic gold – into a series of staging posts, starting with winning the Yorkshire title, then the North East of England and junior England titles.

But first was Yorkshire. Moorhouse had come second the year before, but now Denison wanted him to win. After that, he wanted him to come in the top three in the North East. That aim was broken down into a time goal and a performance goal, which led to highlighting the areas of Moorhouse's technique that needed work. Moorhouse says:

'Terry was giving me the agenda and making it real. That's an important skill in life – going for something big and then working out what you can do in reality today. I'm a great believer in creating the future from the future. Don't shoot low and worry about failing; don't be easy on yourself. Be hard on yourself but know how to deal with failure. Go to win the Olympics and if you don't win, then deal with it. If you ultimately miss it by just a little bit, at least you've still done something great.

'By having milestones or benchmarks you've also got a way of measuring your progress. Lots of people want to do things – lose weight, stop smoking and so on. Okay, they are big things, so how are you going to break it down and plan for them? Don't be a dreamer, be a planner.'

Throughout his competitive swimming career Moorhouse sat down every New Year's Eve and thought about what he wanted to achieve in the coming year. He highlighted each championship and the time he wanted to achieve.

'I would do that myself and then get together with my coach. We'd start breaking the goals down. There were three phases: outcome, performance and process.'

Sally Gunnell began goal-setting from an early age, and once she met her coach, Bruce Longden, they would sit down and agree her goals together. Each year she tried to set realistic goals. Some years the goals weren't achievable, and then Gunnell says she would work out why and what went wrong. On the other hand, when she did achieve her goals, her confidence grew. Achieving her goal of winning the county championships, for example, gave her the confidence to get into junior internationals, then senior internationals and then major championships. Gunnell recalls her goals for 1986.

'The achievement for that year was to get into the Commonwealth Games team. It was probably my first major championship. I got

into the team and then went on to win it. I think that was because I was on such a high.

'In 1988, which was the year of the Seoul Olympics, my goal that year was to get into an Olympic final. I got to the final and came fifth. I came away thinking, "In four years' time I can be the Olympic champion."'

The target for 1992 was to win Olympic gold.

'We planned back from there. We knew that I was going to be at my peak on my thirteenth or fourteenth race. Bruce had worked that out for years leading up to the Olympics. So we would plan every single race and Bruce would know every single training session. Having been my coach for so long he'd worked out what my body needed. He knew how every individual was different. He knew what sessions would add speed and how much strength work I had to do at what point.'

England rugby fly-half Jonny Wilkinson says his goals have developed over time. When he was very young his goals were to play for a particular team, or to play for England. Later on his goals became more individual. What are his goals now?

'I want to be seen as the very best in my field that there has ever been. I want to be captain of this side. I set the goal of winning the World Cup. I put all these down on paper. In my rugby I have set several substantial goals and I am going about achieving them.

'Maybe I will go into a game thinking that I want to show more running, or to make better decisions. But each game in itself is a step towards achieving my ultimate goal of being able to say to myself, "I gave everything". People talk about the greatest player there has ever been, but I want to be among the very best. Therefore, every game I play matters. I can't afford to stand still or go backwards. I want to be able to say to everyone else, "Judge me on what you see". Once you have finished playing, your reputation is all that's left to go on and therefore I want to build mine while I

can. I hate it when people turn up to watch and in one game you're brilliant and then in the next you're not. I believe you can have slightly off days, but you are still in control of certain things.'

David Platt set himself the goal of playing for England's first side after he had played for the Under-21s and then the England B team. Those experiences made him think that playing for the first squad was possible. Platt says:

'You have to set yourself a goal that is achievable. It has to be in touching distance. Once you have got it, nothing says you can't set yourself another goal. For nine or ten years that's what I have been doing. I said to myself, "I want to be an England regular, I want to go to Italy". You just go on and on, setting yourself a goal that you can focus on, that is achievable and that you have a drive and desire to get.'

When Platt scored for England in the World Cup he then set himself the goal of becoming England captain.

'I'd scored against Belgium and people were talking about me. I'd scored other goals in the World Cup too, and there was talk in the papers that there would be a new England captain and there was talk that it would be me. So it became a goal to become captain.'

Achieving that goal and captaining England for three years gives Platt most satisfaction when looking back at his playing career.

'The pinnacle of anybody's career is to play for his country, but to go one step further and captain your country – for me, that was the pinnacle. If I could only keep one thing that I have achieved, it would be the England captaincy. To lead your team out at Wembley was a tremendous feeling.'

Athletics coach Ron Roddan recalls Linford Christie's goal-setting. He says that first Christie wanted to be best in the country, then in

Europe and then in the rest of the world. Once he set himself those targets, he was very positive that he could do it. That said, Roddan believes people who enjoy what they do will naturally want to do it to the best of their ability. You might set yourself the goal of beating someone from another club, but if you enjoy your sport, you will do your best anyway.

THE ROLE OF THE COACH

While sporting champions have to set and be committed to their own goals, the coach plays a vital part in helping them achieve those goals.

Professor Graham Jones says that coaches play an important role in helping athletes to set goals because there is a fine dividing line between having goals which are absolutely fantastic, and goals that are too ambitious and are therefore bad goals. Coaches have an important role to play in helping performers keep their feet on the ground and focus on the things that are important. Winning is important, but there are other things that are going to help people win. Professor Jones says he has come across too many coaches for whom the result has been the all-important thing, with the consequence that they have put too much pressure on their athletes.

When David Lloyd was running the Slater Scheme to train boys showing early tennis talent, he realized that goal-setting was an important tool. As a coach, he tried to encourage the boys to set goals effectively.

'Every six months I made the boys write a list of their goals. Then they had to come and talk to me about them. I would ask them why they had chosen those goals. So they wrote down their goals and we monitored them. I would try to get them to think more around the subject.

'With goals, it doesn't matter whether you are a sportsman or a businessman, you have to revisit them every six months minimum, because they will change. External circumstances might change

and the goal might be unattainable and there's nothing worse than
putting a goal that's unattainable because you just go downhill.

'There are also tasks as well as goals. I would link a goal with a
task, so there's a ladder to go up to reach the goal.

'Sometimes I set myself really tough goals, but I know if you
keep at it, you'll get pretty close.'

Lloyd trod carefully if a child wrote down a goal he thought unattainable. He says coaches must be very careful that the ambition burning in a youngster is not put out. On the other hand, some kids will say they have a certain goal just because they think that is what the coach wants to hear. They might say they want to win Wimbledon, when that doesn't really mean anything to them. Lloyd says that coaches therefore do need to dig deeply to make sure that the stated goal really is embedded in the youngster's heart.

Former national athletics coach Frank Dick has an uncompromising attitude to the importance of goal-setting, believing it absolutely essential. Athletes need to be clear about what their goals are in the coming year. If a 400m runner wants to win an Olympic gold, he needs to work out the performance required to achieve it – say 43.50 seconds. Then he needs to think about the consistent quality of performance and training required in the season in order for 43.50 seconds to be a realistic goal; the fitness parameter for that consistency; and the preparation plan detail to achieve the goal.

When thinking about the consistent quality of performance required, parameters need to be established in terms of the athlete's conditioning and techniques. Then the coach draws up the training plan, breaking it down into six-week cycles, and taking into account the competition programme. Controls need to be built in to test that the athlete is on track and making progress. Although the plan becomes very detailed, it has to be open to adjustment if the athlete performs unexpectedly well.

The plan needs to consider the support people required – the doctor, psychologist, physiotherapist, physiologist, biochemist. Any special training needs for the individual in question should be considered. Is there anything more that could help the person achieve this year's goals? The planning must be comprehensive.

Dick believes that coaches should be so attuned to their athletes and so focused on the detail of the training plan that they can predict how their athletes will perform at a particular competition during the season timetable. He says:

'I find it inexcusable if a coach can't tell me on Monday what he thinks his or her athlete is going to do on the Saturday. It's not good enough to say you are going to do a little bit better. If you really know your business, you should know to within a few hundredths of a second. Daley Thompson's lifetime best in 100m was 10.31 seconds prior to the 1986 European Championships in Stuttgart. Tests over 30m and 60m made 10.27 or 10.28 achievable. He ran 10.26.'

When choosing competitions tests during a season and when building up to a major championship, Dick believes those tests must be truly challenging. Otherwise, why bother with them? Dick says:

'The purpose of competition is to help you perform better. There's no point in finding competition you can beat. I was puzzled back in 2000 when the England football team went to play Malta as their last game before the start of the European Championships. Malta's a very passionate nation about football; in fact, they are an accomplished team, considering the population numbers. But what level of challenge did they really present for England? Hardly testing! That would be like Linford Christie racing local sprinters in preparation for the Olympics. You know that's stupid. You find competition that challenges and pushes you on to even greater things. Otherwise, how do you become that champion?

'You sometimes see pretty useful athletes ducking out of competitions because they would like to have an easy outing to build their self-belief. Come on guys. You want to be the best in the world. If you don't beat someone this time, beat them next time. If it doesn't happen that time, beat them the time after that. You seek them out.

You seek out people who are even better than you are and you keep going at them. You've got to keep the will to win there all the time. It's about your drive, your sense of purpose, your relentless determination to keep going for your goal. You're going to get there, so how do you get there? By being better than you are today. Athletes need to keep their minds on that. You may not guarantee the results at the end of it, because you've only got control over your performance. But if you keep on performing better, your chances of a result are a lot better than if you don't.'

THE JOURNEY

Roger Black believes it is the *process* of achieving the goal that really matters – not the achievement of the goal itself.

'The whole point of setting yourself a goal in life is not the moment you run that race, it's actually the recognition of the journey to that point. When people achieve goals, most will say they really enjoyed the process of trying to get there. That's why, when they achieve the goal, they think "What am I going to do now?" It's not because they have achieved their goal, but they are looking at the process. The process has gone.'

For Black, doing the best he could was essential for his sense of achievement.

'Many people think if you don't come first, it's not worth taking part. In 1996 I went to the Atlanta Olympic Games. I had never had a good Olympics. I missed the one in 1988. I was injured in 1992. I had never actually made an Olympic final.

'I was 30 years old in Atlanta, which is quite old in athletic terms and I knew this would be my last Olympic Games. But I had learnt so much over the 12 or 13 years of my career that in 1996 I was about as good as I was ever going to be. When I stood behind the line I was absolutely ready to become an Olympic champion, but Michael Johnson was in the race.

'When I crossed the line I came second and about an hour later they put an Olympic silver medal round my neck. But for me, that was my Olympic gold medal. I had learnt so much in my career and the most important lesson I learnt that night was when I stood on the rostrum with Michael Johnson, the only difference was that he was a little bit higher than me. We both felt the same. I learnt you don't have to have a gold medal to feel like an Olympic champion. When I went into that race I wasn't really thinking about anything apart from running as fast as I possibly could. That's all it was about.

'In that race there were athletes who were as talented as me, if not more talented, and on paper I should have come fourth or fifth. But I got it right. I ran within a hundredth of my personal best.'

Black feels he ran 'the perfect race'. He says: 'It was the fourth race in four days under enormous pressure and I ran about as hard as I possibly could.'

Javelin champion Steve Backley also values the journey involved in achieving goals. 2002 was a busy year for Backley, containing both the Commonwealth Games and the European Championships. After a good start in training, Backley caught an inner ear infection which lingered on and hampered his preparations.

'At the lowest point my goal was just to get through the Common-wealths, to just win that and then do my best in the Europeans in Munich. In my more confident moments I might think I could do alright in the Europeans. I'm never really comfortable with expecting the best. I think about accessing the required state and performing. The journey is far more important than the result. For example, if I'd have accessed the state I desire, which I know is difficult, and thrown 90m in Munich and come third, I'd be happy.'

As it was, Backley threw 88.54m in round five to take gold.

When it comes to personal satisfaction about his performance, it isn't just the colour of the medal that counts. Backley says:

'You have your own mountain to climb. If you set a plan and make good decisions about everything in your control, and the plan's gone well as a result of that, then wherever you come, you can't be disappointed. There are some warriors who come second or third who I respect more than some of the guys who've won.'

In the 2000 Olympics, Backley was struggling to overcome injury. He had undergone knee surgery the year before, and was still vulnerable to swelling. As a result, his silver medal represented a massive achievement.

'The physio knew what I'd gone through to get that silver medal. He told me that silver was a platinum. And I look at that silver and think it's a platinum – it's better than gold because of the journey and the achievement and what it means to me.'

Achieving a goal is a great feeling – for sporting champions as well as ordinary people. And like ordinary people, champions also often have heroes – people who have inspired them to aim high and give their all. But who are these heroes?

Chapter 8

HEROES HAVE HEROES TOO

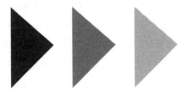

EVERYONE NEEDS A SOURCE OF INSPIRATION. Most often it is the acts of others that inspire us to try new things, undertake challenges or simply do better than we thought possible. And, not surprisingly, sporting heroes have heroes too.

THE VALUE OF HEROES

Sports psychologists believe that interacting with heroes can be helpful. Research in cricket has found that giving talented youngsters access to world-class players increases their belief that they too can succeed. Sports psychologist Steve Sylvester says:

*'In Australia, the best in the world – Shane Warne – will go down
to his club and bowl in the nets with an 18-year-old young starter.
We need more of that crossover in the UK – between the amateurs
and the professionals – because it makes being a world champion
become more believable, more real. It's about providing a clear
signal that you can achieve; you won't block yourself, because you
see a world champion right in front of you; they drink coffee the
way you drink coffee. Heroes need to be normalized – they are real
and touchable. In cricket we've brought people like Mike Gatting,
Derek Randall and Neil Foster and put them in a game situation
with our best young players. Suddenly those players are feeling and
thinking more like somebody who feels and thinks like a world
champion.'*

Sports psychologist John Syer also believes that heroes can be useful
for aspiring champions – to a certain degree. Heroes are valuable for
the lessons they give us about what it is we value in them. However,
Syer says it is important to guide the athlete to see that creating
someone in the image of a hero is not reality. Nobody is really a hero
– or we're all heroes. Syer says it is important to identify what the
qualities are that make someone a hero to a particular person. What
quality is it the athlete admires? Then the sports psychologist can
guide the athlete back to invoking those qualities in themselves.

WHO ARE THE HEROES' HEROES?

When 400m runner Mark Richardson was 11, American sprinter
Carl Lewis was one of his heroes. In fact, Lewis shaped Richardson's destiny.

*'As a child, sport was my first love, but it was a toss up whether I
concentrated on athletics or rugby. When I was 11, I watched Carl
Lewis win his four gold medals. I thought he wasn't only a fantastic
athlete, but he was also so graceful and he made his achievement
look so easy. It really instilled in me a desire to be an Olympian. I
wanted to be like Carl Lewis. It was my dream.'*

Later, when Richardson was coming up through the athletic ranks, 100m sprinter Linford Christie also became an inspirational figure. Richardson says:

'He was beating everyone there was to beat at the time. He was taking on the Americans at their own game – he was encroaching on their territory and bettering them. That was inspiring.'

As an adult Richardson still has heroes who inspire him, such as Muhammad Ali. Richardson says:

'He's such an icon and won against all odds. Some of his fights are just incredible. If you fail to be inspired by that man, then I think there's something wrong with you.'

Middle distance gold medallist Sebastian Coe also names Muhammad Ali as an early sporting hero. Coe says:

'I think anybody who grew up during his career would choose him, as well as people who didn't. Kids down at my athletic club a quarter of my age would give the same answer. The impact he had on the sporting twentieth century was mammoth.'

In athletics, Coe says that Brendan Foster, former 3000m world record holder, had a big impact on his career:

'I was brought up in the north of England and Brendan had quite a large impact in that he was the first athlete within my frame of reference who could be seen winning major titles overseas. It was a relative rarity. My athletic career started in the early seventies and by the early eighties we still hadn't got anybody who was consistently winning championships overseas. Brendan was the first of that breed to come through. He broke world records and was the equal of any of the Kenyans.'

Three times Olympic gold rower Matthew Pinsent admits that his fellow rower and team mate Steve Redgrave was an early inspiration. Pinsent says:

> *Steve was a bit of a hero, because he'd won two Olympic gold medals before I met him. My heroes now are people who are really consistent – guys like Tiger Woods and Michael Schumacher. People who are winning time after time.'*

David Platt, former England Under-21 football coach, also finds Tiger Woods a source of inspiration. Platt says: 'It's the way he can handle all the pressure and win the way everybody expects him to win.'

Tiger Woods is also a hero to Michael Lynagh, former Australian rugby captain, as is another great golfer – Jack Nicklaus. Lynagh says:

> *Jack Nicklaus has been playing for 45 years at the top of his profession. To be on top of your sport for so long is great. He is somebody I admire.'*

Basketball player Michael Jordan also commands Lynagh's respect:

> *That's not so much for all the hype that surrounds him, but the sheer athletic ability of the guy. You forget that he is six foot seven tall and there are things he can do on a basketball court that I really admire.'*

Lynagh also certainly had sporting heroes when he was growing up. He says:

> *Because I grew up in Australia, most of my sporting heroes come from there. When I was a child, cricket was my main game and the heroes of that time were batsmen: Greg Chappell, Dennis Lillee, Jeff Thompson. Then when I was 11 or 12, rugby league was the main game in Australia; it got all the coverage. Certain fellows like*

Bob Fulton and Mick Cronin were great Australian rugby league players around that time. Arthur Beetson was a big forward. So most of my sporting heroes when I was growing up related to my own environment in Australia.'

As far as Dr Stephanie Cook, modern pentathlon Olympic gold medallist, is concerned, there is one man who stands above the rest – Eric Liddell. Liddell won a 400m gold medal in the Paris Olympics in 1924, but famously put his religious faith before his running. His story featured in the film, *Chariots of Fire*:

'A friend who was doing pentathlon at university gave me his biography, The Flying Scotsman. *At that time I had quite a reputation as a runner and I was actually born in Scotland. He wrote inside it, "To the flying Scotswoman". I'd never seen the film about him and so it was a big inspiration – the way he kept his principles and values in life, and still achieved great things. That was very important to me.'*

England football manager Sven-Göran Eriksson's hero as a young boy was Brazilian football legend, Pele. Eriksson says:

'He was the best player ever. He was a role model for me when I was a young player.'

Golfing great Nick Faldo was inspired by Jack Nicklaus to take up golf, but another early hero was multiple Wimbledon tennis champion, Björn Borg. Faldo says:

'I loved the way he handled himself; the way he handled poor decisions. He was totally focused on the tennis court. He's a very shy guy like myself. He'd play a shot and he'd have his head down. Then he'd go to the service line and wait for the next shot and play it. Later in life, through a sports psychology friend, I learnt how Borg used to train. He trained with the attitude that every single shot he played in practice was match point. I tried that in golf. It

blows your brains out – to think this is the shot to win the Open, with the last shot on the eighteenth. Can you imagine the mental strength to practise like that, day in, day out?'

Former sprinter John Regis had a hero who became a source of great advice, as well as inspiration. Regis says:

'My hero as an athlete was a Jamaican sprinter called Don Quarrie. I thought he was poetry in motion. To me he epitomized the perfect 200m. He ran a great turn, had great style, was fluent, strong and quick. Over the years we got to be good friends and I would pick his brains on what he thought about when he ran and how he used to avoid negative thoughts. He told me you've just got to block everybody else out and do what you do in training. Your coach tells you to do something in training, and then you try to do it in the Grand Prix circuit. Then one of the main things he told me was that there is no difference between the Grand Prix circuit and a major championship because you're racing the same people. In my early years I used to think you had to act differently in a major championship. But it's the same athletes. There are just more people in the stands.

'That realization was one of the major things that helped me understand how to relax and become happier with what I was doing.'

Former badminton champion Gill Clark had three sporting heroines as a youngster, starting with pentathlete Mary Peters.

'One of my first recollections as a child is of being on holiday in Scotland and watching the 1972 Olympics on television. I can remember Ron Pickering doing the commentary on the 200m. He talked about Mary Peters being this down-to-earth, ordinary girl from Belfast. He said, "Come on Mary, you need the race of your life". Several times I've actually said to myself, "Come on Gillian, you need the race of your life". Mary inspired me because I was an ordinary little kid from an ordinary little village in Kent.'

Lucinda Green was Clark's second heroine as a youngster, inspired by the fact that her family had a pony. Green won the Badminton horse trials six times on six different horses. Clark says: 'I really admired Lucinda Green. Nobody could say she had won because of the horse she was riding.'

Clark's third inspirational heroine was tennis legend Martina Navratilova. Clark says:

> 'She seemed to take tennis, and women's sport in general, to a new level. It became more acceptable for a woman to be openly seen trying to be a success at sport. It's still a problem with girls in schools that they think it's not feminine to show the qualities that are needed to be successful at sport – like guts and determination.'

For former Davis Cup tennis captain David Lloyd, tennis star Pancho Gonzales was a hero. Lloyd says:

> 'My father didn't stop talking about Pancho Gonzales, and I happened to play him when I was 17. It was one of the best matches I my life. I lost 10–8 in the third set at Wembley. Pancho was 43 and he won the tournament. I think I played my best match because my father kept saying, "You know he's the greatest player".
>
> 'Pancho was a giant, very tall, and he had a beautiful serve. He used to tape his fingers meticulously for hours before a match. Each and every finger was taped in white. He also used to put white tape around the top of his racquet. His shoes were all lined up. He was absolutely meticulous.'

Breaststroke champion Adrian Moorhouse was first inspired to win an Olympic medal by swimming great David Wilkie, who won one gold and two silver Olympic medals for 100m and 200m breaststroke in the 1972 and 1976 Olympics. Moorhouse says:

> 'He embodied what I wanted. I didn't know much about the way he did it, but the year after he won the Olympics he ran a weekend swimming school in Liverpool for 40 kids. I asked my mum if

I could go on it. She signed me on and I went to the swimming school for the weekend. I played five-a-side soccer with Wilkie and asked him lots of questions and tried to impress him. I was trying to learn what I could from this person. I remember him showing a video of the Olympics and asking the group, "Who wants to do this? Who wants to be an Olympic champion?" I said, "I do. I want to do what you just did."'

At swimming meets, Moorhouse's coach would point out the talented swimmers and Adrian would then watch them closely. Moorhouse says:

'I watched one guy – Salnikov – all weekend to see exactly what he did. I trailed him. I spent a lot of time when I wasn't racing just walking behind him. I saw what he did and started to do what he did when he came to the pool.'

Moorhouse also read biographies of other successful sportsmen, picking up advice and tips – anything that he thought would be useful. His coach also gave him photocopies of articles that had helpful insights. It might be a piece in an American swimming magazine, or even an article in the *Financial Times*. Moorhouse soaked it all up.

However, Moorhouse says he tried not to have heroes, as such. Instead, he used to collect inspirational quotes. One of his favourites is: 'If you follow in the footsteps of somebody, you'll never overtake them.'

As Moorhouse explains:

'I always thought, "I've got to try and beat these guys, even though they are people I look up to. If I want to beat their times and what they have achieved, I can't follow them. I've got to be different."'

Olympic hurdler Sally Gunnell had a similar viewpoint. As a youngster she didn't idolize other athletes. As Gunnell says: 'Before you know it, you're running against them and you want to beat these people.'

However, she does admire people in other sports, such as former tennis champion Steffi Graf. Gunnell says:

'I like seeing a woman who's quite aggressive and determined. It annoys me when I see women in sport who haven't got that determination.'

Similarly, round-the-world yachtswoman Ellen MacArthur didn't have heroes when she was a child. She says:

'I never carried someone's picture around in my pocket saying I wanted to be like them. There are people I respect enormously though. They can be people from all walks of life, and you can be inspired by all sorts of things.'

For example, MacArthur says her grandmother was an inspiration to her because she achieved a university degree in European languages at the age of 83. 'It's never too late,' MacArthur says.

Ron Dennis, boss of the McLaren racing team, believes his life has been greatly influenced by psychologist and author Edward de Bono, who became famous for promoting lateral thinking. As Dennis says, 'Success is about what's between your ears.'

However, in general, Dennis believes that role models need to come from inside your team. He says:

'You have a few people who, through their own achievements, can be the key motivators. I'm not a great one for looking at the outside world. I prefer to have these champions or inspirational characters inside your team.'

Heroic inspiration can clearly come from many sources – from famous people and from family and friends. As long as we don't put these people on a pedestal that could limit our own achievements, there is no harm in inspiring ourselves by marvelling at the qualities and achievements of others. This final source of motivation closes Part II.

Analysis II

MOTIVATIONAL MATTERS

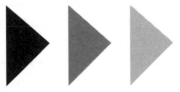

Acknowledged sporting champions clearly need the physical talent and the trained skill to succeed, but they also need motivation to keep them going when times are tough. Something has to keep them training even when their limbs ache, it's 6 o'clock in the morning and they would rather be in bed. In Part II we looked at champions' motivations – what it is that drives them on.

CHAPTER 5

In Chapter 5: The Success Magnet, we found that many champions have a strong 'need' to win. Coming second simply isn't good enough. In particular, they want to win the really big occasions

– world championships and the Olympics as compared to ordinary international contests.

Many sportspeople are motivated to put in the hard training required because they want to experience the feelings that come with being a winner. They are attracted towards the feelings of esteem and elation that come from winning gold. For some of our interviewees, achieving success in their sport as a child gave them a sense of esteem. Olympic swimmer Adrian Moorhouse was a small, shy child, but swimming made him a winner.

However, the emotions associated with winning vary from person to person. Some feel great elation; some describe feeling great relief that they have achieved their goals; many are moved to tears.

These differing emotions are not surprising given that, in simple terms, there are two different types of motivation: the desire to move 'towards' and 'away from' certain feelings. Champions who thrive on the feelings of elation are pulled towards those feelings; the desire to experience them again motivates them during the preparatory training required. However, many sportspeople are also motivated to train because they don't want to fail, or to let people down. Their drive is underpinned by needing to avoid feeling something. We looked at this group in more detail in Chapter 6: Fleeing Failure.

As Ceri Evans from mental conditioning specialists Gazing Performance explains, in practice most sportspeople are motivated by a mixture of the 'towards' and 'away from' drivers, though one theme may dominate at any particular time. The common denominator is the intensity of *emotion* that is involved in these drivers. For example, rugby players may want to win the World Cup, but the underlying significance of this will vary from player to player. The reason lies in the emotional associations. It may be that winning the World Cup will enable that rugby player to say, 'I am the best'. For another player winning the World Cup may mean they are part of a winning team and so they feel accepted, because they belong to that successful group. For other individuals the key factor may be that they are moving away from the feeling of letting anyone down. When the team wins, they feel they haven't disappointed anyone and the dominant feeling may be one of relief.

The champions we interviewed were strongly motivated because they wanted to enjoy certain feelings and they really didn't want to experience others. Without a strong emotional response to winning or losing, the people we talked to wouldn't be champions; they simply wouldn't have the motivation to do what needs to be done to achieve their goals.

Renzie Hanham from Gazing Performance points out that in a business environment it is useful to know what drives the members of your team. Are the goals of the group aligned with the drivers of the individuals involved? If not, then the likely result is disharmony and resistance to what you are trying to achieve. Similarly, in your personal relationships, if you and your partner don't share similar goals and drivers, what Renzie calls the 'themes' of each person's life will become quite different. Eventually this can create a wedge between the two of you, potentially driving you apart.

These drivers are closely related to how we define ourselves. Ceri Evans notes that people can define themselves in many different ways. An elite sportsman might define himself as 'the world champion' or 'the best in the UK'. Such status may be so important to their sense of self that they will endure great hardship to maintain it. The way that we define ourselves will generally change over time, as our lives develop and our priorities change. This process can have important implications for sportspeople as their careers progress, in the way that they come to define themselves more strongly in terms of the level of their achievement and ambition.

A final motivational force we found amongst our sporting champions was the desire to beat their own previous best performances. They weren't just competing against their competitors, but against themselves. In fact, once middle distance runner Sebastian Coe realized there was nothing left that he could do to improve his performances, he decided the time had come to retire.

This kind of attitude is one that can be applied in all walks of life. You don't need to be competing in a sporting environment. You can compete against yourself to improve your performance at work, in your hobbies and anything else you want to do well.

Applications

- Think about times when you achieved something that meant a lot to you. Maybe you passed an exam, managed to hold a conversation successfully in a foreign language or gave your first major presentation. How did that make you feel? Were you elated? Did you feel like jumping up and down with joy? Were you simply relieved that you didn't let yourself down? In fact, you probably felt a bit of both, but was one stronger? By thinking about your reaction you can get a better understanding of what motivates you – 'towards' or 'away from' feelings.
- Think about something you want to achieve in future. What is it that motivates you? Do you want other people to acknowledge your achievement? Will you feel relief that you have done something you always said you would? Are there similarities with how you felt about the things you have achieved before?
- Whenever you decide to achieve something challenging, make a note of what it is that motivates you. Refer to it whenever you need a boost to keep you going.

CHAPTER 6

In Chapter 6: Fleeing Failure, we looked specifically at champions who were driven by the desire not to fail. For these people the emotions that came with being beaten felt so bad that they were highly motivated to do all they could to make sure they didn't have to suffer them.

For example, 400m champion Roger Black talks of the 'great pain' that he feels if he looks back and knows he didn't do something properly.

Sometimes it isn't just your own feelings that matter. Yachts-woman Ellen MacArthur hates to think she has let down all the people in the support team working with her; she feels she has to do well for their sakes.

Other people can also provide a motivating force for our sporting champions – by telling them they can't do something. For some people, being told you will fail provides huge motivation to prove that person wrong by succeeding. This was the case for Sally Gunnell early in her sporting career when she was told she would never be good enough to be a top hurdler.

Champions who are driven to avoid feelings of failure generally feel relief as the dominant emotion when they win. There is euphoria too, but relief is the major sensation.

As we noted in considering the findings in Chapter 5: The Success Magnet, the emotional response that comes from winning – or not losing – is absolutely key to the motivation of successful people. These feelings and emotions really matter. They can't be easily shrugged off or ignored. Without this strong emotional response, no one would spend hours every day practising a skill or improving fitness, perhaps in addition to holding down a full-time job. This would be madness, if it wasn't for the powerful emotional impact that becoming an Olympic medallist or winning Wimbledon has.

The same applies in everyday life, though perhaps on a less dramatic scale. Renzie Hanham from mental conditioning specialists Gazing Performance suggests that if we understand our drivers, how they relate to our emotions and underpin our motivations, then we can be more deliberate about the choices we make. This in turn will allow us to feel more in control of our lives.

Applications

- In the applications for Chapter 5: The Success Magnet, we suggested you recall the emotions you felt when achieving success in the past. Now try thinking about some goal or task you want to complete now. Imagine how you will feel having completed it. Imagine the feelings of joy and imagine how you will celebrate. Sense the wonderful feeling of relief you will have. (This is particularly relevant if the task is something you don't necessarily want to do, but need to do.) Revel in how good it feels, then think about the goal or task itself. Do you feel more motivated to achieve it now?

CHAPTER 7

Goals play an important part in motivating any athlete, a topic we considered in Chapter 7: Goals Galore. Goal-setting is in fact an invaluable tool for anyone seeking to achieve a particular ambition, be it a sporting challenge, a career ambition or a personal dream.

Renzie Hanham of mental conditioning specialists Gazing Performance says that having clear goals can help drive certain behaviours which can keep you motivated in the most difficult situations. It's not the goals themselves that are necessarily significant; it's what those goals represent, what significance they have for the individual. This significance 'drives' the individual to achieve the goals they have established. The more meaning the goals have, the more the individual will be driven to achieve them.

All the champions we spoke to set themselves goals. Many did so from an early age and it was something that they did naturally.

The goals that champions set are commonly divided into three types: outcome goals, which set the target, such as winning the gold medal: performance goals, such as the time required to win the race; and process goals, which address how that performance will be achieved – perhaps by focusing on a particular aspect of the technique involved.

By formalizing a goal and writing it down, you can develop a sense of commitment to achieving it. Once you have established the ultimate goal – the outcome goal – you can work backwards to establish the steps you need to complete to achieve it. The individual steps keep you focused on the processes you need to follow in order to achieve your ultimate goal, while the emotions associated with that ultimate goal keep you motivated when the going gets tough.

The goals that are set need to be realistic and achievable. If they are too hard, they will have no motivational impact. If they are too easy, then achieving them means nothing. They should be flexible and can be changed if your rate of development suddenly alters. In fact, goals should be reviewed regularly and adjusted as necessary.

Coaches can play an invaluable role in helping emerging champions to establish realistic goals, and in ensuring that the individual really does want to achieve that goal. If the thought of achieving the goal doesn't trigger strong emotions, it is a waste of time to try to achieve it.

Renzie Hanham stresses the importance of alignment between an individual's goals and values. When there is misalignment between the goals and values that athletes have, they often sabotage their own performance. In contrast, the greater the alignment, the greater the chance of success.

Top sportspeople generally use goal-setting much more effectively than people with non-sporting ambitions. In the business world, for example, people often overcomplicate matters by trying to achieve too many things at once, rather than focusing on three or four key objectives. Most sportspeople have far more clarity about their goals. That clarity is important for maintaining motivation and focusing on what needs to be done to achieve the desired goals. We can all learn from sporting champions by trying to be more precise about what it is we are aiming to do and the steps we must take to succeed.

Secondly, top sportspeople typically are far more disciplined than other people in terms of completing the processes they need to complete in order to achieve their goals. As Ceri Evans from Gazing Performance says, many people performing in domains outside sport, such as business, aren't as organized as elite sportspeople. Some initiate good processes by doing a lot of work on outcomes and targets, but then don't follow it up on the preparatory work. Goals are only useful if you have discipline behind them.

Applications

- Identify one or more outcome goals or ambitions that you have. This could relate to your work or private life. It might be to achieve a promotion or even to change careers. Perhaps you want to be

able to move up your squash ladder or be able to paint a picture of
your child – one that you would be proud to hang on your wall.

- Take each goal and think about what you need to do to be able
  to achieve it – your performance goals. For example, if you want
  to be promoted to sales manager for your area, what kind of performance do you need to deliver? Perhaps you need to increase
  your sales by a certain amount or demonstrate your ability to
  manage other people.

- Think about the process goals that will support your outcome and
  performance goals. If you need to display staff management skills,
  what does this mean? Do you need any extra training to be able to
  delegate effectively or coach members of your team well? Identify
  the things you need to do to start working towards your ultimate
  outcome goals.

- Set your goals in a timeframe. When do you want to achieve that
  promotion? Work backwards to establish the timescale you need
  in order to achieve the supporting steps along the way.

- Review your plan. Is it realistic? Is it too easy? If you need to
  adjust the timescale, do so. Your aim should be to come up with
  a plan that inspires you to achieve it and that you believe you can
  achieve.

- Consider taking advice from someone with relevant experience
  whose opinions you trust. They may be able to comment on
  whether your performance and process goals are appropriate.

CHAPTER 8

In Chapter 8: Heroes Have Heroes Too, we decided to find out
whether our sporting champions had their own heroes, just like
ordinary people do.

We found that most people were inspired by someone. This could
be an elite performer in their own sport, who inspired them in their
childhood to try to become a champion themselves. For example,
Olympic swimmer Adrian Moorhouse was highly motivated by
meeting David Wilkie at a swimming school. It was then that he
decided he wanted to be an Olympic medallist himself. In general,

sporting champions who work with talented youngsters can have a big impact on their future success. Not only can they teach them good techniques, they can also help talented youngsters to believe that they can become champions too.

Many of the champions we interviewed were inspired by individuals from completely different sports. Muhammad Ali, for example, is widely respected. Sometimes the champions deliberately avoided thinking of people in their own sport as heroes. If they idolized them, how could they beat them?

Ceri Evans from mental conditioning specialists Gazing Performance believes that heroes can play a useful role if the desire to emulate the hero leads to better application to effective training and conditioning processes. If the individual wants to emulate the hero, that desire can provide an added motivational pull to encourage them in their endeavours.

One of our champions, yachtswoman Ellen MacArthur, never really had heroes as a child. She does, however, believe that all kinds of people can be sources of inspiration, such as her own grandmother.

Without doubt, heroes can be useful in the sense that they provide inspirational examples of human achievement. They can encourage champions and everyone else to do better or act in certain ways. However, they should never be put on so high a pedestal that they leave us feeling inadequate, particularly if there is a chance of competing against that person one day.

Applications

- Who inspires you? These could be sportspeople, public figures in general or members of your friends and family.
- What is it about these people that impresses you? Can you try to emulate these characteristics or attributes in your own life to positive effect?

Part III

MENTAL TRAINING

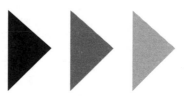

Chapter 9

MENTAL REHEARSAL

VISUALIZATION IS AN IMPORTANT TOOL that any athlete can use when preparing for competition. Champion sportspeople use it expertly to give themselves the greatest chance of performing at their absolute best when it counts.

WHAT IS VISUALIZATION?

Visualization is the process of seeing yourself doing what it is you need to do – whether running a winning race, throwing a record-breaking javelin distance or kicking the perfect penalty. To make the visualization as powerful as possible, you should be seeing the experience through your own eyes – rather than watching yourself as if on a screen. You should also engage all your senses.

For this reason sports psychologist John Syer prefers the term 'mental rehearsal' to 'visualization', because visualization suggests that the process or experience is totally visual, when it is not. The most important component is kinaesthetic.

Recalling the 'feel' of the action is vital. This is an aspect that multiple javelin champion Steve Backley learnt when working with a sports psychologist. He has always used visualization to great effect when preparing for competition, but he has improved his technique over the years. Backley says:

'I was lucky – I did it automatically as a kid and I've always been quite visual. Then I met a psychologist, Dave Collins, around seven years ago. He picked up on the fact that I did visualize but that I did it externally, as if watching myself on TV. Dave was more feelings based. We did a lot more on the rhythm of the run, how it feels, the surging of acceleration and so on.'

The trick to visualization, according to 400m runner Roger Black, is not to see yourself doing the desired action, but to see inside yourself as if you are doing it. As Black describes it, you are not looking at yourself, but you are 'actually in yourself, feeling'.

Black practised his visualization of a race so that it became extremely vivid.

'I could lie down and see it, hear it, smell it. It never included the results, though. I believed that I could only influence my perform- ance, not the results. My performance was under my control, the result wasn't. The magic was to get the performance right; the result would usually follow.'

Black really believes it is possible to recreate a competitive environ- ment in the mind and so prepare for a big event. Black 'visualized everything' in preparation for his 1996 Olympic Games.

'Visualization in sport is crucial. For the Olympic Games I walked round the stadium four months prior and I kept that picture in my

mind every day. I ran it from every lane. I could close my eyes now and run the 400m race and I would feel how I would feel.'

Sports psychologist Ian Lynagh feels that using visualization techniques, or mental rehearsal, is an essential part of any sporting preparation. As he explains, most of the things we do in our lives start with us imagining them in our heads. What the mind imagines usually creates a capacity for the body to do it. Therefore it makes sense to train athletes to visualize their golf swing, kicking the ball or whatever it is they are going to do. They can even visualize achieving their goals.

Anyone who enjoys watching athletics will have seen competitors using the technique of mental rehearsal during competitions. When high jumpers, for example, are preparing to jump they mentally run through what they are going to do just before they do it. As Lynagh says, you can see them talking themselves through the jump one step at a time – setting off, building up momentum, hitting the board and taking off. While they go through this mental rehearsal you can often see their bodies moving. As Lynagh explains, this is an ideo-motor response. In other words, the idea of the movement produces a motor response.

Former national athletics coach Frank Dick believes that athletes should adapt the basic visualization process to ensure that it works effectively for them. Although the visualization process can be made to sound complicated, it isn't. Dick has found that each athlete has their own sense of what visualization is. When someone is trying to learn a new technique, but finding it difficult, visualizing it, or as Dick says 'feeling it with words', can help. He recalls a long jumper he worked with. When she described how she geared herself up before a jump she said she liked to sense she was 'collecting', just as she would 'collect' horses. Dick says that her background included horse riding, so using that term worked for her.

Dick explains that choosing the right word is important for giving the right mental image or sensation of what the athlete is trying to do. He explains:

'A lot of coaches used to talk about "driving" off the bend in the 200 metres, but that's not a very effective thing to do. If you think "drive", you think about a longer period of contact with the ground. But longer contact with the ground actually slows you down. An expression Don Quarrie used was "lift off the bend" – so you think about touching the ground very lightly. That actually gives you a sense of acceleration. It's not just a mental thing, it's a factual thing. You accelerate off the bend, but that acceleration's not done the way you would normally accelerate from the blocks. It's done by being light and using a different configuration of sprinting technique.'

POSITIVE RESULTS

Visualization is an important element of Neuro-Linguistic Programming (NLP), which is looked at in more depth in Chapter 10. NLP trainer Graham Shaw explains that the reason why visualization works from an NLP perspective is that the mind doesn't actually know the difference between a real or an imagined experience.

Shaw recalls a story told him by his skiing instructor. A man turned up for a ski course a year after attending the previous one – but he had vastly improved during the year's gap. The instructor asked him where he had been skiing in between times, and was told he hadn't skied at all. What the guy had done was to think about skiing and he had found that he could remember the route he used to ski down. He told the instructor he'd skied down it a hundred times in his head. Of course, in his head, he had skied it perfectly. According to Shaw, if we imagine an experience powerfully enough, we have the opportunity to programme our minds to do something successfully every time.

Shaw gives another example involving basketball genius Michael Jordan. When being filmed for an advert, the director wanted him to miss the basket a few times, but Jordan couldn't do it. He was so programmed to get the ball in that he had to spend some time practising before he was able to miss. Only then he could do it for them. Shaw gives another example involving an entire basketball team. One section was asked to improve their game by visualizing and imagining, as well as by doing their regular practice. The other section of the team just practised. The two groups then came together in a dunking competition. The team that did the visualizing and spent a lot of time sitting on the bench imagining the game consistently outperformed the others who had just physically practised.

Shaw says that one of the ways visualization helps athletes is by creating positive 'filters'. Everyone automatically creates their own filters through which they view the world. These filters can be supportive or limiting, depending on the individual's past experiences and response to those experiences. Shaw explains:

'In life we experience the world in different ways, so we create our own mental maps. We create pictures and sounds in our minds, self-talk, and feelings that are all component parts of our internal experience. In NLP we call that your "map". One of the reasons people often don't communicate well is because they're on different maps.

'We filter the world and our experiences and create different maps. That means we don't notice everything. If two people see the same film they might notice different bits or the music would have different effects on them. How does that apply to sport?

'Say two people decide to learn tennis. Player number one has begun to talk to himself about learning tennis. He turns up for his lesson and he's already said to himself in his mind 100 times "I was never any good at tennis at school, therefore I can't learn tennis. I was always last in the running race and I'm no good at sports." Even before he begins his lesson he's got a set of filters on the world; it's as if he's put a special pair of glasses on and he sees everything through those. He starts the tennis lesson and hits three balls over the net and seven into the net. He says to himself, "That's awful. I've hit seven balls into the net." That's what he noticed. He started with the belief that he was no good at tennis and now he's reinforced it. Then he notices how he hits even more balls into the net.

'Another player comes along who has never played tennis. He thinks, "I've learned a lot of other stuff and I can't see why I can't learn this." He also hits seven balls into the net and three over. He says to himself, "I've hit three balls over already. I wonder if I can get five over? Perhaps I can learn this."

'So visualization works because you set your filters up in advance.'

RE-EDITING THE PAST

Mental rehearsal can also be used to minimize the impact of poor performances and negative associations. Sports psychologist John Syer says that visualization can be used to re-edit a bad mistake. This is helpful because if someone has made some bad mistake, they may unconsciously replay it mentally, which actually makes it more likely to happen again in a similar situation.

Syer explains how he leads a visualization exercise with athletes.

'I ask for the background, what immediately preceded the action to be visualized. I then lead a relaxation, followed by the beginning of the visualization. I ask the athlete to be aware of the scene, who is there, the colours, the sounds, any movement and the atmosphere. I then repeat the beginning of the story I have just heard, in the present tense. I then ask the athlete to continue the action, aware of how it feels to perform like this, and to move one finger on completion.'

When the person has finished the visualization, Syer doesn't ask them to open their eyes immediately. Instead he asks them to come up with a verbal description that is linked to the visualization. For example, Syer might ask the athlete to complete the sentence 'I feel as if I …' When they are ready and can complete the sentence, they open their eyes.

'That can be turned into an affirmation. An affirmation is a sentence that is connected to a past, positive experience, begins with

*the word "I" and is in the present tense. It can be repeated inter-
nally or written on to a piece of paper that is put into one's bag or
wallet or stuck on to the fridge door. The affirmation is connected
to the visualization.'*

Recalling that affirmation associates the individual again with the
positive outcome, encouraging them to anticipate and achieve the
positive result they want.

Sports psychologist Professor Graham Jones also sees visualization as a useful technique for correcting problematic aspects of a
sporting performance – but one that needs to be used properly, otherwise it can just reinforce the existing problem.

*'I worked with ice-skaters earlier in my career. There was one in
particular who before he went on the ice would sit and visualize a
particular jump where he always fell over. It was never successful.*

*'I took him out on the ice and had him go through some of the
basic movements. I'd have him imagine he had just done the jump
and was in the position he would be in afterwards. I would put him
in that position and say, "Now close your eyes and just imagine
doing the jump and now experience this – being in this finishing
position." You have to coax some performers through sometimes.*

*'I ask some performers to watch videos of themselves and think
how they could have done it better. Then I ask them to visualize
it.'*

VISUALIZATION IN PRACTICE

Modern pentathlon Olympic gold medallist Dr Stephanie Cook
worked with a sports psychologist once a week when she was training.
They would work on various mental aspects of the sport, including
visualization techniques. This meant that when she learnt something
new in a coaching session, she was able to rehearse it mentally for
herself before actually putting it into practice. 'You can put things
into practice much more easily when you have gone over them in
your head a few times,' she says.

Dr Cook practised her visualization regularly.

'It's the sort of thing you might do at odd moments when you're waiting around – say you're waiting for a fencing lesson. You can sit down quietly and go through a few things. But it is important to set a time when you will do it as well. I would make a conscious effort to make that time.'

Michael Lynagh, former Australian rugby captain and renowned fly-half, would rehearse his kicking mentally the night before a match. He would do so having already visited the ground he would be playing on and practised kicking in the local conditions. He practised kicks at Twickenham the afternoon before the 1991 World Cup final.

'That night, when I was going to sleep, I would mentally rehearse those kicks. I had the picture of the ground in my mind. I even knew the publicity boards. I knew what the posts were like. I could visualize all that.'

Lynagh had begun using mental rehearsal techniques early on in his career, back in the early 1980s.

'I have done it for a long time. It was part of my pre-match routine. When I was doing a mental rehearsal I would lie down and I could see lots of fine detail – even seeing the referee giving a penalty. It would include the position, the people in front of you, the sand boy coming out and giving me some sand, setting the ball up, walking back, visualizing where the ball was going to go, then coming in and kicking it and seeing the result. I would see the linesman putting the flag up. It would take a while to go through it all. I could see it very clearly.'

Lynagh found it important to 'feel' the process of the kick as well as see it. He says you have to involve your senses in sport. The more you involve, the better. He says you need to feel it, see it, hear it – use all your senses.

Champion 400m runner Roger Black made good use of visualization techniques during his sporting career.

'For every championship, as soon as I arrived the first thing I would do was go to the stadium and walk around it three or four times. I'd walk around most of the lanes and I would see myself running. I could smell the place, I could touch it.

'I had worked out that this was food for the brain. I was into visualization.

'I found that if you go into an empty stadium and walk around it, and then two days later you're there running, you're brain goes, "Oh yeah, I was here a few days ago", and that's a big help. If you walk into that environment and your brain thinks, "Oh. I've never been here", you're in trouble.

'And because I'd walked round the stadium when no one was there, when it came to the final I could almost do it as if there was no one in the stadium.'

Visualization is essential for success in motorsport too, as Ron Dennis, boss of the McLaren racing team explains.

'Most drivers will visualize not just the course, but every blade of grass. For Monte Carlo, the top drivers will also be driving it in their dreams. It's so fast. It calls on every sense. They'll be visualizing the things they have to do to become fluid. With a top driver the whole process is fluid, in harmony. There is a tranquillity about them, a rhythm.

'Top drivers will visualize and train themselves to make sure there's almost a delicacy in what they input to the car. A racing car reacts to what the driver tells it to do. If a driver puts in too much brake, too much steering, too much throttle, that takes away energy. If there is too much steering and the car skids at the back, you are taking away energy. If there is too much throttle and the rear wheels spin, they are not pushing the car through the air. So the driver's inputs have to be tremendously controlled. If you talk about a driver over-driving a car, he's almost certainly going slow.'

Former England Under-21 football coach David Platt believes visualization can help, particularly in terms of strengthening the sense of familiarity that players develop with their home ground. He says players can picture the scene when the team walks out, whether at Villa Park or wherever their home ground is. They see in their minds how a game is going to develop – they play the game in advance in their imaginations. Platt describes this as 'positive thinking in your mind'. If players see themselves being successful and doing well, he believes that does play a big part in how they actually play in the real game.

David Lloyd used visualization when preparing to play in Davis Cup matches. The Davis Cup was different to other tournaments because there was no doubt about when the players would be going on court, and this certainty helped with preparing to play. Lloyd says:

> *'The whole week was geared up to walking on the court. I imagined walking on the court, serving first. I imagined serving for the match. I imagined it all before it happened.'*

Lloyd did this naturally, without being taught to do so.

> *'I visualized every match. I visualized the food I had before I'd go on, because I always used to have the same food. And I'd have a cold bath about half an hour before I practised. I went to the practice court and sweated like a pig. I'd walk straight on the court hot. And I imagined winning. Then when you walked on it was like seeing an action replay.'*

Lawrence Dallaglio, England rugby captain, starts visualizing the competition he's up against during the last few days before the match. He puts himself in the match environment, so that when the whistle blows he knows he's been there before.

> *'You can teach yourself visualization, but it's something you have to practise. You have to coach yourself. It's a whole new world*

– how the body reacts to the mind. But there is a lot to be said for walking around a rugby pitch two or three days before you play on it, and visualizing yourself doing everything perfectly – making a perfect pass, a perfect line-out and perfect tackles. Seeing yourself in the arena. Then when you go home, when you have got a bit of time to yourself to meditate, you might do the whole process again. As a result, when you go back on game day, you are not there for the first time and you know you are going to play well because you already have done.'

Sprinter John Regis used visualization and mental rehearsal when preparing for a major championship.

'I'd always have two or three days beforehand just rehearsing the race in my head. I would rehearse every facet of the race until I got bored, and then I did it some more. I did it so that when I got to that particular situation, I didn't need to think about anything. I just did it.

'All I did was visualize winning. It didn't matter what lane it was because I knew what I had to do. I was imagining the perfect race and the feeling I got when I was running the perfect race. When that happens it's called being in the zone, because you just don't seem able to lose or run badly. Even if you try to run badly, you can't because you're so tuned to what you should be doing and how you're supposed to perform, no matter what's going on around you.'

When on the blocks, waiting for the gun to go off, Regis kept his mind blank.

'I'm just thinking, "On any sound – go". I already know what I'm going to do, so I don't worry about it. When the gun goes, my body will take over with what it's been trained to do. The gun is the trigger that brings back the memory of all the mental visualization I'd done before, two days ago, a day ago, even two hours before.'

SCENARIO PLANNING

One great benefit from using visualization or mental rehearsal techniques is that they enable the individual to prepare for unexpected eventualities or unfamiliar situations. As NLP trainer Graham Shaw explains, visualization enables people to create a sense of familiarity in new situations, thus removing the shock of the new. Even if you don't know exactly what's going to happen, you can practise reacting to unexpected events. For example, a presenter with a business audience who doesn't want to handle awkward questions can imagine in advance how he's handling the questions to which he doesn't know the answer. He can imagine himself doing so successfully, and so improve his chances of actually performing well at the real event.

Sports psychologist Professor Graham Jones says that close to a race athletes should be visualizing in a very positive way, drawing on past successes so that they are building confidence and belief as the race approaches. A few days beforehand, you should go through all the 'what ifs'. You identify all the different scenarios and what might go wrong and you work through them. This helps you to be thoroughly prepared for anything that happens.

Former national athletics coach Frank Dick recalls that Olympic decathlon gold medallist Daley Thompson liked to use visualization for problem-solving. Dick says:

> *'That's an important use. You can think through something that might happen and then work out how you would deal with it. You end up going into the arena with a whole bunch of solutions in your mind to problems that have never occurred, but should one occur, you are better equipped.'*

Early in her career, Olympic hurdles gold medallist Sally Gunnell simply used visualization the night before a race. Then, in the run up to the 1992 Olympics, she began using visualization much more intensively and placing herself in a wide variety of different situations. She estimates that from October 1991, leading into Barcelona in 1992, she would go through the race on average 11 or 12 times a day.

David Hemery, former 400m hurdle Olympic gold medallist, helped Gunnell with the technique when she met him a couple of times in the year before the 1992 Olympics. Hemery was so expert at his visualization and experienced it so vividly that he could actually make himself sick at the end of visualizing a race.

'Hemery taught me how to visualize, starting around September 1991. He told me I had to visualize myself in every situation that could happen in that one race – the Olympic final. He taught me to make sure I went through the race including every scenario – whether I was in lane one with tight bends, whether I hit a hurdle, and seeing my competitors outside me. I had to make sure I got through the situation, corrected myself and got back into the stride pattern, making sure that I ran that perfect race.

'The key was making sure I crossed the line first in every situation. I'd find my brain telling me negative thoughts, but I had to see that tape and stop it – rewind it, making sure I crossed the line first every single time.

'I did it repeatedly during the day. I'd be sitting down at home watching television, or maybe I was training – but I'd go through the situation. It was hard at times to start with, but then I found it began to come naturally and became a way of life.'

Repeated visualization gave Gunnell the comfort of familiarity, whatever happened in the race.

'It felt comfortable; it felt familiar. If something happened – if I hit a hurdle or came off the eighth hurdle and wasn't in the lead – it felt familiar and I knew I should get back in the race. The race that I won – the 1992 Olympic final – I had visualized so many times. I included every situation and different athletes, whether they were on the inside or the outside of me.'

The visualization technique became so much a way of life that Gunnell still uses it, even though her athletics career is over.

'I use it, for example, when I'm going to do a big talk. I've just done one to 5000 people, which scared the life out of me. But I visualized myself standing on the stage, delivering the perfect speech and people enjoying what I was saying. It really helped and allowed me to control my nerves. I still find that live TV gets nerve-racking, but I visualize myself beforehand talking and feeling confident. You can use the technique for whatever you are doing in life. If you want to lose weight you can visualize how you want to look. So many people on diets don't actually see themselves how they want to be, getting into certain clothes. You can draw on that picture on days when you lose your motivation.'

Adrian Moorhouse, Olympic gold medallist in the 100m breaststroke, also used visualization to enhance his own competitive performance. He used to imagine various 'what if' scenarios – not necessarily positive ones.

'My race is two lengths. So, what if at halfway you are in last place? What do you do? I would visualize the start of the race and then swimming through and coming to a successful outcome. I would visualize different scenarios during the race, but it was always a successful outcome. The idea was that whatever the eventuality, you'd been there before so that it wasn't a worry – you knew what you would do.

'I was also a big fan of visualizing the race with a stopwatch – starting the watch at the same time that I started the visualization and trying to get the same time as when I swam. I used to get within half a second.

'I also used to visualize training. I would invent training partners swimming next to me. I imagined when we were kicking, leg kicks, it really hurt them.'

When the 100m breaststroke final arrived in Seoul in 1988, Moorhouse found that his visualization practice paid off.

'I remember swimming into the first turn, touching the wall and going under the water. I remember having a quick look and thinking, "Shit, I'm behind, but I've visualized what I've got to do now. I've got to catch that Russian guy. The same thing happened in my visualization. I was behind in the first length and I caught him." I remember thinking I'd left it too late. But I thought, "Keep going, hold the stroke, hold the stroke ..." and I remember it being very painful.'

Moorhouse stole the lead and won gold – by a hundredth of a second.

Champion National Hunt jockey Richard Dunwoody used to visualize his races in advance, both to improve his familiarity with the fences and to prepare for any eventuality.

'If the horse goes down on his head, you want to slip your reins and get back. In racing so much of it is anticipation. You want to be ready for the mistake almost before the horse has made it.'

Dunwoody found that his ability to visualize improved over time.

'I got better at it through my career. With a race like the Grand National, even when your mind ran that race a thousand times, there would be so many eventualities – horses coming from left, right and centre ... But I would study the colours of all the opponents and know everything about their form and their horses' form.'

Round-the-world yachtswoman Ellen MacArthur spends time before a race considering what might go wrong.

'When we're racing across the Atlantic there are lots of different things that could go wrong. You could break your arm, you could lose the hard drive on your computer, you could damage part of the rigging or your engine could stop working, which could mean

you're out of the race. So our preparation is both physical and mental.'

When yachtsman Sir Chay Blyth's catamaran capsized at Cape Horn, Blyth put into practice the actions he had rehearsed beforehand.

'You've gone through exercises in the event that you capsize – what you've got to do – so the actions just click in. It's like if your clutch goes on the car, you just pull into the side of the road and put your indicators on. You know what you've got to do in that situation and you just click into it. There's never any panic.'

Three times Olympic gold rowing medallist Matthew Pinsent knows the importance of mental rehearsal to prepare for any eventuality in the race.

'You mentally rehearse all the time. You imagine what the race is going to be like, what the opposition is going to do and what the feeling on the start line is going to be like. You imagine the weather conditions, the lake, the crowd and then you superimpose on that any amount of race outcomes or eventualities. You're constantly asking yourself, What happens if we do this? What happens if we make a good start? What happens if we make a bad start? What happens if New Zealand are half a length up on us when we don't expect them to be? What happens if we get within 20 strokes of the line and we're not leading? You go over and over them again and again. It's an illusion to think that you only think about winning because it's not true; you think about losing the whole time and you try and examine what the factors are that are going to make you lose or what mistakes you could make that would make you lose.

'Then it's important that if you ever don't know how you would deal with a scenario, that you talk to the other guys in the crew. There's very little communication that can go on during a race, so you've got to be able to deal with every eventuality with a very limited number of words or calls. The closer the competition gets, the

more often you have these discussions. During the heat, the semi-final and the final, you're looking at the opposition and trying to figure out what's going to happen and who might have something up their sleeve.'

Pinsent accepts that mistakes can be made in a race, but they don't necessarily mean you will lose.

'Sometimes it's not making no mistakes that determines the winner, but recovering from the mistakes you do make better than other people. That's quite good psychologically because it gives you some room to manoeuvre. You're not going out desperately trying not to make a mistake, because that almost becomes a self-fulfilling prophecy; soon you do make a mistake and you think you've blown it.'

Having a number of plans is vital to cope with all eventualities. As Pinsent says, you can't rely on the A plan all the time. If you *can* win the gold medal with the A plan, that's great, but more often than not you're pretty quickly down to plan B and then C. For Pinsent, the transition isn't panic stricken. He says:

'It's more like, "Okay, this is what they're doing, so this is what we're doing." If that doesn't work, we've got something else. You've got multilayers of tactics and confidence and ideas; as soon as you run out of ideas or you're taken by surprise by something, then you're in trouble. Then you're being defensive or waiting for them to make a mistake to hand the impetus back to you again.'

Pinsent says that the mental rehearsal before a competition provides a means of reinforcing your own strengths. You might also be examining and understanding your own weaknesses, but you don't reinforce them. Pinsent says he has been lucky enough in the Olympics to know that if the boat he was in rowed its best, it would win. He knew that he was a member of the best crew in the event and that if they rowed well, they would win. However, competitive life isn't necessarily that straightforward. Pinsent says:

> *'As it happens, in a couple of Olympic finals, we haven't rowed our best, so it's been close, but we still won. That's because it's no good just having a game plan that you must row your best. I think it's a weak psychological point to go out saying we have to row our best to win. It comes back to the old maxim about ordinary athletes training to give themselves a chance of winning, and true champions training to eliminate the chances of losing. What we're trying to do is first, narrow the band of performance we're in so the difference between our best and our worst is very small, then if you possibly can, you're trying to move that band away from the opposition's band. You know that your boat is better than their boat. You also want your worst to be better than their worst and, if possible, your worst to be better than their best – but you can't get that. You can't beat everybody all the time.'*

Javelin champion Steve Backley realizes the importance of being prepared for unexpected eventualities. He says it is essential to have a solution for any possible problem that could arise.

> *'For the 2002 Commonwealth Games in Manchester I made a trip up to make sure the run up was long enough and that there were no obstructions. Sometimes there's a drain, for example. One exercise I do is to make a snag list and write down anything and everything that could go wrong – for example, that the freezer breaks when I'm away or someone breaks into the house or my shoe lace snaps on the run-up.*
>
> *'I make a list of anything that can happen and then over three months come up with answers. I do that every year. I came a cropper once because there was one thing I hadn't put on the list. It was in Florida. I underestimated how hot it would be. I knew it would be hot, but didn't realize what effect it would have on my contact with the javelin.'*

This kind of preparation may seem like common sense, but it can still set champions apart from the rest. It isn't just the fact they make these preparations that counts, but the detail and quality involved. In the next chapter we look at some particular techniques that can help champions perform at their best, when they want.

Chapter 10

ANCHORS AND TRIGGERS

WHEN TRAINING THE MIND FOR COMPETITION, top athletes know that they can learn ways of creating certain desired mental states. In this way they can improve their ability to remain focused, to stay calm or to increase their determination – whatever the state they need to help them perform well.

NLP

This type of training is used in Neuro-Linguistic Programming, or NLP. As the name indicates, NLP is to do with the mind, language and programming: how to programme your mind for success. It was developed in the 1970s by Richard Bandler and John Grinder.

NLP trainer Graham Shaw explains that NLP is the study of what successful people do. In fact, NLP could be described as the art and science of human excellence. One of the principal uses of NLP is to model excellence. As Shaw explains, that essentially means that an NLP practitioner could take anyone in any field – an athlete, a footballer or a saleswoman – and analyse what it is they do that makes the difference in what they are doing. It might be to do with their sense of identity, what they believe about themselves, their values, what their skills and capabilities are, and their behaviours. Also, Shaw says, their environment has an impact. People who are successful tend to have all those elements in alignment. NLP therefore enables you to learn from anyone who is very good at something. Shaw says:

> *'You could take David Beckham and look at what he physically does, what he believes about himself, what his sense of identity is, what he does and what the component parts of that are that make the difference in terms of him being successful in pressurized situations. What is it he does that is merely idiosyncratic? That's not necessarily the bit you want to copy; that's just their foible.*
>
> *'You often find that there are certain key pieces that make the difference. It could be physical, or to do with mental strategy, with visualization or with how they prepare. You then look at the person you want to transfer those skills to and you create their own kind of model. It's not going to be exactly the same. But hopefully you have enough pieces in there that it's going to make a difference to them.'*

NLP techniques overlap with other areas of sports psychology. For example, NLP involves goal-setting, visualization and managing your state – getting psyched up or keeping nerves at a level that supports performance, rather than hampering it.

ANCHORS AND TRIGGERS

NLP provides a technique for creating desired states, such as a feeling of confidence. This technique is called 'anchoring'. If someone says they have never felt confident on the starting line, that may be true, but they probably have felt confident in another situation. NLP enables someone to draw on that other experience and transfer it to the experience where they need it. Shaw explains:

> *'With NLP you would ask the person to think of a time when they felt really confident. As a coach, you could say, "Go back to a time when you felt really confident. It might be on holiday, at school or at work. A time when you felt you could do anything. Be there now. Are you there now?"'*

Shaw says it is important to use the present tense when speaking to the individual who is recalling the experience. To help the person recreate the past sensations fully, you can ask questions such as: What are you seeing? What's the picture like? What are you hearing? Are the sounds loud or quiet? In this way, Shaw says, you can build up what are called the submodalities – the finer distinctions of the experience. When the experience becomes more real the physiology of the person changes; the person's breathing may change, for example. This is a sign that tells you they are really back in the experience and reliving it fully.

The aim is to get the person into an associated experience, rather than a dissociated one. This means that the person is seeing the experience through their own eyes, rather than watching themselves having the experience. They are feeling the same sensations they felt before, in the same way.

When the individual is fully experiencing the desired state it is possible to create an 'anchor' that becomes associated with the state. This could be achieved by simply squeezing a certain finger, or touching them on a certain point on their shoulder. If the anchor is firmly established, it is possible to 'trigger' the desired state at will and on command in future – simply by squeezing the same finger.

Anchors can take many forms. They can be words, memories, images, feelings or even pieces of clothing. Shaw says:

> *'When you go for an interview you might put on a particular tie because that tie makes you feel great. That's an anchor. You might put a piece of music on in the car when going to a difficult meeting because it buoys you up a little.'*

Once you know what triggers work to create positive states for you, you can use them deliberately when needed. You can trigger them at will.

Shaw recalls an example of a word-based anchor told to him by a sports commentator.

> *'A basketball player had an anchor that he used in big tournaments so that he could put balls in the basket. He previously was very nervous. In training he could always put balls in the basket, but he couldn't always do it on the real court.*
>
> *'So he was asked what feeling he would like to have in those situations on the basketball court and to recall a time when he had experienced that feeling in the past. He remembered a time when he was at the beach, sitting with his girlfriend on a wall overlooking the sea and eating soft ice cream. He said he felt great and that was how he wanted to feel on the basketball court. He was asked to get that feeling and then think of a word that would bring it back. His word was "soft ice". When he said "soft ice" to himself, he went back to that feeling. That association was built into him.*
>
> *'When he went out onto the basketball court and the fans were screaming at him and he had to take a free shot, he could say "soft ice" to himself and he went into a different state. He created that sense of peace.'*

Former 400m champion Roger Black used to listen to music for inspiration before a race, choosing the music he needed to create the desired mental state. This music was his trigger, but it took him some time to find out what music created the most appropriate mental state for him.

'Lyrics of songs inspire me. I listened to certain songs before I ran and some of them were really motivating for me. The lyric that motivated me most was written by a band I was a big fan of when I was younger, called Aztec Camera. A guy called Roddy Frame wrote all the songs. There was a lyric in one of his songs that really crystallized everything for me and I played it all the time. It said: "The secret is silver, it's to shine and to never simply survive." I always thought, "If I am going to do this I am going to shine and not just simply survive, not just do it because I am good at it." That song had a big effect on me. He was right because I got a silver medal!'

Black recalls a great sense of peace just before the Olympic final in 1996.

'For most of my career I would stand behind the line just before a race and like most athletes, you are supposed to be really agitated and really nervous. You are supposed to be aggressive, but it never really worked for me. It took me ten years to work that out. I used to have aggressive music in my ears when I was warming up. I used to think I'd really got to "get up" for this. I worked out in 1995 that that wasn't the right state for me to be in before I performed. For me it was about being at peace, really being calm. Of course you've got nerves, but it's about not letting them take over. When I walked into the Olympic stadium I smiled, I was very focused and inwardly I was very calm. I realized that for me this was the best way to be. That was how I could really come into myself and be incredibly focused, rather than aggressive.'

Sports psychologist John Syer works with sportspeople to help them develop useful triggers. Syer explains that triggers are a way of providing an association. For example, when you evoke an image or touch something it is often related to a particular feeling. However, when Syer is working with an athlete, the process is the other way round. Syer says:

'I ask what feeling they want in a particular situation. Working with cyclists, they may say that the feeling they want at the beginning of the race is different to the feeling they want when they are two thirds of the way up a steep hill. Once I know what feeling is important for the athlete in a given situation, I look at the triggers. I ask for the situations that evoke that feeling. What people? What clothes? What music?'

The same technique can be used in many situations. NLP trainer Graham Shaw, for example, uses it to help youngsters who get too nervous before taking exams. He asks them to choose the resource they want to have available to them in the situation. This might be a sense of calm, for example, or a feeling of relaxation with a bit of anticipation thrown in. The resource identified, Shaw asks the person to identify a situation in the past when they had that resource – when they experienced the desired state. He says:

'You ask them to go there and fully experience it, so they can step forward into it, visualize it, imagine it, experience it fully. Then you get them to step back out again. Then get them to go back in. You do that about four or five times. Then they can more or less do it when they want. They can access that resource.'

Before relying on the anchor in a real situation, Shaw recommends giving it a test to check it works. Take the teenager who is nervous about exams and develops an anchor for calmness. He can test this anchor by imagining walking into the exam room and then asking himself how he feels. If he feels nervous, he should try using his anchor and then ask himself how he feels again. If he feels calm, the technique has worked.

As we have said, triggers can take many different forms. Music can be a valuable trigger for encouraging creative thought. Shaw says:

'If you want to improve at a stroke your ability to study, or to be creative when you have to write a project, play some baroque music in the background very quietly. Baroque music goes at a

rhythm of about 60 beats per minute, which roughly equates to the average heart rate. It slows down the heart rate and increases blood flow to the brain. It also begins to increase the flow or the doorway between the left and right sides of the brain. Why is that helpful? It puts you in a kind of trance. You find you're able to focus and you get into the flow. You're able to come up with lots of ideas very easily. And if you've got to learn something, that's the sort of music you want in the background.'

PRACTICAL USE

Breaststroke gold medallist Adrian Moorhouse worked with a sports psychologist during his career, learning about the power of the mind and techniques for manipulating the body with the mind. Part of this involved looking at ways for dealing with pain, and also for turning pain into a trigger to release extra adrenalin.

'I worked on this quite a lot before the World Championships. I did a lot of trigger work related to pain, so that when it hit me, that was my trigger for "go for it". It was my trigger for: "The pain will release a surge of adrenalin in me and I will be the fastest swimmer in that pool." I actually felt myself lift in the water when it happened.'

Dr Stephanie Cook also found triggers useful when she was competing in modern pentathlon, which requires completing five events during the course of a day.

'There's not much time to prepare between each event. You go directly from one to the next and you have to be able to switch straight away into the next mode. So I certainly used to use triggers. For example, every time I went to fence and put my mask down, that was a trigger for a certain mental state. That would be my cue to focus entirely on what I was doing and to forget all the distractions around me. It was a similar idea with putting on my goggles and getting up onto the blocks before the swimming event. These were all triggers.'

In order for these triggers to become automatic, Cook had to practise them regularly.

*'Unless you've practised something like that, you can't expect it
to suddenly work in competition. When you go to a competition
you're not actually expecting to do anything completely out of the
ordinary. The chances are that you may; people end up surprising themselves because of that extra adrenalin. They might run
that bit faster. But at the end of the day, you're not going to suddenly change what you do in practice. So you're not trying to do
anything different; you're trying to perform to your potential – and
you should be training at your potential as well. For me, that's how
you go into competitions. You have the confidence to know what
you're capable of doing – and that's what you're trying to achieve.
Hopefully you'll do a bit better.'*

Anchors and triggers can be used to create the right mental state
in training, as well as when competing. If you don't have the right
mental state when training, it doesn't have the same effect. Former
Sunderland manager Howard Wilkinson says:

*'We've got to get footballers to recognize that preparing for train-
ing is as important as preparing for a match. If you're going to
maximize your training there's a warm-up period mentally and
physically. The best preparation for getting the most out of your
training is not to turn up at five to ten, throw your kit on and take
a call on your mobile phone. You have your living zone and your
training zone and in between there's a zone where you go from
one to the other. You do that physically when you go out on the
pitch. But mentally, the warm-up has to be done before that. It's
something we've got to educate players about. If you're going to get
the most out of training, your brain has got to be in training mode
when you start.'*

Getting the best out of training also requires players to try to recreate
mentally the conditions they would face in a real game. Wilkinson

says: 'If it's Friday morning and I've said there's to be no tackling, you've still got to train as if there is tackling.'

Mental training, and in particular techniques such as anchors and triggers, enables sporting champions to boost their performances. In the next chapter we look more widely at how elite sportspeople train their minds and bodies to cope with the pressure of competition.

Chapter 11

PREPARING FOR PRESSURE

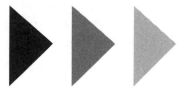

WINNING RACES OR SCORING MATCH-WINNING GOALS doesn't come without some degree of pressure. The top quality sportspeople are those who show themselves able – time and again – to rise to the occasion and hold their nerve when it really counts. In fact, they thrive on that pressure – and they train themselves to make sure they perform well under it.

LEARNING TO HANDLE PRESSURE

Sports psychologist John Syer explains that excitement and anxiety are the same sort of emotion. An athlete learns that discomfort is necessary to a good performance. Sportsmen need to be excited and it is possible to turn anxiety into excitement. Syer says:

'I was in a plane crash once and as a result I didn't fly for a long time. But I eventually found a strategy for dealing with my fear. This was to pay precise attention to my sensations in the moment. Fritz Perls, the colourful co-founder of Gestalt Therapy, used to say "when you have one foot in the past [what happened] and one foot in the future [what might happen] you are pissing on the present." Once I'd mastered this, I discovered that each time the plane I was in was about to take off, I was excited. I had found a way to redefine my sensations I was experiencing.'

Professor Graham Jones has completed research that shows the importance of dealing with the pressure of competition. He says that thriving on the pressure of competition is a must for top sporting champions. They know that the pressure is going to be there and know they can handle it. They accept that anxiety is inevitable and know they can cope with it. As Professor Jones says, you know it's going to be tough, you know there are going to be times when you don't want to be there but you come through because you've done it before.

In the course of his research Professor Jones has found that elite and non-elite sportspeople experience the same things in terms of physiological build-up, but elite performers interpret that differently to non-elite performers. The first group experience facilitative anxiety, while the second experience debilitative anxiety. In other words, Professor Jones says, elite performers see what's happening to them in a very positive way.

'You might, for example, have a 100m sprinter who has a massive physiological build-up. A sprinter came to me once saying, "I don't want this, I don't like it. I want you to help me relax and calm myself down." I said, "That's fine, but let's think about what you're doing. The hundred metres is about explosive power. What your body is doing is building itself up to help you produce that. So I can help you compose yourself a little bit, but you don't want to lose that stuff either. So let's think about the way you think about it, and see that's it's actually helping you."

'That sprinter, during the build-up, began thinking that "this is brilliant – let's have some more" and that the build-up was helping. It was just a completely different psyche to the same physiological response.'

As Professor Jones explains, what matters is how people interpret what is happening to them. If you put yourself in a stressful situation you can interpret it in one of two ways. You can see it as a real threat and get all the negative things that go with that, or you can interpret it as a real opportunity – you can look forward to it and accept it. The same things happen to you, but you have a completely different response. For example, Professor Jones says, you may not have got enough sleep the night before a major event, but that's OK. You can interpret it as meaning that you know the event is important and you are focused on your performance in it.

THRIVING UNDER PRESSURE

Former Australian fly-half Michael Lynagh was one of the greatest ever rugby kickers. For him, extreme pressure was a normal part of his sporting life. The whole match result could hinge on his ability to get the ball between the posts. Lynagh recalls one such situation when he was playing for Queensland against Ireland at Ballymore, Brisbane.

'The full-time siren had gone and we received a penalty to win – and that wasn't an easy one. Nothing else mattered but me kicking that goal and nobody else could have an influence on the match. I remember saying afterwards, "Yes, that's why you are a goal kicker".

'That time I got it, but I have missed kicks as well and that's pretty tough. But that's what you are there for. That's actually the performance. Performing under pressure, making decisions that influence outcomes, making actions that influence outcomes – that's one of the great things about sport.

'For me, those moments are why you play. That's why you are a goal kicker. As I say, I haven't always been successful in terms of making the last goal to influence the decision – I have missed some. There was one where we lost the Bledisloe Cup. I had a kick to draw or win – it wasn't an easy one, but I missed. And that cost us the Cup. All my team-mates said, "Nah it wasn't on a kick, we played poorly". But I remember that being a pretty low point in my career, though I wouldn't have had it any other way looking back on it. You take the responsibility and you take the accolades that come with it, as well as the disappointment.'

England rugby fly-half Jonny Wilkinson admits that he doesn't enjoy pressure in his normal daily life, but somehow it is different when playing rugby. When he is kicking, he says he doesn't think of it as a pressure. He sees it as his opportunity to do something for his team. He understands that there is pressure involved, but he deals with that during the week before the match.

Wilkinson deals with it by practising his kicking over and over again. He's not someone who just takes a few kicks on the Friday, then turns up on the Saturday to play. He can't allow himself to think that he could have done more to prepare and that, as a result, he has let his team-mates down.

When putting together his dream team, England rugby head coach Clive Woodward looks for players who will, as a group, rise to triumph in pressurized occasions.

'You've got to try and find those players – and you do need 15 of them – who are absolutely going to rise to the occasion. Say it's a World Cup final, we're five points down and we've got a scrum on their line. Is their mindset going to be "Yes, fantastic, this is our moment", or "Oh my God"?'

Anyone in the 'Oh my God' camp shouldn't expect to put on an England shirt in the near future.

Sprinter John Regis says he always felt under pressure before a big race – a championship that came round once every four years. When competing on those occasions he knew that he had one chance to get it right. Everything before the big race was just fine tuning and didn't matter. As Regis says, if you made a mistake in the big race, you had another four years to wait. That in itself created a lot of pressure.

How people cope with that pressure is a key factor in determining whether they become a champion or not. Champions relish the chance to rise to the occasion when it matters, Regis says.

'You want to be in a pressure cooker situation. You want to be there and to show the world that you can rise to the occasion, even if you've had a bad season. For the champion, the only race that means anything is the big one. In the others he could come fourth or fifth, but he knows he's preparing for the one big race. I knew that I wanted to be at my best for the European Championships, the Commonwealth Games, the World Championships, the Olympics. The rest was irrelevant. People don't remember that John had a great race in Zurich. To me that's what makes a champion – it's the person who can raise their game when everybody's there competing in a major championship. I wanted to be the man standing tall at the top.

'Talent gives people an ability to perform, but if all the guys on the line have the same amount of talent, then it's the mental strength that determines who crosses the line first. It's the person who doesn't panic under pressure who wins. It took me three seasons in athletics to learn that. I just used to come to meetings and run hard to win. But at the top level you can't just run hard and win. It's like driving a car with your eyes closed. After the first full three years all of a sudden I opened my eyes.'

THE BIG FREEZE

Former Davis Cup captain David Lloyd recalls playing a Davis Cup doubles match with Mark Cox against Czechoslovakia. The Czechs were a pretty good pair and the match was a great one, Lloyd says, recalling the battle.

'We struggled. We got to 5–4 up in the fifth set, with Coxie to serve. I was waiting, waiting and nothing was happening. I turned round and Coxie was on the baseline like a statue. I went up to him and asked if he was all right. He looked at me. He was left-handed and so he looks at his right hand and says, "I can't get these balls out of my hand". I said, "Just throw the f**king things up". He said, "Oh, alright", and he did – down against the line. He was actually frozen. I couldn't understand because that never happened to me – not until about ten years ago. I was serving and I couldn't get the balls out of my hand. In the end I threw them up but I didn't get them above my nose and we lost the game.

'With Coxie, I shocked him and told him to hit the balls and off he went. He threw the balls up and we won the game. But it's strange when you've fought all the way and you're on top, that that happens. You should be thinking you're a million dollars at that point, whereas nine times out of ten you think the opposite and it's the worst game you play. Mentally we sometimes freeze.

In contrast, champions want the pressure. They love it.'

TRAINING TO THRIVE UNDER PRESSURE

When under pressure, champions manage to keep thinking clearly and correctly. They are able to make the right decisions, regardless of the intense stress they are under. As Dr Ceri Evans from Gazing Performance Limited says, it is clear thinking that drives effective action; ineffective thinking leads to ineffective action. Anybody can think clearly in moments when they are under control, but it's thinking clearly under pressure that is difficult.

Whether seeking to maintain skill levels or to think clearly under pressure, there is no substitute for training.

Dr Ceri Evans and his colleagues at Gazing Performance advocate building in pressure situations to the skills acquisition and training process. In Gazing's recommended skills ladder, the first level of training should be focused on mastering the technical aspects of the skill, which often involves breaking it down into its component parts. Level two involves rehearsal of the skill with some intensity and pressure, indicative of playing or competing conditions. Level three of the training introduces diversions. Dr Evans says:

> *'To be successful under pressure you have to have experienced conditioning at all skill levels. Mental conditioning conducted solely in classroom-type settings is likely to have limited effect. It is better when it is integrated with the technical and the physical. Players need conditioning to keep their attention focused on the task.'*

Dr Evans gives an example of a player practising a throw to a line-out in rugby. The skill components would include technical aspects such as how to stand and how to hold the ball, while the whole technique involves the whole throwing action. Intensity can be introduced by repetition, rehearsal when physically stressed, and by using opposed lineouts. Pressure can be introduced in various ways. Evans says:

> *'Before handing over the ball you could dunk it in water. You can distract the player with unexpected noise. The player's goal is to stay on task and not get diverted – stay with the rituals they have put in place.'*

Players need to practise maintaining their process focus during real training sessions. These enable them to experience what Gazing calls 'world lessons'. In contrast, learning something in a classroom is more a 'word lesson' and not as powerful a learning experience.

Evans gives the example of a karate drill. A young practitioner may start out learning and practising some hand combinations. They may have been told to keep their hands up to protect themselves and to maintain awareness for the opponents' attacks, but how well do they learn the lesson? Dr Evans says:

> *'As a trainer you could get them doing some combinations, and when they let their guard drift down the trainer can counterattack with the focus mitt. That focuses their attention on keeping their hands up and defending themselves. If they drop their hands again the trainer can attempt to counterattack with the focus mitt again.*

Once they've got that idea, the trainer could unexpectedly attack with a leg kick. The student may drop their hands in surprise, thinking that they weren't warned about this possibility for the drill. Their response may let the trainer attack the exposed head again. Then they may finally understand what is meant by the concept of deliberately placing their attention on certain important tasks, and maintaining this focus in the face of predictable and unpredictable diversions. This can induce a heightened sense of awareness and improved control of attention. That might give them a "world" lesson, one they have experienced for themselves.'

Dr Stephanie Cook practised techniques for dealing with anxiety, such as breathing and relaxation techniques. She and her coach tried to recreate a sense of pressure in practice. She says:

'In shooting you want to be very calm and controlled and have a very steady hand. In a competition environment you have to deal with the affects of adrenalin, which causes a real physiological response. You have to know what to expect and then know how to deal with it. So when I was training we tried to simulate the competitive environment – we would have regular competitions so that I could train in ways to deal with competitive situations.'

England rugby head coach Clive Woodward and his coaching team try to up the pressure during training sessions to see how players react.

'You want to try and create pressure situations. When it happens for real, you want the players to react positively. There are all sorts of ways you can try to create these pressure situations in training. The idea is that when it comes for real they will have rehearsed for it mentally. They've handled it and it should become a lot easier. So you can coach for coping with pressure, though I do believe a lot of it is innate. It's in there somewhere.'

Former England Under-21 coach David Platt felt that the England Under-21 football team needed to be put under pressure in training, to see whether they had what it takes to play at the highest level.

'I thought I could put them under pressure, because if they were going to become what they should with their ability, they had to be able to handle that pressure. When I was at Nottingham Forest I might not load somebody up with a great deal of pressure because I might be unsure whether he'd be able to handle it. At international level, you might still be unsure whether they'll be able to handle it, but they're going to have to if they're going to go on and play for the full England side in a World Cup. So you may as well find out. It's about stretching people.'

AUTOMATIC PILOT

If players are to perform well under pressure they need to be able to switch into an 'automatic pilot' mode. They need to be able to function without having to think consciously about what they are doing.

Athletics coach Ron Roddan would train his athletes to run on automatic pilot. He would tell them how to run the 200 metres, how to start, run the bend and come off the bend. Every time they would get told the same thing. When they came to run an actual 200m race, Roddan would tell them to do what they did in training. In effect, he says, he basically brainwashed them. He told them what to do in training and then they didn't need to think about it in the race. As Roddan describes it, 'You have programmed the computer'.

It is important to be able to perform on automatic pilot right from the start of a race. Roddan says:

'Once the race starts it's a matter of making sure everything you have practised comes in automatically. Once the gun goes, your aim is just to get to the finish as quickly as possible. That's all you think about. You concentrate on one thing: move on the B of the Bang. That's the only thing you think about.'

England rugby fly-half Jonny Wilkinson, when kicking for goal, relies on all the work he has done in training to put him on autopilot. He goes into his kick routine, a procedure he has rehearsed over and over again.

> *'As soon as you know you are going to kick you fall into that routine, which more or less shuts you off from everything. So I would set the ball up, move back a certain number of steps, check everything is in line, do a visualization of the path of the ball – where it's going to go and where I want it to go. Then I move to the side so I am now ready to kick. The routine then continues in a visualizing kind of way, but it's actually more of a sensation; I imagine the feeling I have when the ball hits the foot, the perfect feeling of how I want it to feel when it hits my foot, where I want it to hit my foot – what it's going to feel like when it goes right.*
>
> *'Then I find a tiny dot dead centre between the posts, or wherever I am aiming. I visualize the line of the ball to that dot, as if the ball were on a wire attached to it. Then I have a kind of "centring" response, whereby I visualize all the power going from my central point down to where it needs to be, down my left leg and exploding from my left foot. I really feel that sensation. Then I really focus on the exact point on the ball I am going to hit and the part of my foot that I want it to come off. Then I send the ball up that wire.*
>
> *'So I don't stand by the ball and say, "I am going to kick this, I feel fantastic". It's that as soon as I am given the kick I go into the routine I have done a hundred times a week in practice.'*

Spectators can see the outward signs of this routine.

> *'I tend to push my left foot and toes to the floor. That's what's happening as I am getting the sensation of the ball and the part of the foot I want it to come off. It's a reaction to what I am thinking, but that's also how I foresee my foot being as I hit the ball. You do visualize how it's all going to pan out.'*

Wilkinson also has an unusual hand movement but this, he says, is just what happens to him when he is imagining all the power and the energy coming from the central point down to his leg. Similarly with the way he bends his knee – that's just the shape he finds himself in when thinking through the kick in advance. As Wilkinson says, the movement is a by-product of what is really important – which is him feeling strong and powerful and confident in what he is about to do.

Going through this routine also gives Wilkinson a sense of protection, despite the huge numbers of people watching.

> *'It's a very individual thing, and you are very much on your own out there when you are doing it. It's the way it has to be for me to be engrossed in what I am doing and shut off from everyone else and what they are doing. It allows me to get on with something I really need to succeed in. It makes me feel a bit protected and secure in the routine.'*

Wilkinson says he prepares for each kick the same way, and always with the same thoroughness.

> *'I'll never move towards the kick unless I am completely ready. That means if I miss, I miss because I didn't get it right, not because I wasn't prepared. I believe there's no excuse for that. If I get it wrong because I slipped a bit or I was absolutely knackered, fair play. But if it's because I'm not well enough set in my mind, that's no excuse. I can control that.'*

Former Australian fly-half Michael Lynagh also relied on his automatic kicking routine in a pressure situation. He recalls a penalty awarded to Australia against England in the 1991 World Cup at Twickenham. Lynagh describes himself as going into 'an almost dazed state'. He says:

> *'I focused and concentrated on the routine – down to how I kneeled, how I would place the ball, the line I would see from the seam of the ball through to the middle of the posts. I wasn't*

thinking about the crowd because I was thinking about the task at hand.

'Focusing on the outcome often causes failure. Focus on the task at hand and the outcome will look after itself. The ability to be able to do that as a team, as an individual and as a goal kicker is absolutely crucial to performance. If we start worrying about where we are going, what the score is going to be, and whether we are going to win – forget about it. If you do each individual task well and then go to the next one, the scoreboard will look after itself.

'It was all about routine, getting my routine right and then just jumping into that routine. It gets disturbed every now and then. In the 1987 World Cup semi-final against France the lead changed six or seven times. France ended up winning. Five minutes from time David Campese scored a try in the right-hand corner. I had got to kick to go into the lead by one point. An eight-year-old kid brought the sand out. Part of my routine was picking up the bucket and saying "Thank you." It was just part of the routine and normally the kids just go back again. This one stopped and looked at me and said, "Pretty important, this kick." I said, "I know that, I know that". I ended up getting it.'

THE PRESSURE OF PENALTIES

One of the most pressured situations in sport has to be the penalty shoot-out. As England football manager Sven Göran-Eriksson says:

'The walk from the middle circle to the penalty spot is a long walk, incredibly long. How many thoughts do you have during it?'

The only way to succeed at penalty taking and deal with the intense pressure is to have developed a secure penalty-taking routine. Eriksson says:

'You must be focused. You must know exactly what you want to do. Don't let the opposition goalkeeper play tricks on you. It's a

*war with the goalkeeper, and he will do everything to try to disturb
you.*

*'Don't go to the spot early. Wait until the goalkeeper is more
or less where he will be. Put the ball right on the spot. Don't try to
cheat because then the referee will come and disturb you. Be sure
where you want to put that penalty, and then do it, whatever happens.'*

The penalty-taking routine starts when the penalty takers enter the
centre circle. It involves who players stand next to, what they do while
they wait, what they think about and what the trigger is that gets them
absolutely focused when it's their turn. Howard Wilkinson, former
Football Association technical director, says:

*'Do you leave the centre circle when the goalkeeper's got the ball,
or when the referee's got the ball, or when the ball boy has got it? If
you leave the centre circle when the goalkeeper or the ball boy's got
the ball, you're not in charge; they are. If you go when the referee's
got the ball, then you're in charge.'*

The combination of good technique and strong mental approach
makes a good penalty taker. Wilkinson believes that Alan Shearer
has always inspired confidence when he steps up to take a penalty
because he has both attributes. Wilkinson says that Shearer is not
aware of his opponents or the crowd. He has no sense of anything
else going on apart from his penalty kick. He just has the ability to
focus entirely on the task in hand.

David Platt, former England captain, had a firm penalty routine.
He recalls his attitude to taking penalties:

*'I'd go to sleep the night before knowing what I'm going to do,
having practised what I'm going to do, knowing where I am going
to put that penalty. I would replay it in my mind. I could take the
goalkeeper out of the equation because I knew that if I connected*

right and I put the ball where I wanted to put it, at the right velocity, then he wasn't going to get it anyway.

'Technique is important because everybody will have a negative thought. So you need the ability to block out those negative thoughts. I want to be in charge of the whole walk. I would never jog up – I think people do that because they are nervous. When people put a ball down and turn round, to me they're nervous. It's like they are turning away from the situation. But if that's their routine and what they're familiar with, then it's right and proper that they do it. But for me, the fact that you're strolling out means you are slowing it down because you're in control.

'There was one boy who took a penalty recently who I thought really had some balls. He put the ball on the spot and then he tied his bootlace before he took the penalty. That is being in complete control of the situation.

'I believe I can trust my technique to score a goal and I don't want anything else in my mind when I'm going up from the half-way line to the penalty box. I know exactly where I'm going to put the ball and I won't be changing my mind. I made the mistake of changing my mind in 1990.'

PENALTY PRACTICE

With penalty taking, practice is vital. And the situation needs to be as realistic as it can be, including trying to simulate the distractions and the pressure. As England football manager Sven Göran-Eriksson explains:

'You should try to be as prepared as possible. We practised penalties during the World Cup and we told the goalkeeper to try to distract the penalty takers. If they didn't put the ball exactly on the spot, the referee – Ray Clemence – told them to wait. It's difficult because you can never do it 100% realistically, because you can never put on the same pressure during a practice. Imagine if you meet Argentina and go to a penalty shoot-out. You are the last man

up and you know that if you score, you stay in the tournament, but if you don't score, you go home.'

Trying to add pressure into the training practice can only help players when it comes to the real thing. Eriksson believes that even though you can't recreate the same pressure 100% perfectly, you can get part way. He says:

'In football practice you normally play seven against seven or eight against eight for ten minutes. Instead of a team having two corners, they have a penalty. Even though it's a practice, every player wants desperately to win that game. They want desperately to win it.'

Sports psychologist Professor Graham Jones believes it is 'absolutely crucial' to practise penalty taking. He considers the requirements for successful penalty taking:

'First of all you make a decision on where you're going to put the ball, and then it's all process. If you've got any doubts on where you're going to put the ball, stop. Be quite certain. Don't just hit it as hard as you can.

'Once you know where you're going to put the ball, it's process. You work through beforehand what you do. You place the ball on the spot, walk back a certain number of paces. Do you turn your back? Whatever you do, you do it in the same way.

'The keeper will come out and try to distract penalty takers, so they need to have worked through that as well. They might think the keeper is doing it because he knows they're going to score and therefore they should feel great about it.

'It's about having complete control. The process is absolutely crucial. It's the people who forget the process and try to do things differently who get in a mess.'

Former Leeds and Sunderland manager Howard Wilkinson notes that the perfect penalty taker is someone not remotely aware of the crowd, the police or anything else apart from the process of taking that kick. Wilkinson's advice to players is:

> *'Develop a good swing. Get a reliable swing, because under pressure the swing will stay with you. You won't even have to think about it. You've got to get that groove well-honed, well-practised, well-oiled. It's about routine.'*

David Platt believed it essential to practise penalties and he made sure the England Under-21s did so, given that international games could be very tight:

> *'I couldn't recreate the pressure, but they could practise the technique. They could practise the walk from the halfway line to the penalty box. The more you practise, the less you leave to chance. They could visualize it – from the moment the referee gave a penalty.'*

NLP trainer Graham Shaw has no doubt that there is plenty that can be done to improve performance in penalty shoot-outs. It is also possible to recreate the sense of pressure. Shaw suggests how penalty practice could be built into training:

> *'The first step would be to have the players go out and practise kicking the ball into the net in exactly the way that would be their ideal penalty shot. Then you could sit them down and have them imagine that they're doing that every single time. Then they go out and do it again for real. You would probably have them keep a record so they can prove it to themselves that it's working.'*

After that, you can develop strategies for dealing with the pressure of the real situation. Take a scenario where the final whistle has gone and the match is to be decided on penalties. Say that the sound of the final whistle, followed by the manager asking if you're ready to take a penalty, normally results in feelings of nerves and being scared. NLP can be used to identify those kinds of triggers and then develop a strategy for dealing with them.

For example, in this case the stimulus for the nervous response is the manager asking if you're ready to take a penalty. By putting something between the stimulus and the response, the performance can be improved. Without this, the nervous response can seem automatic. In fact, Shaw says, our responses are not all automatic; they just seem that way because we have done them so often. What we want is to have a choice about our response.

Shaw suggests getting players to practise their response, perhaps by having them waiting in the centre circle not knowing who is next up to take the penalty. This is where anchors, as referred to in Chapter 10, can be used to get players into the required state.

SELECTING THE PENALTY TAKERS

Sports psychologist Professor Graham Jones believes that choking during a penalty shoot-out is a sign of mental weakness. He says that mental toughness provides a barrier against choking, so choking is a function of not being mentally tough. Mentally tough people may have negative thoughts, but they get rid of them straight away, Professor Jones says. However, when people start to choke, when things are starting to go wrong, they lose some control of the environment. There's a snowball effect and things just get worse.

This means that when selecting players to take penalties, alongside basic technical ability there has to be mental toughness. Jones says:

'There has to be a combination of the two, but if selecting players, I would go with the people you think can handle the situation. They're not necessarily the people who step forward either, because a sign of mental weakness is actually stepping forward and thinking "I should be taking this, I'm expected to take this. I don't want to, but I'm going to." Mental weakness can be taken for mental toughness.'

Reliability is also what every manager wants in his penalty takers. Sometimes those initially reluctant to put themselves forward to take penalties do the best. Former Leeds and Sunderland manager Howard Wilkinson recalls one player who was initially the least willing to consider it.

> *'He finished up being the most reliable player. He was reliable and a quick runner. He had a steady personality. He wasn't one to panic, he wasn't impetuous, he wasn't a depressive. He put every penalty in the same place, but providing the goalkeeper didn't cheat, it went in. He could put the ball there 99 times out of a 100 at a pace that was impossible to deal with.'*

There is no doubt that those who are chosen to take the penalties need to be happy to do so. England's players were asked if they were willing to take penalties before the World Cup. England football coach Sven Göran-Eriksson says:

> *'First we talked about it and asked them if they wanted to take a penalty. Most of them wanted to. Then we practised.'*

A HOCKEY EXAMPLE

A team can significantly strengthen its ability to perform well in penalty shoot-outs. Sports psychologist John Syer was asked to go to the Netherlands to work with the national men's hockey team before the 2000 Olympics. Although one of the top teams in the world, they had a record of losing major competitions on penalties. These only come into effect in the semi-final or final, when the two competing teams are level at the end of extra time.

> *'Mauritz Hendriks, the national coach, was determined to leave nothing to chance. He asked me to work with the team over a period of two weeks just on penalties. I began by having a long discussion with Mauritz to discover his precise objectives, with whom I'd be working and for how long. I found that he wanted not only to improve individual technical ability through mental training but also to build a strong team within the team, that would*

take responsibility for winning the match if it went to a penalty shoot-out.'

Syer got the players to complete a number of exercises. He describes the first of these:

> *'I asked the players to move all the furniture to one end of the room and then to stand against the walls. I then put a hockey bag in the centre of the empty space and asked the players three questions. After each question they placed themselves in relation to the bag, beside the bag meaning "a huge amount" or "very much" or "very" and against the wall meaning "none" or "not at all". The first question was "How many penalties have you taken?" and the second was "How much do you enjoy taking penalties" and the third was "How good are you at taking penalties?" After each question and self-placement the players looked around to see where the others had placed themselves. After the final question, each player spoke in turn about his experience of taking penalties. At the end, they brought their chairs back into a circle and said what had struck them as they listened to each other.*
>
> *'This was an introduction to my sessions with them and did two things. It allowed each player to reflect on his attitude to taking (or, in the case of the goalkeepers, defending against) penalties and it made him more aware of other players in this "team". The exercise also resulted in one player dropping out of the group. He was willing to continue but didn't relish the idea and Mauritz decided not to insist.'*

Syer then led a series of team-building exercises. He wanted to create the sense that there were two teams: a team that played the full match and a sub-unit that took over when extra time had not produced a winner.

> *'We developed a strong team identity through a variety of exercises and a number of discussions. There was dialogue between the players who took the penalties and the goalkeepers, particularly*

with regard to what distracted them. We did different visualization exercises of taking penalties or saving penalties. Players each spoke of their physical and mental routine. And the team reviewed their hitherto unspoken norms of being together, as well as deciding in minute detail what they would do from the minute the umpire signalled the end of extra time. The more they talked, the stronger they became as a team, as they increased awareness of themselves, each other and their complementary differences.'

The exercises paid off. At the Olympics, the Netherlands team reached the semi-final, played through extra time and then had to play penalties. They didn't miss one. Having made it to the final, again the match was decided on penalties and again they didn't miss. The gold medal was theirs.

As this chapter has shown, champions understand the importance of training themselves to cope with pressure. They also understand the value of reviewing performances and learning from mistakes, a topic we turn to next.

Chapter 12

REVIEW AND REVISE

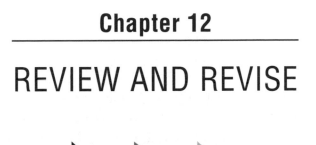

LEARNING FROM MISTAKES – and successes – is a key element of all top sporting champions' training routine. They review their performances and use that information to revise future training schedules or preparatory routines, all with a view to improving future performances.

Champions can always learn something new. England rugby captain Lawrence Dallaglio learnt some valuable lessons early on in his career, and has continued to do so. Dallaglio found some of his early club games quite challenging, when for the first time he felt he was playing against fully grown-up men.

'It's not a bad thing to be thrown in at the deep end because you learn a lot about yourself. It might not always end with the best result, but you feel you have achieved something anyway.

'But it doesn't matter how many games you've won, or what you have achieved in the sport, without doubt you can always learn more. It doesn't matter whether you are Tiger Woods, Sebastian Coe or Steve Redgrave. If you approach sport with that attitude, provided you are physically in form, you are just going to get better and better.'

REGULAR REVIEW

Sports psychologist Ian Lynagh says that after every performance athletes need to evaluate how they did. Then they need to review their goals. They might look at what they are doing well in their golf game – perhaps their drives are working well. However, they realize they need to work on their chipping and so they put that down for work during the week. Lynagh says that sportspeople might also review their emotional control, concentration, confidence, arousal control and so on – whatever the skills they want in their package. Lynagh says:

'A lot of athletes are encouraged to keep journals where they record their performances and their feelings at the time and learn from that. I would develop little ratings scales for athletes to rate themselves after a performance.

'Athletes can only improve by being self-reflective. Athletes who don't do that can be on an emotional roller coaster. When they win they are euphoric and forget what made that possible; they don't learn from it. If they lose they get depressed and don't talk to anyone for days and again, they never learn anything.'

Former national athletics coach Frank Dick believes that debriefing after an event is a matter of personal responsibility. Sportspeople have to 'take personal ownership' of the review process. Dick has worked with football club Ipswich Town's academy. He recalls how one particular lad had a moan one week after he had received 'a right bollocking'; he complained that no one said anything in the weeks they did well.

Dick is not impressed by such complaints, noting that a professional sportsman won't just sit back because the coach doesn't say anything.

'You should ask yourself, "Was I OK?". If you don't know the answer you should ask the coach. If the eleven people working together in the team got the right result, that's fine, but does that mean your performance was 100%? It may not. There may be something you should work on. You should score yourself out of ten for each aspect of your "game". Whether you've won, lost or drawn, you should be able to look yourself in the mirror and ask what you could do better next time. Winning is about being better today than you were yesterday. It's ridiculously arrogant that, having won, you walk away and don't look at your performance.'

Dick believes that the debriefing should take place immediately after the event. As a coach, he knows that athletes will sometimes try and tell him what he wants to hear, rather than what they really think. The more time they have to compose themselves after an event, the better prepared their answers may be. But Dick doesn't want people to give him a cosmetic answer; a neat explanation in hindsight. He wants to know what they were really thinking or trying to do in the arena under pressure and that's more likely to happen sooner after the event than later. As Dick says, he wants to catch people when they are 'still expressive'.

Sprinter Mark Richardson also believes that a post-race review is invaluable, but he prefers to allow a little break before conducting it.

'I don't think you should do it straight after a race because it's the wrong time. If you've run badly, for example, you're too emotional. You need to come to terms with it first and analyse it with a logical mind, not an emotionally charged mind. Any post-race critique

should happen a couple of days later. And if something went wrong, you talk it through with people who are close to you – your coach or manager.'

Olympic hurdler Sally Gunnell would have a relatively quick review of her performance in races in the run up to major competitions, but then move on to focus on the next race.

> *'My coach, Bruce Longden, would always find something good from a race. He might say, you could have done this at the seventh hurdle, but he always found something good and that gave me the confidence to move on.*
>
> *'I don't think I ever ran the perfect race. Probably the nearest I got to it was in the World Championships in 1993, but there was probably a bit more I could do somewhere.*
>
> *'I was always very good at forgetting about the last race and moving on – even straight after the Olympics. You had to look at it, learn quickly and move on.'*

Yachtsman Sir Chay Blyth sees the value in reviewing situations that occur in order to learn lessons from them. How that review is performed depends on the situation in question, he says.

> *'If it's a one man thing, you just sit down and make a few notes. If it's a team situation, you sit down together and say, "Right, what the hell did we do wrong here?" In the first Whitbread Around the World yacht race we had a specially designed boat and when we arrived at Cape Town we were third. We should have been first. We got the team round and looked at what had happened, so we could refocus and regroup.'*

Blyth recalls this period, arriving third in Cape Town, as perhaps the toughest of his life.

> *'The reason was because I had a group of people on board who in themselves were winners, who in themselves had total belief and*

yet I was not delivering for them. I was letting them down. It was a really tough time for me. When you're letting down your peers, it's extremely tough. At those times what you have to do is sit down and have a self-assessment with yourself. You take yourself off and sort through it to get some understanding about it. Then you can get the team together and admit you've made a few cock-ups and discuss the way forward.'

CONTROLLABLES

England rugby captain Lawrence Dallaglio notes that it is important to focus your review on factors that are within your control. He believes that too many people get worried about things they can't influence and can't control. As Dallaglio says, you only have a certain amount of energy and if you expend some of it on things that you can't directly affect, you're wasting something that you could channel in the right direction.

Hurdling Olympic gold medallist Sally Gunnell also recognized during her career that it was a waste of energy to worry about what the competition was doing. She concentrated on her own training and preparation. Gunnell says:

'Former Olympic gold medallist David Hemery taught me that there's nothing you can do about anybody else, so why even worry about it? That's what a lot of athletes do. They worry about the competition, but there's nothing you can do about that. It's important to accept you can only make a difference to yourself.'

Former 400m champion Roger Black learnt to focus on the controllables when he took advice from David Jenkins. Jenkins was the 400m British record holder for many years in the 1970s and number one in the world for a year, who was imprisoned after being caught trafficking steroids across the USA–Mexico border. Black knew Jenkins, but had no idea he was involved in such activity. The two kept in touch after Jenkins went to prison. Black says:

'In 1995, before the Atlanta Olympic Games, I felt I needed a bit of guidance and it could only come from someone who had been in the same position and messed up. I often think you can learn more from people who have tried to do what you want to do and have failed. You can learn as much from them as you can from people who have tried and have succeeded.

'I asked Jenkins to help me and he changed my way of thinking. He asked me what my goals were. I had been taught that you must be very clear about your goals and you must write them down. I had a performance goal – to run 44.3 seconds and my outcome goal was to win an Olympic medal. I was quite impressed with my goals and Jenkins said, "Great". Then he told me to put them on one side. He said: "From now on I want you to have only one goal, and it's a very powerful goal, but a very simple goal. It's the most effective goal anyone can ever have. I want you to carry it with you on the track when you are training. I want to carry it with you when you are in competition but I want you to carry it with you when you are off the track as well."

'He said: "I want you to focus on running your perfect race."'

The key point Jenkins was making was that Black should not let himself get distracted by worrying about what his rivals might do, but to concentrate on the factors he could control. For Black, the advice hit home. He says:

'Jenkins said to me: "I spent my whole career worrying about what might happen. Don't overanalyse it. Just enjoy it and do the best you can and really focus on that."

'A weight came off my shoulders. I started to smile. I thought, "What's the worst thing that can happen if I don't do well at the Olympics? It is not the end of the world." I just became very focused on simply running a 400m race as fast as I possibly could. I took the advice with me all the way through Atlanta. It was the best advice I have ever had.'

In the Olympic final in Atlanta Black faced an extremely tough line-up, including Michael Johnson. Black says:

> *'Before the race I never thought about where I would come. I just thought that if I executed my perfect race, where I came would not be in my hands. I could come first, I could come seventh. I couldn't control how the others performed. If all things went equally I would probably come second, third or fourth. Fortunately, I came second.'*

MISTAKES HAPPEN

Champions see mistakes and setbacks as learning opportunities. England rugby captain Lawrence Dallaglio recognizes that sports-people can face all kinds of setbacks – on and off the field, in social terms as well as in their performance.

> *'The key is to learn from your mistakes. If you have had a setback, normally it's as a result of a mistake that you have made or some-one else has made or you have made jointly. The key to succeeding after a setback is knowing why you failed, accepting the failure – not necessarily publicly, although you might in certain situations – and then learning from that.'*

Even great champions can make bad mistakes during their careers. Olympic hurdler Sally Gunnell proved her champion's quality when she came back from disappointment in the European Champion-ships in 1990.

> *'I was the fastest in Europe going into that race. I'd won all the races leading up to it and I guess I just got too confident. I got too blasé about it. I just thought I'd got to turn up, run it and win it, and I ended up fifth.*
>
> *'That was my first real setback. I was absolutely devastated. I went off the track and cried my eyes out for probably 24 hours. I felt it was the end of the world; it was going to finish my career. I*

couldn't work out where I'd gone wrong. Then my coach, Bruce Longden, sat down with me and said, "You can't pack it all in. You've got to work out where you went wrong." I learnt a lot from that. Whatever happens, you've got to accept it to a certain extent, but then work out what went wrong.

'I realized that I'd missed a big chunk of training because I'd gone down to Auckland, New Zealand, for the Commonwealth Games in the preceding December and January. Once I had found the reason I realized I had to move on, and make sure it never happened again.'

The next year, going into the World Championships in Tokyo in 1991, Gunnell was one of the favourites to win gold.

'I found myself in the lead going off the ninth hurdle, with one more to go. Then I made a massive mistake again. I stuttered into the last hurdle and the Russian athlete, Tatyana Ledovskaya, came charging past me. She went on to win and I came second. I threw that world championship gold medal away. I thought, "I can't make a massive mistake like that again."'

The two major disappointments in 1990 and 1991 made Gunnell reassess her support team.

'I realized I needed more help around me. I realized I couldn't do it all on my own. You need a team around you. So I found a nutritionist to tell me what to eat. I was eating pretty much rubbish at that time; it was like I was trying to put diesel into a Formula One car. So I needed a nutritionist to advise me what to eat to create energy so I could go out there and run 100%. I also needed a physio to help me prevent injuries, rather than waiting until I had those injuries and then getting one. If I got a niggle I went straight off and found him. And then I had my coach, Bruce Longden, who was running all my track sessions and feeding me information. I also had my husband [Jon Bigg], who was doing all the training sessions with me. So it was a big team.'

Gunnell also decided to make use of a sports psychologist.

'I made that mistake in the 1991 World Championships and I had to make sure it didn't happen again. That mistake happened because I wasn't mentally prepared. So I met David Hemery, the 1968 Olympic gold medallist. He asked me how often I visualized before a race. I told him I sat down and did it the night before. He told me I couldn't be an Olympic champion like that; that you literally had to visualize it a year beforehand. This is where the difference is probably made between getting silver and gold medals.'

For more on Hemery's visualization advice, see Chapter 9.

Sebastian Coe looks back at the Moscow Olympics and his two finals – one a disaster, the other a triumph. Coe says that in the 800m he learnt how not to behave 20 minutes before an Olympic final, and in the 1500m he learnt the right way to do it.

Coe recalls:

'Forty minutes before an Olympic final you are led from the warm-up track down the tunnel which normally connects the track and the stadium. There are eight or nine of you and you are all put in a holding room. There are also eight or ten officials checking shoes and putting numbers on you. The one thing I remember about the holding room at the Lenin stadium in Moscow was that it was right next to the kitchen. The last thing you want to smell 20 minutes before going out to an Olympic final is rancid dumplings.

'It's quite an experience because you are sitting there with these people and you know only one of you will emerge and have a pleasant evening. You will have done your warm-up by this point and you have to keep warm, loose and stretched in this small area. It's like a Jane Fonda video gone mad.

'Ten minutes before the start you are led into the stadium and there are 100,000 people sitting there. At the age of 18 that was quite an experience to go through.'

On paper Coe was two seconds faster than anyone else in the 800m and was the world record holder. The expectation was that Coe would win the 800m final and Steve Ovett would win the 1500m. However, things didn't go to plan in the 800m. Coe describes it as 'an appalling race' and he finished second. His father, who was also Coe's coach, wasn't best pleased.

> *'He said he felt ashamed for himself because he had a major contribution in it. He is a fairly brutal, honest bloke. We had not spent ten years working two or three times a day from the age of fourteen onwards on windswept Yorkshire moors and rainswept tracks for me to run as badly as I did.'*

The newspapers wrote critically about Coe's performance, but this acted as a spur for the 1500m. He received the UK Sunday papers in the Olympic village three days late. The front page of the *News of the World* displayed a photo of him on his training run the day after the 800m with 'Coe's trail of shame' written underneath. The criticism increased his motivation to come back with a win in the 1500m.

Mary Peters, the team manager, also helped to inspire Coe.

> *'Mary was great. I knew her really well and she was quite tough about it. She said, "You have run an appalling race. There is no point telling you that because you know it. You are lucky because if you had been another athlete – such as Jim Ryan, the American world record holder who was tripped up in 1972 by an unseeded African competitor – your Olympic career would be over. But you can get back onto that track in four days' time and go out and win another title. You don't have to wait four years to do it." She was quite right.'*

When it came to the 1500m final Coe was psyched up for the task. He describes himself as in the best shape of his life and knowing that he had to win it. Happily for Coe, he did. The gold was his.

One other race that didn't go too well for Coe – one that he looks back on as the most important race of his career – took place in the

800m in Prague. Coe came third, but he feels that he learnt a huge amount from the experience.

'A great fallacy in sport and other walks of life is that people think it's only when you win that you succeed. They think failure is automatically linked with losing, and it's not. I learnt more in finishing third in that one race than I learnt in the ten or twelve years leading up to it. In the 800m in Prague I was running against Steve Ovett for the first time in my career. I decided the only way I could beat him was to try and run the legs off him from the front, because I wasn't quick enough at that time in my career to outkick him.

'I ran the first lap faster than anyone had ever done in an 800 metres. I got to 600m feeling quite good and then I got to 610m and I thought the world was caving in. I remember Steve came past me in the finishing straight and then to his complete shock an East German came past both of us.

'I then realized two things. First of all, you never ever go into a race thinking about just one competitor; you recognize there is a race and there are other people capable of doing things. You have to think about the whole field. Secondly, most people said I was mad to have gone through the first lap in the time I did, but I probably would not have got a medal if I hadn't gone at that pace. The one thing I knew was that I had one year, two at the most, to get myself in training to not only go through the first lap slightly quicker, but then to hold on for a second lap. That is exactly what I did in the winter of 1979.

'I completely changed my approach to the distance work I was doing and the kind of speed and endurance work I was doing on the track. I broke the world record nine months later. So if you ask me what was the foundation stone of my career, it was that race in Prague.'

SUCCESS MATTERS

It isn't just poor performances that provide good learning material. Former national athletics coach Frank Dick believes it essential to review your winning performances too. He believes that it is as important to know why you have won as it is to know why you haven't. As he says: 'If you don't know why you won, it was an accident.'

Professor Graham Jones agrees that analysing success can give valuable insights for a sportsperson. He says that people tend to forget the things that have gone well. Instead they focus on what has gone wrong. Professor Jones says that his approach has always been to build on what's going well – to understand why someone is doing really well at something. After Wales beat France in Paris in the 2001 Six Nations, Professor Jones advised Graham Henry, the Welsh coach, to spend a session before the next game on working out what was great about the match. He says:

> *'The players split up into small groups and worked out what was good and what they needed to make happen again. Then they could work on things they needed to do to build on it, rather than things that weren't good. For me, it's crucial that you build your foundation from what's good and you revisit your successes every single time.'*

Mark Richardson, 400m Commonwealth silver medallist, also notes that there is value in reviewing why a race has gone well: he says he is always aware of what made a race successful. He doesn't believe you need to go into as much detail in the analysis, but stresses that it is important to recognize why you performed well. As he says, if you don't, how on earth are you going to recreate that performance at a later date?

OPEN TO INNOVATION

An important aspect of the review and revise process that champions use is their willingness to try new things. You might look at what went wrong, for example, but unless you can come up with a solution or a new approach to try, you can't do better next time.

Former badminton champion Gill Clark believes that 'being an innovator' is one of the undersung characteristics of a champion. She was always looking for new techniques that she could use in preparing to take on her badminton opponents.

> *'Champions are always looking to do it a bit better, which means not necessarily using the same training methods that everybody else has used. How can we do it a little bit differently? What is it that means I can get the edge over somebody else?'*

Introducing new ways of doing things can often meet some resistance, partly because changing habits can be hard. Michael Lynagh, former Australian rugby captain and renowned fly-half, notes that it isn't always easy to just try something new. He believes people need to have a certain level of intelligence to be able to accept new things. He admits that he was never a great one for accepting new ideas. However, he would listen to what was being proposed and then make up his own mind about it. Once he accepted the new ideas, he embraced them wholeheartedly.

In the mid-1980s and 1990s in Australia, sports psychology was in its infancy. It was far from accepted that rugby players needed to think about the mental aspect of the game. Lynagh was lucky in that his father Ian was aware of its importance. His influence did have an impact on his son's success. Michael Lynagh admits that he probably wouldn't have achieved what he did so easily without paying attention to the mental side of the game. He says that he was taught how to think about things – the mental side of performance – from an early age. He believes that not only made him more successful, but also prolonged his career. As Lynagh says, goal kicking was a big responsibility. Refining his mental approach made him feel a lot more comfortable about doing it.

In some sports the only way to make it to the top is as a result of some kind of quantum leap – a complete, radical revision to how things are done. This is the case in motorsport, as Ron Dennis, boss of the McLaren racing team, explains. Motorsport requires a particular approach when a racing team is not doing as well as it might and trying to get back on top. Dennis says:

'Motorsport is different from other sports where the sporting equipment has generally remained unchanged for years. In motorsport, you get dramatic change. So to go back and look at what you did two years ago is immaterial. You can learn from the past, but Formula One doesn't respond well to this sort of systematic approach. If you are successful, as Ferrari have been, then you are only making incremental changes.

'The only way to catch them is to make a quantum leap, for example, by changing supplier or radically redesigning the chassis or engine. You have to be entrepreneurial in the way you make progress.'

Experimentation and being willing to try new things is important for achieving success in all walks of life, not just sport. The ability to adapt increases our potential not only to record one-off winning performances, but also to repeat our success time and again.

In training themselves to achieve repeated success, sporting champions often call on coaches to give them advice and support. We examine the nature of the relationship between sportsperson and coach in the next chapter.

Chapter 13

COACHING RELATIONSHIPS

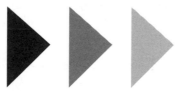

BEHIND EVERY GREAT SPORTING CHAMPION there is often a great coach. That coach may or may not have worked with the athlete throughout their career. However, successful coaches always have the qualities the elite sportspeople need to perform at their peak on a consistent basis.

COACH SUPPORT

Clive Woodward, England rugby head coach, says that his role, and that of his support staff, is to give the England players every opportunity to achieve, win matches and be the best in the world.

Woodward knows that success on the field requires the right supporting environment off the field.

'I've never seen things going right on the pitch unless they're going right off it. When I walked into the England coach role there was nothing going right off the field. I had to change everyone's thinking in terms of how we were going to operate and how to be a high performance team. I got involved in getting the environment right.'

England football manager Sven-Göran Eriksson also believes that coaches need to create supportive environments that encourage footballers to try new things, without worrying about the repercussions of making mistakes. This is part and parcel of daring to win – taking appropriate risks that make winning possible.

'I am not a psychologist, but I try to use what I have learned: be calm, be positive and give courage to your players.

'If you are a winger, you have to try to beat the fullback. The risk is that you may lose the ball. Okay, we take that risk, because if you never try, you will never beat the opposition.

'Sometimes you have players who are afraid of making mistakes. But if you are afraid of making mistakes, you will never try something difficult. You don't want the ball. You're hiding. You never try to dribble, or to make a cross, or to try a shot on goal. You have to give players courage so that they aren't afraid to fail. As a coach, if you start shouting at the player who gives a bad pass, then you take him down – you don't help him. A football player never goes out meaning to give a bad pass, or to do bad things. He always tries to do good things. So it's important as a leader that you don't start shouting once he makes mistakes.

'You must always be positive and never lose your temper. If a player has failed, makes a mistake, forget it and try to be positive.

'The player must feel secure. You defend the player against the press, directors, friends or whoever.

'Of course, if the player always makes the same mistake, then you have to tell them they can't do it every time. You can't risk doing difficult things in the midfield because you create problems for the whole team. If someone does stupid things five or ten times in every game, then you have to show it's not acceptable.'

Sometimes Eriksson's wisdom alone has not been sufficient to give a player the courage to take the necessary risks – the courage to risk making a mistake. In such situations he calls on the services of a sports psychologist.

> *'For example, one of the players I had in Italy was afraid. He was a centre forward and extremely good, but during the big games he was afraid of failure, afraid to be kicked. I worked with him for one year and he didn't improve. I recognized that I couldn't help him any more. So I took him to see Willi Railo [a leading sports psychologist] and after six months he was the best centre forward in Europe. He became a great, great player thanks to Willi's involvement.'*

Of course, a coach cannot make an athlete or sportsperson believe in themselves if the individual doesn't have an inner core of self-belief already. Former sprinter and coach John Regis says belief has to start with the athlete, but is then reinforced by the coach:

> *'It comes initially from the athlete. The individual has to believe that they can – they have to believe that their talent and ability and mindset can get them where they want to be. Then the coach manipulates that so the athlete can call on their belief to get the best performance at a particular point. It's about the individual having the courage to believe in themselves, and the coach rein-forcing that, saying "yes you can, you are good enough, you've done the training".'*

Sometimes a coach needs to encourage the athlete to stop training and relax. Sports psychologist Ian Lynagh says that athletes can burn themselves out. They can become too narrow, too obsessive. They can think about training 24 hours a day because they haven't learned to have a balance. He says:

> *'I work with athletes in terms that they switch on when they go to training, and they switch off when they leave – just like someone*

leaving an office, putting the files away and going home and being a person. It's really important. Recovery and rejuvenation is critical in sport. A lot of younger athletes do too much and lose balance at an early age and usually burn out or bomb out or become overstressed or fanatical about it.'

QUALITIES IN THE COACH

If a coach is to be able to bring out the best in talented sportspeople, then the coach requires certain characteristics and qualities. What does it take to be a good coach or manager?

Sven-Göran Eriksson believes that for a manager to be successful, he has to be true to himself.

'As a boss, as a leader, you have to be yourself. You can't go and play another role. The Italy manager Giovanni Trapattoni's style on the bench is fantastic to see. It's worth the ticket. His whistling is fantastic. That's his style. But I can't do that because I would feel stupid. I have to be myself in front of the players. As a player you want your manager to be genuine, in whatever way that is.

'I always keep a certain distance from the players, and I don't know if that's good or not. But I never thought a football player would want to go out eating with his manager. I don't think he's comfortable doing that. You need to keep a certain distance, but on the other hand, players should never be afraid of coming to you with a problem they have, whether it's on the field or off the field. And I'm always happy when a player comes to me saying, "Boss, do you think we could do this in another way?" Then you know you have involved them. I never thought I knew everything about football, so if players come to me with opinions, that's excellent. As a coach you have to ask what players think, because if they get involved, they will play much better.'

Sometimes it can be of help if the coach has been through similar experiences to those of the athlete. Former Davis Cup captain David Lloyd believes that having a coach who has been through similar experiences can be helpful to a player. With Tim Henman, for example, he believes that Stefan Edberg would be a great inspiration.

'He doesn't need Edberg to coach his shots, because Edberg has basically the same game. Tim has two technical weaknesses. One is his forehand that he tries to hit too hard under pressure, and the other is that he tends to have a lot of double faults. Edberg was exactly the same. But Edberg learned, through his strength of mind, to loop his forehand in and to kick that serve so high that, although it was slow – about 90 miles an hour, it came up very high and he didn't serve any doubles. To have someone like that around you who has won Wimbledon would help. To have a player so similar to you sit in your corner and believe – I think it would rub off.'

Former sprinter John Regis tries to pass on the benefit of his experiences to the athletes he coaches, but he accepts that they sometimes need to learn some things for themselves. Even so, being given a suggestion about how to look at a problem or tackle an issue can help young athletes to get over whatever it is more quickly. That means they can perform at the desired, high level more quickly or more consistently.

Regis believes that coaches need to speak to athletes in plain and simple terms, rather than making what they say too technical.

'The athlete has to understand what you are saying and have belief in what you are saying. I'm fortunate because I've been there, done that and got the T-shirt. So I can demonstrate what I'm looking for and the athlete can see it vividly. Then he can absorb that and adapt it to his technique.'

Adrian Moorhouse had a long-standing relationship with one particular coach – Terry Denison. Denison expected Moorhouse not only to train, but also to learn about physiology so that he understood the body's system. Then they could have a proper dialogue about the training. Moorhouse says:

'Terry didn't just want me swimming up and down, he wanted intelligent talking feedback – a protégé if you like. The more I knew about physiology, the more we had conversations.'

If a coach needs to be able to communicate effectively, what about other characteristics? Does the gender of the coach matter? Former badminton champion Gill Clark doesn't think so. She says:

'The coach needs to be able to recognize the faults of the athlete and the strengths of the athlete, and get the weaknesses to become strengths – to make the athlete a better athlete overall. It is totally illogical for anybody to assume that a man can do that better than a woman. But there aren't a lot of women coaches and part of it is that sport is a very macho thing as far as male athletes are concerned.'

RELATIONSHIP DEVELOPMENT

Former national athletics coach Frank Dick believes that the relationship between sportsperson and coach develops over time.

'As a young athlete you start off accepting. You get told by your coach, "this is what you do". Then after a while you start having the courage to ask questions and exploring. That's your curiosity coming through. You shift from being an "acceptor" to an "explorer". Then, once you start to explore enough, the bit of drive and ambition in you encourages you to challenge. You develop self-confidence and you become a "challenger". Once you feel really strongly about it you want to be a "winner". Once you've won a couple of times you want to be remembered forever because of your quality of winning and you try to become a "champion".'

Those who go on to become legends in their sports don't stop at simply becoming a champion, Dick believes. They are driven to achieve real greatness. Those people have a level of self-belief that they continue to contribute towards a greater dynasty.

Champions' single-minded determination means they aren't afraid to challenge their coaches, Dick says. Their sense of self-belief and single-mindedness can lead them to feel they need to know all there is to know about what they are doing. Therefore, challenging the coach is a natural thing to do. Dick says that he was quite comfortable with Olympic decathlete Daley Thompson, Boris Becker (tennis), Katarina Witt (skating), Gerhard Berger (Formula One), Ronnie Irani (cricket), Justin Rose (golf), and other top performers, challenging him on almost every programme they worked on together.

Sports psychologist John Syer also believes the relationship between a coach and the athlete should change over time.

'The athlete certainly needs technical coaching and it is primarily up to the coach to establish a productive relationship. However, success depends on the initial relationship developing into that of a two-person high performing team. This means reaching the stage where they are able to challenge each other. When challenges are well expressed and well timed, they allow the relationship's potential to emerge, as together they find new ways of doing things that neither of them might have discovered alone. Eventually, the athlete may need new input and the coach may also feel it is time to move on.'

Former badminton champion Gill Clark feels that the requirements of the coach change over time as the sportsperson develops technical skill. Clark was able to analyse her own game effectively when playing a match. If she kept missing her smashes she had the technical knowledge to be able to work out why. She was therefore able to try to adjust what she was doing immediately, without having to wait for her coach to have a chance to tell her. She believes that a good coach in the classical sense of the term should make himself more and more redundant – because a coach should teach the athlete how to self-analyse. The role of the coach therefore ought to change as the athlete develops. As Clark says, over time the coach should provide more moral support and mental back-up, rather than being a coach in the technical sense of teaching a forehand and backhand.

Sports psychologist Ian Lynagh also feels that professional athletes should be able to analyse their own performances and progress. As the athlete's ability to do so improves, so the demands made of the coach change. Lynagh says:

> *'It's critical for a professional athlete to be able to monitor how they are going. As an athlete matures and stays in the sport, the coach becomes more of a consultant for the athlete to talk to and get feedback. They consult and organize the programme together.'*

The relationship that former sprinter John Regis had with his coaches developed as he became more experienced. He also changed coaches when he felt he had learnt all he could from them.

> *'Once I'd got all the information I could from a coach, I felt we reached a plateau. We were both at the same level. So I would move to somebody who had more information. I always needed someone there I could look at, who would give me the information I required. When you're good enough you know technically what you're doing, but for things like block starts you still do need a coach. You try so hard to generate power and speed that you may do something wrong that may need tidying up. I had about six coaches in my career. I needed somebody who was keeping me on my toes, who knew more than me.'*

When advising young sprinters, Regis gives them a chance to identify areas for improvement. After a competition they sit down together and go through what happened. Regis gives the athlete a chance to give his own analysis of what he did right and what he did wrong. With top athletes, 95 times out of 100 they come up with the correct analysis, Regis says. This comes in part from the athlete's knowledge of their own body. Regis notes that top athletes know their own bodies inside out. They also know great technique from poor technique, whether in terms of arm action or knee lift. As Regis says, a good athlete should in each stride know what they're doing.

Before a race Regis doesn't give a pep talk as such. He explains:

'I just listen. I say, "Go and do what you do best. You've trained for it, so just go and do it." At the end of the day the athlete holds his career in his own hands – or in his own feet.'

Former 400m champion Roger Black feels that many athletic careers are curtailed because of a bad coach. Coaches have to be able to let go of their athletes.

'If you're lucky enough to have a good coach and a happy relationship, that relationship must evolve. It's going to be painful at some point. You have to both share the same goals. It's tough because most coaches believe their way is the right way. Of course they do. But one thing I learned was that there's no right way. There are many ways of doing things.'

What is most important, Black feels, is that the athlete believes he or she is doing the right thing. As he says, it isn't anyone else who walks out there and performs.

In general, sportspeople need to be independent-minded to be successful. Michael Lynagh, former Australian rugby captain and renowned fly-half, feels he was 'very lucky' with his coaches.

'I became very close to most of them and worked closely with them. Some would say I was very pig-headed and hard to change, which I would probably agree with, but I would always talk to the coaches. I would never just say they were wrong and not talk to them. I would explain why I thought what I did.

'I had certain ideas of how I operated on the pitch and that might have been pretty intimidating for some coaches and players. But I thought I was always pretty fair and my sole goal was to get the team to perform better and to win. I thought my motives were right.'

Former badminton champion Gill Clark believes that as sport has become more professional, so full-time coaches are taking too much control.

> *'They are arranging travel, telling the athletes what time to practise, setting up their training programmes on a daily basis. The athlete is becoming a zombie. But the ones who are really successful think for themselves. Michael Johnson is absolutely spot-on. He thinks for himself, and that's why he's been so successful.*
>
> *'Players need to be encouraged and taught to take personal responsibility. The coach is there to help, but you know the old expression – you can lead a horse to water but you can't make it drink. I could tell a player what to do, but they're the ones who have to go out and do it. They've got to perform, and if they've got to perform, they've got to believe 102% that what they're doing is correct, instead of just thinking the coach told them to do it.'*

Athletics coach Ron Roddan certainly encourages his athletes to think for themselves. He believes that everyone needs someone they can bounce ideas off, but that sportsmen have got to be independent right from the start of their sporting careers. They have got to think for themselves because when they go out on the track, Roddan knows that he can't do anything for them.

Roddan is critical of some coaches who make their athletes so dependent on them that they have to travel to all competitions together. He believes it is to the detriment of the sportsman if they are relying on someone else. In his experience Roddan has found that sometimes athletes are shy and won't initially push themselves forward. However, once he has encouraged them to think by themselves and go to race meetings by themselves, that shyness goes away. As Roddan says, you can't go to an Olympic final being shy.

QUALITIES IN A GOOD RELATIONSHIP

Sports psychologist and former national volleyball coach John Syer believes that a successful coaching relationship requires certain qualities. He says there must be respect, trust and the opportunity for each of the people involved to discover things they didn't know. As Syer says, this is only achieved when those concerned are self-aware, aware of each other and able to appreciate their differences.

Sports psychologist and performance specialist Professor Graham Jones has a similar view, that having trust and confidence in one another is key to the coach–player relationship. It's got to be reciprocal. Nobody knows an athlete better than the athlete himself or herself. Professor Jones says that when you talk about the world's top performers, they know themselves much better than anybody else and so the coach almost has to fit in with them.

> *'The coach plays a key role in helping to build performance self-belief, the ability to handle pressure and so on. The performers then have to take that on board.*
>
> *'I believe that coaches empower athletes, yet I still come across coaches at a very senior level who take a very transactional approach in terms of "This is the way it's going to be". In this day and age you don't get many of those coaches working with the world's best, because the best in the world know what they want, they know what's best for them. At that top level the coach almost becomes a mentor rather than a coach, and that's a very different relationship.'*

Former England Under-21 coach, David Platt, recalls being impressed by former England manager Graham Taylor's ability to inspire trust and belief in his players. Taylor, he says, was able to speak to players in a manner that was respectful, whether one-on-one or in groups. He put pressure on players, but they always felt he was on their side. Platt says that Taylor got into his psyche. He delivered his words in a manner that meant he and the other players actually believed what he was saying.

> *'For me, too, I have to portray to my players that I believe they can win, that it's not just words. That's what Graham could do.*

The way he spoke, you thought it wasn't just words – he actually
believed it.

   'Sven also gets the players to believe that he's with them and he
trusts them. He puts great trust in his players. He doesn't ask them
to do things; he puts them under pressure to perform. When he
speaks to them he demands things of them in a respectful way, but
he believes in them.'

At Nottingham Forest, Platt worked hard to understand his players.

   'I had different characters at Forest. By the end of a two-year
period I could influence the players I had in the club. I knew what
made them tick and I could make them tick. It might be knocking
them down or picking them up. It might be handling them respect-
fully, it might be tolerating their deficiencies without embarrassing
them. Everybody has got a different character and as a manager
you can't treat everybody in the same manner. You have to find out
what makes the player tick and then you treat the player in the way
that means you can get the best out of him.'

From the age of 15 onwards, Sally Gunnell had the same coach
throughout her career – Bruce Longden, who was also the coach of
Daley Thompson. Gunnell feels that having the same coach gave her
extra stability. By the peak of her career, the relationship between
Gunnell and Longden had naturally matured, but still retained
essential characteristics of trust and belief. By the top of her career
Gunnell had amassed a wealth of personal knowledge, but she still
found she needed Longden to be there. She needed him to be 'saying
the right things' and she needed to believe in what he said. As Gunnell remarks:

   'A lot of coaching relationships go wrong because the athletes end
up not believing what the coach says. With Bruce, I always knew
that every single training session he set me was right and that it
would make a difference. He planned every session. I would do it

and he would watch me and time me. And as long as you believe that you're doing the right thing, you're halfway there.

'If I had run a bad race, Bruce would find a reason why, and he was right. That was fine because then I could move on. I believed everything he said. He was quite a hard coach and a lot of people couldn't get on with him. But I guess it's hard training people and he expected a lot of an athlete.'

A TOUCH OF TOUGHNESS

Whatever the duration of the coaching relationship, whether at the start or many years down the training line, coaches do need to be prepared to be tough in their athletes' own interests. Former national athletics coach Frank Dick was prepared to be tough with athletes who didn't commit wholeheartedly to their training regime and who didn't understand that training was directly linked to performance in competition.

'You've got to make a commitment. That means every time you train, everything you do is in line with the objective you're going for. I remember falling out with an athlete I was working with in preparation for the AAA Championships. We'd agreed the squad was going to be out there training every night of the week. On the Monday night the squad was all ready to go except this athlete, who turned up a bit late. He got a bollocking for that. Then he said he'd forgotten his shorts. So I wouldn't let him train.

'Every time you train it's a rehearsal. It has to demonstrate the unshakeability of what's going to happen in the arena. Learn to live with no second chances.'

Dick believes that training must always be conducted with the same attitude required for the day of competition. Giving your best and doing things the right way has to become instinctive. Champions understand the importance of such training. Every player, whether in football, athletics or any sport, has to know why they are going to training, Dick says. At the end of the training they should also know whether they achieved what they wanted, and what they have to work on next time.

Dick believes that coaches need to develop a strong, disciplined framework for the sportspeople they work with.

'You start off with your values. You've also got to agree your vision. And you make your journey towards that vision. Attitudes and behaviours are shaped out of that. It's because of the notion of personal discipline in your code of values that behaviours begin to shape.'

Olympic gold medallist Adrian Moorhouse recalls how his relationship with his long-time coach wasn't always an easy one. Moorhouse says:

'I had lots of coaches, but Terry Denison was my main coach from when I was 14 to 28 – for the whole of my career. I was a pupil, he was a teacher. He told me what to do. He'd write a session and I did it, but I was very stubborn. I answered him back a lot; I got kicked out of the session a lot. He told me never to come back one time. I was actually being quite denigrating about people in the squad, taking my frustration out on them, and he was trying to take a hard line with me. So he told me not to come back but the next morning I was there and he kicked me out again. I think he kept doing that until he got tired of sending me home.'

At the 1984 Olympics, Moorhouse went to compete in Los Angeles as Commonwealth and European 100m breaststroke champion, and came fourth. He went to Hong Kong to train, spending three months with Dave Haller. When he returned, his relationship with Denison entered a new phase. It became a more adult relationship. From then on Moorhouse would spend a month here, a month there, three months here, three months there – working with different coaches to broaden his outlook.

In the world of football, managers bear huge responsibility for how their players perform. This means that they tend to demand more control over what their teams do on the pitch. Jack Charlton, former Ireland manager, says:

> 'You're the manager. You're the one who takes responsibility for all the performances and how the game goes, so the players have got to do it exactly the way you want them to. When you see managers yelling at people on the field, 90% of the time it's not because a player is not trying; it's because they're doing it differently to what the manager wants, or take up a different position or go in a different direction. That's why the managers stand up.'

Charlton remembers the difference that Don Revie made when he arrived at Leeds United, bringing coaches such as Sid Owen and Les Cocker with him.

> 'Suddenly we weren't allowed to go to Leeds for the whole of the day or the dance at the Mecca in the afternoons or go to the bookies. Two or three days a week, if we hadn't got a game, we would call in and work on the pitches. I would be the centre back and people like Mike O'Grady or Eddie Gray would have the ball and come at me. I would have to push them left or right, depending on which way I was told to go. You were taught how to tackle and where to push people, how to stop them coming at you and where to direct them. In other words, we had a coach and we listened and learnt. It was repetition, and we did it.'

Charlton has great respect for Revie, who would be firm but fair with players.

> 'If he promised you something, he would move heaven and earth to make it work, to keep his promise. He also introduced rules. The number of times me and Billy [Bremner] got hauled in front of him because we used to go and play dominoes on a Thursday night in the pub on the other side of Leeds. We only had a pint of beer all night – or maybe two – and we played dominoes. At half past ten we would go home but somebody used to report us, Don

*would haul us in and say, "You have been told you cannot do this".
I told him we only played a game of dominoes and had a couple
of beers, and that I would rather do that than sit at home drinking
Coca-Cola or lemonade. Don said, "Fine, as long as you don't
abuse it". That was Don's motto – "Don't abuse it and you can do
it". We didn't abuse it and he accepted that.'*

Sometimes coaches do need to give some tough talking to the sportspeople they work with. Athletics coach Ron Roddan considers how
to deal with athletes who have suffered some form of setback – perhaps a disappointing race result. He says:

*'You know they'll bounce back in one or two days. If their slump
lasts longer than that, bollock them. If you want to do something,
do it. If you don't, don't. With a setback you have to forget it – it's
gone. You can't do anything about it. You have to think about next
year and start working to prepare for that. As a coach you have to
find the right switch to push. You have to know the person well. You
could push and push and it wouldn't work.'*

CLOSE RELATIONSHIPS

The relationships that form between coaches and their athletes
often become extremely close. Middle distance champion Sebastian
Coe was coached by his father. Did that make a difference?

*'I always thought it made it much easier. There are probably more
pressures if it is a father–son relationship. A coach–athlete relationship is probably the closest you are ever going to have with
somebody, outside of a marriage. It is equally as volatile on occasions.*

*'We used to unnerve the press because I often used to refer to
him in interviews as Peter. The press would say, "You mean your
father?" and I would say yes. My old man would often refer to me
as his athlete in the same way he would refer to three or four other
athletes he was coaching at the same time. They used to think this*

was quite odd. We were able to deal with it a lot easier than they were.

'The one rule we always had was that we would never allow a family issue, which inevitably there are from time to time, to spill over onto the training track, and we would never take the training track back to the supper table. If we ever did I had brothers and sisters who would sit there chiming in unison "Boring!" That used to have quite an effect.'

Coe believes his father was a great coach – 20 years ahead of his time. In fact, he doesn't believe he would have been as good an athlete or a competitor if he had had a different coach. He says that the testimony to his father's coaching is the fact that Coe held the 800m world record for as long as he did – from 1979 (though Coe broke it again himself in 1981) until 1997. Coe says of his father:

'He has the arrogance of an engineer who believes that most things have to be tested to destruction before they work. That's a bit unfair because he also recognized, like a good manager, that you don't waste assets early on in the lifecycle of a career. My training was geared very much to 10 or 12 years down the road.

'As a good scientist, which effectively he was, he was also honest and sharp enough to recognize that you can't be skilled at every discipline. Although he had a good understanding of physiology, it would have been wasteful of his time to spend hours figuring out the physiological underpinning of what I was doing. So he went out and found who was the best physiologist around, who happened to be an American, and he brought him onto the team back in 1983. The guy worked with me right the way through to the end of my career.

'Then my father wasn't a great expert on nutrition, so he found somebody at my old university, Loughborough, who was a nutritionist who used to balance my diet. He wasn't a biomechanics expert so we found a guy from Leeds University who was able to do the balancing work I needed. He brought this team together and then set the schedule. My dad put together the first management

team in athletics, which is now commonplace. The only thing he didn't have much time for was the sports psychologists. They never made it onto his team.'

While a close coaching relationship can be an important ingredient in an athlete's success, that doesn't mean other relationships can't also provide extremely positive influences. Former 400m champion Roger Black feels that his relationship with fellow runner Kriss Akabusi was also crucial to his success. Black believes that neither athlete would have achieved what they did without the other. That's because they wouldn't have made the decisions they made if they had been on their own. As an example, Black says that the two athletes took the decision to leave the UK and train in California together, a move they would not have made alone.

Training together had a big impact on both runners. Black believes that training companions are as important for determining success as the coaching relationship.

> *'You can have a great coach working one-on-one with an athlete, and the athlete won't perform as well as he can. Then the athlete changes groups and goes in with somebody he can respect and suddenly he comes on.'*

Black says he is often asked whether the most important thing about training is to have a great coach, but he doesn't think it is. He explains:

> *'Coaches are obviously terribly important, but I think your training partners are the most important – the people with whom you surround yourself every day, who you share the same goals with, the same dreams and aspirations. If you are thinking about being the best in the world, it helps to have somebody around you who is also trying to be best in the world.*
>
> *'I was very lucky because my training partner for the first half of my career was Kriss Akabusi. Kriss is totally mad, but great fun to have around. Behind that jovial person is somebody who is so*

focused, so dedicated, so disciplined – he's incredible. He changed events. He went from being a very good 400m runner to an event he really couldn't do, the 400m hurdles. When he won his Olympic bronze medal six years later it was a fantastic achievement, because most people never make that transition, or they start and then give up.'

Athletics coach Ron Roddan always coaches athletes in groups, rather than individually, but for slightly different reasons. Roddan believes that group coaching works well because no one is special. No one gets big-headed. He says that anyone who does seem to be becoming big-headed is soon brought back down to size by the rest of the group. Linford Christie, for example, wasn't allowed to develop airs and graces. The rest of the group made sure his feet were kept firmly on the ground, just like anyone else.

Analysis III

MENTAL TRAINING

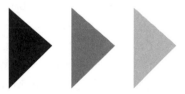

THE BUILD-UP TO SPORTING COMPETITION is key to success under pressure on the day. In Part III we looked at the mental training processes and techniques sporting champions use to prepare themselves effectively.

CHAPTER 9

Many of the sporting champions we interviewed used visualization techniques to help them prepare for competition. In Chapter 9: Mental Rehearsal, we looked at how they practised visualization and how it helped them achieve their sporting goals.

Although people talk about visualization, the process is actually much more than simply visualizing yourself completing an action.

Effective visualization involves recreating the sensations of the action – the feelings of running on the track, the sound of the crowd, or the other runners beside you. It draws in all aspects of the experience. It requires regular practice; it is a skill that needs to be learnt just like any other.

Visualization is a useful element of the sporting champion's armoury, when combined with training and skills acquisition. It can be used to reinforce the individual's physical talent and skills by enhancing their mental strength. However, it should not be seen as the single route to delivering world-beating performances. Without talent and skills already being in place, the value of visualization alone is limited. As Ceri Evans from mental conditioning specialists Gazing Performance says, visualization is potentially useful but it is not an answer for everything, nor is it enough on its own. You can't just lie down on a couch and imagine things and expect they will all just happen for you. They are not going to happen if you haven't got the necessary skill base, the skill acquisition framework and the confidence derived from gradually acquiring competence.

Sporting champions use visualization techniques to experience in their minds a perfect performance, with the aim of being able to recreate this perfect performance in the heat of competition. The individual needs to feel totally involved in the experience – seeing the things they would see in a race, hearing the same sounds, smelling the same smells.

The technique can also be used to re-edit a past experience so as to dampen its impact on the individual. This can be helpful if an athlete made a mistake in competition and then keeps reliving that experience in the mind. Re-editing the visualization so that it ends positively can reduce the chance of the athlete making the same mistake again – because the mind is reprogrammed to expect a different outcome. Renzie Hanham from Gazing Performance says that when people have had a bad performance they often replay it in their head in a way that retraumatizes them. Visualization can help because if people change the way they run through the experience in their heads, the impact is diminished.

Visualization can also be helpful in encouraging individuals to feel more at home in a strange environment. For example, 400m champion Roger Black would visit a stadium before a competition and walk round it, seeing himself running there. In this way he felt more comfortable in the environment when it came to the day of the real race.

When preparing for a competition, visualization can also be useful as a form of scenario planning. The individual can consider different situations that could arise and then visualize themselves dealing with them successfully. This can encourage the feeling of confidence before a performance, because the individual believes that every eventuality has been considered and that they are prepared to deal with anything that happens.

As Renzie Hanham points out, there is a difference between expectation and anticipation. When people expect something to take place, the implication is that the future is carved in stone. This approach doesn't allow for the unexpected and makes adaptation difficult; it can lead to denial – 'this can't be happening'. Anticipating what might happen allows for flexibility in the way we respond to a situation. We adapt, deal with it and then get back on track.

Applications

- Think of a positive experience that you have had where you did well, and that you want to recreate. To visualize the experience again, make sure you are sitting comfortably and are relaxed. Close your eyes and put yourself back into the experience. Try to see it through your own eyes, rather than seeing yourself as if you were watching a film of yourself. What did you hear at the time? Were there any smells you remember? Go through the experience in your mind from start to finish. How strongly were you able to recreate the experience? Do you feel more positive about being able to recreate it? Think about whether there are any more sensations you can introduce to enhance the experience. For example, how did the wind feel on your face? Was the racquet rough or smooth in your hand?

- You can use such visualizations for scenario planning. Think about things that could happen unexpectedly during the experience you are recreating. What if someone starts heckling you during your speech? What if your slide projector breaks down? Before starting the visualization come up with some solutions for how you could deal with such situations effectively and successfully. When you have the solutions, go through the visualization, but include the unexpected situation and your successful reaction to it. Make sure that the end is a positive one where you come out on top. At the end you should feel increased confidence in your ability to deal with such situations if they arise.

- There may be a past event which bothers you and where you would like to diminish the impact that the memory of it has on you. Perhaps you were in a situation where you felt humiliated. You may be able to reduce the impact of the memory by using certain techniques that create a sense of distance between you and the memory. For example, when you recall the past event, imagine you are seeing it played out on a cinema screen. See yourself sitting in a chair in front of the screen watching the drama unfold – with you as one of the 'actors'. In this way you have removed yourself somewhat from the direct action. See the event played in black and white. (Colour tends to make experiences more vivid.) Now try giving the characters silly, high-pitched cartoon voices. You might add in the sound of a honky tonk piano for added comic effect. Perhaps you could give some of the characters huge mouse ears. Play around with the images. You can speed the film up and run it backwards. If you can make yourself laugh at the screen, the negative impact of the memory should be hugely reduced; if the memory comes to mind, the chances are it will trigger a humorous association rather than the negative emotions of before.

CHAPTER 10

In Chapter 10: Anchors and Triggers, we looked at how sporting champions can use techniques to recreate desired mental states at will. We looked at how Neuro-Linguistic Programming (NLP) can be used to programme your mind for success.

Useful techniques for this include anchors and triggers. Athletes can anchor feelings of confidence that they have experienced in the past and use triggers to experience them again at will. Anchors can take many different forms, such as images, sounds or even pieces of clothing. Olympic swimmer Adrian Moorhouse even used the pain he felt during a race as a trigger to release a surge of adrenalin. When modern pentathlete Dr Stephanie Cook pulled down her mask before a fencing match, that was her trigger to create the mental state she needed to fence well.

The experiences of our champions and experts show that anchors and triggers are useful tools to help maintain an individual's focus on the processes required for their sport, rather than becoming distracted by other things – the crowd, their nerves or other competitors. They can also be of use in everyday life, to help us maintain our attention on what we are doing.

Renzie Hanham from mental conditioning specialists Gazing Performance describes anchors and triggers as 'useful parts of the sportsperson's toolbox'. They enable individuals to put their attention where it is going to be most useful. This can be particularly valuable for specific situations, such as kicking in rugby, enabling attention to be focused on the current process that really matters.

If such anchors and triggers are to be effective, they need to be practised regularly and used in training as well as in the heat of competition.

Applications

- Think of a mental state you would like to be able to recreate at will. For example, perhaps you want to be able to maintain a sense of calm even in situations you find stressful, such as visiting the dentist. The basic way to do this is to relax in an environment where you feel comfortable and think back to an occasion where you felt this sense of calm. Perhaps it was when you were floating in the Mediterranean sea on your last holiday. Maybe it was when you were planting out spring bulbs in the garden. Recreate that experience by reliving it in your mind. See with your eyes the things you saw then. Feel the same sensations. Bring the experience vividly to life. Try making the images larger and brighter and see whether that makes the sensation of calm even more powerful.

- When you feel absolutely calm and fully involved in the sensation, the next step is to anchor it to a particular part of your body. For example, you might squeeze the tip of the little finger on your left hand. In this way you create a link between the feeling of that squeeze and a calm mental state.

- When you have squeezed your little finger once, return your focus to reliving the calm experience. Recall the sights, sounds and sensations again. Make them vivid and then once again, when you are fully reliving the experience, squeeze your little finger in the same place as before.

- By repeating this process several times you are reinforcing the link between the squeeze on your finger and the feeling of calm. This should mean that in future, if you find yourself getting worked up or anxious when you don't want to be, you can squeeze your little finger and trigger that feeling of calm.

- You can, of course, use the same technique to anchor a range of mental states, such as enthusiasm or determination. Just make sure that you use different triggers for each, i.e. don't anchor everything to the tip of your little finger! Ideal places are those that you can access easily but other people can't.

CHAPTER 11

In Chapter 11: Preparing for Pressure, we looked at how top sportspeople learn to handle the pressure that comes with top level competition, and even thrive on it.

Part of this involves simply accepting that competing at the highest level inevitably brings pressure. However, top athletes over time also develop the belief that they can handle that pressure because they have come through similar situations before.

One interesting finding was that top performers who clearly perform well under pressure in their chosen sport don't necessarily enjoy pressure in other situations. Jonny Wilkinson, England rugby fly-half and scorer of the winning 2003 World Cup drop goal, admits that he doesn't enjoy pressure in his normal daily life. Yet he can not only handle it but also deliver top performances under high pressure on the pitch. Wilkinson practises his kicking over and over again, building up his confidence and belief that he can kick accurately in pressure situations.

Renzie Hanham from mental conditioning specialists Gazing Performance notes that the ability to function at an optimum level is often contextual. He says that an individual may be able to cope with stress in the sporting domain and yet not be able to deal with pressure in a relationship or in the workplace. This is partly because we have trained ourselves in one context and developed the necessary skills, but we haven't developed similar skills in another context. Our processes may not be as highly tuned in that other area because the context does not have sufficient significance for us to make the kind of effort required to perform at our best.

Our research amongst our sporting champions found that the key requirement for any champion is to be able to think correctly under pressure. This is what England rugby head coach Clive Woodward looks for in his players. However, it isn't just a natural ability to think correctly under pressure that counts; champions learn how to do it and practise their skills in pressurized situations to do so. By trying to recreate the feeling of pressure that they experience on the pitch or on a running track, sporting champions become increasingly able to perform well regardless of the pressure they may feel.

Ceri Evans from Gazing Performance notes that top performers repeatedly drill themselves and practise their skills. They establish competence and then subject it to pressurized situations in training, perhaps by being subjected to a lot of noise or having to perform the skill when tired. They drill it so that they can remain focused on the process.

Some athletes and coaches, such as athletics coach Ron Roddan, describe this ability to perform regardless of the pressure as going into 'automatic pilot'. Athletes learn their skill or technique so well that they can produce it automatically – almost unconsciously – as needed. They 'over-learn' the skill; it becomes so embedded that they don't need to think about how to do it. England rugby hero Jonny Wilkinson, for example, has practised his kicking so thoroughly that when called on to kick in a game, he just automatically goes into his kicking routine.

Penalty taking, whether in rugby, football, hockey or any other sport, is one of the most high-pressure situations any sportsperson can experience. Yet some people love nothing better than to step up to the mark. Successful penalty takers are keen to put themselves and their reputations on the line, but they can't just rely on a gung-ho spirit. They practise their routine – from the moment they walk up to the spot – over and over again.

Some people may appear naturally good at coping with pressure, but that doesn't mean we can't all learn to do so. The first step is to frame the experience in a positive way. For example, if you can see pressure as exciting and stimulating rather than threatening, you are more likely to view it as a positive experience.

Most importantly, there is no replacement for practice. If you have to do something under pressure, you must practise it repeatedly. Once you have the basic skill and can perform under relaxed conditions, then you must increase the pressure little by little to reinforce that skill. You need to develop the ability to go into automatic pilot mode, regardless of what is going on around you.

Applications

- Is there some skill that you want to apply in a situation where you feel under pressure? Perhaps you are nervous of public speaking, but would like to be confident that you can do this well. One solution is to practise your skill in environments of steadily increasing pressure; start gently and build up gradually, increasing your confidence as you go.
- There is no substitute for rehearsal. Using the example of public speaking, start out by simply practising giving a talk in the pri-

vacy of your own home, where you are your only audience. Then try yourself out in front of someone you trust, such as a family member or friend. Make the most of any positive suggestions they make. If possible, take advantage of any situations where you can talk in front of a small group of people – perhaps a group of colleagues at work. If you build up your confidence gradually, you will find that you are more comfortable with speaking in front or larger and larger audiences.

- Seize opportunities that come your way to practise your skills. Think of them as positive learning experiences that are helping you to develop in the ways that you want.

- Accept that you will probably always have some nerves when speaking in public – or doing anything else where your performance matters to you; virtually everyone does. In fact, those nerves can help to sharpen your performance.

CHAPTER 12

In Chapter 12: Review and Revise, we looked at how sporting champions review their performances and learn from their successes and their mistakes.

A regular review of performance is invaluable for checking that an athlete is on track in terms of their performance and outcome goals. Coaches clearly play an important role in giving feedback on what went well and what could be improved.

The timing of these reviews depends on the individual and the circumstances. Some people need a breathing space before they pick over their performance; their emotions may be running too high immediately after a competition to be able to think rationally about their performance. Some people prefer to look at the performance when it is still extremely fresh.

A key lesson that emerged from our champions was that the review should be focused on things the athlete can control. Worrying about what your competitors did is unhelpful.

Another key lesson is that mistakes can be learning opportunities. In a sense, there are no mistakes, only learning opportunities. Pretty much everyone slips up sometime, but the champions look for what they can learn from these experiences. Is there something they can do differently next time? Olympic hurdler Sally Gunnell suffered two major disappointments in 1990 and 1991, but moved on from the experiences by strengthening the support team she had around her.

Renzie Hanham from mental conditioning specialists Gazing Performance says that a useful way to perceive setbacks is to not think of them as failure, only feedback. It is more useful to think of a mistake as feedback, because feedback is useful information; it doesn't have the emotional response associated with the word 'mistake'. However, Hanham notes that feedback is often couched in negative terms such as 'Don't do this' or 'What do you think you were doing?', which is often inappropriate. Giving instructions in the negative implies the individual is doing something wrong and this can lead to an unhelpful emotional response, Hanham says. Feedback should be given as clear, specific instructions about what the individual can do. This allows the individual to stay focused on process and on improving the quality of the task. There are, however, occasions when giving instructions in the negative is useful, especially when individuals/teams find themselves mentally 'stuck'. Sometimes when people 'freeze', a sharp shout or comment can liberate them from this state and get them back into a meaningful process and on task. An example of this can be found in Zen: when trainees' attention starts to wane, the 'teacher' will utter a shout or strike them to 'unlock' them and get them back on task.

The key word here is 'trust' – between coach and athlete – and trust is something that is built up over time. Along with trust comes consistency of behaviour. That said, sometimes the unexpected comment or action can work to refocus the athlete, but if there is no trust then such interventions may be perceived as abusive and you can encounter resistance or withdrawal from the athlete.

Some of our interviewees, such as England rugby coach Clive Woodward, believe that winning performances deserve even more review and analysis than losing performances. If you focus on what you have done right, you are more likely to be able to reproduce that winning performance again in future.

Being open to innovation was also a characteristic that many of our top sporting champions displayed. They were willing to consider new ideas and training techniques that could improve their performance in any possible way. Perhaps people in other areas of life could learn from sporting champions here. Renzie Hanham notes that people in the business world are generally less interested than sportspeople in psychological issues and learning about how mental conditioning can give them the edge. Business people tend to be more combative and less open to such ideas, perhaps because they don't feel particularly secure in the working environment.

Applications

- If there are areas of your life where you want to improve your performance, develop the habit of reviewing what you have done and how you did it. What was it about your performance that pleased you? Why did this go well? How can you try to ensure you do this similarly well in future? What aspects do you think you could have handled better? How could you try to improve these in future? Are there extra skills you can develop or existing ones you can improve?

  Try to conduct such reviews in a calm frame of mind. Don't perform them if you are feeling upset. Give yourself enough time that you can apply a slightly detached, rational approach, but don't leave it so long that you can't remember the details well enough.
- Consider seeking feedback from other people you respect. If you do, be prepared to give their comments a fair hearing and try not to react emotionally. See such feedback as a chance to learn and improve.

CHAPTER 13

Few top sportspeople achieve their success entirely on their own. All of them will have worked with a coach, if not continuously, then at some point in their sporting career. In Chapter 13: Coaching Relationships, we looked at how these coaching relationships can work most effectively.

The role of every coach, and all support staff, is to create a supportive environment in which champions feel confident and encouraged to give their best performances. For example, England football manager Sven Göran-Eriksson believes that his players need to feel confident to try new things, knowing they will not be criticized unfairly for daring to be brave on the pitch. Managers such as Eriksson will defend their players from the press and other critics and see that as part of their job.

However, this doesn't mean a coach shouldn't be tough if required. Coaches need to be able to tell their athletes if they aren't putting in the effort and commitment required. Coaches do need to inspire loyalty, trust and confidence to be effective. This means they need to adopt a coaching style that is true to themselves, and reflects their own personalities.

Most coaching relationships don't stay static, but develop naturally over time. When a sportsperson is younger they may need more guidance, but as they develop confidence and belief, they may start to challenge the coach. This can be a positive, productive relationship if both parties are willing to discuss their ideas openly. Renzie Hanham from mental conditioning specialists Gazing Performance says that some coaches are very directive all the time. Others are directive at the beginning of the relationship, but later on are keen for the athlete to take more and more responsibility. It depends on the processes of both the coach and the athlete.

Sometimes a champion will want to move onto a new coach in search of new insights. Sometimes the relationship will endure throughout the champion's career. There is no right or wrong approach.

Even though the coaching relationship can be an extremely close one, as with middle distance champion Sebastian Coe and his father, athletes will always need a sense of independence. In the end, they are the only person who can achieve the winning performance, and must have the self-belief and determination to do so.

Applications

- If you want a coach, whether for sporting purposes or as a life coach, make sure you find someone you respect and trust. You need to have confidence that the advice you are given is appropriate and well-founded.
- Don't be afraid to make your own suggestions or challenge your coach if you want to. A dynamic relationship can be extremely fulfilling for both parties.
- If you feel that your coach is no longer helping you, don't be afraid to end the relationship. You may have reached a point where you can do well on your own, or perhaps someone with a fresh perspective can be more useful.
- Try not to make your coach the scapegoat for your own shortcomings. In the end it's up to you to achieve your goals; no one else can do that for you.

Part IV

PEAK PERFORMANCE

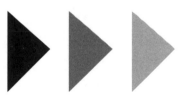

Chapter 14

NERVE CONTROL

NERVES COME WITH THE TERRITORY of competing in top-level sport. Even the greatest champions can suffer from them. The question is, how do they cope with them effectively so that they can put in winning performances? The people who do that best are the people who become the world's champions.

CHAMPION NERVES

Former gold medal hurdler Sally Gunnell admits to having been so nervous that before a race she would sometimes end up in tears. She experienced so many emotions as a big competition drew closer but the worst day of all was perhaps the day before the heats. Once the heats got underway, Gunnell didn't feel so bad because the competition had finally started. She would tell herself that there was no going back: 'This is your chance; if you don't do it now you're never going to get this opportunity again.' At the same time she would tell herself that whatever happened, people would still love her and be there for her.

When trying to relax Gunnell would lie on her bed, deep breathing and visualizing the coming race. She recalls the build-up to the 1992 Olympic final:

'I ran well in the semi-final. Then we had a rest day, which is awful, because you want to get on with it at that point and you're just waiting. It's the longest day in your life, just sitting around because you're scared of using up energy. I'd just try to sleep or go through the visualization. I was feeling quite confident, but at the same time quite nervy.

'Jon [Sally Gunnell's husband] never used to come out, except at the last minute, but he was always on the end of the phone. We would talk a lot. Bruce [Longden – coach] was also good. We would chat and he would always be very light-hearted. We wouldn't particularly chat about the race.

'As the race got nearer I got quieter and quieter. We'd do a little jog the day before. Then I'd try and sleep. But I couldn't sleep that night – your mind's very active, going through the race. I got up as late as possible, and had some food – force-fed myself. I was feeling so sick but I force-fed some bread and banana down my throat. Then I tried to give myself some quality thoughts again.

'I went back to my room. I had this routine of getting myself ready an hour beforehand – showering, doing my hair. Don't ask me why you do your hair and put make-up on, because you're only going to get all sweaty, but I suppose it's to do with wanting to feel good about yourself and building your confidence up. Once you start getting ready it's not so bad and you just stop yourself from letting any negative thoughts come at you. Then I'm meeting my coach and getting on the bus to go down to the track. I would go very much inside myself and sit there totally nervous, but at the same time having to say to myself, "You can do this".

'Once you get to the track and start jogging around it's quite reassuring, because you've done the warm-up so many times. You have your routine of doing strides and stretching and so on.

'Of course, once you reach the track you start seeing all your competitors, and that's where the whole confidence game starts. That's where the arrogant side of me would come out. I would walk on tall and confident and I wouldn't sit in the corner. You can't let the others know you're as scared as they probably are. You're jumping around and saying "I can do this", not so much in words but in your whole attitude.

'I remember watching Sandra Farmer-Patrick hit a hurdle and thinking, "Eek, you could get hurt", and then doing a stride, telling myself it felt good. Bruce might then time me, but he'd lie like hell.

'All the time you're telling yourself you can do it. Negative thoughts would constantly come in, but you have to stop yourself thinking them. You tell yourself you've done everything right.

'The hardest part is when they call you and you have to go into the room to wait. All of a sudden you are on your own, without your coach. At that point you probably feel the loneliest person in the whole world.

'I used to think, "I don't want to do this. I'll go and hide." In Barcelona there was a little gate on the far side of the track. I remember thinking, "Why don't I just go out of that gate? No one's going to know. I could sneak out there and hide in the forest until it's all over." I was asking myself why I didn't have a normal nine-to-five job, and why I was putting myself under all this pressure. I wanted to be anywhere else but there at that moment, but I knew that the bottom line was I had to go through with it. All of a sudden you just want to get out there and just do it.'

As the organizers go through the required procedures of checking competitors' numbers and spikes, Gunnell concentrated on keeping calm.

'You see people who can't cope with the nervous situation, and that's what makes the difference between being a champion or not.

'Then you're marching out onto the track. You walk up to the start in front of 60,000 people. I kept my head down. I didn't dare look up and see the British flags, the people cheering me on. I didn't want to break my concentration. I was starting to get within myself.

'I walked up to the line and thought, "I've still got five minutes to go. What am I going to do with myself?" It was the longest five minutes ever in my whole life. I could hear people shouting my name: "Go on Sally, you can do it". I started to think about all the people at home.

'Then the whistle goes and you strip off down to your leotard, put your stuff in the box and are standing on the line. There's probably a minute to go and you can feel every heartbeat.'

That's when Sally's foundations of belief kicked in – and she had her sense of knowing that she would win.

'I'd been constantly saying to myself, "You can do this. You have done everything right. You've eaten well. You've done every training session possible. You've not been injured. You are 100%." Just before they said "On your marks" something inside me said, "This is it. This is your race. You can do this." And I really believed in those final seconds that I was going to win.'

Before competing in the Vendeé Globe for the first time, yachtswoman Ellen MacArthur sailed the newly-built *Kingfisher* back from New Zealand to the UK, completing the first leg to Cape Horn with a crew, then continuing on alone. The journey of around 10,000 miles gave her more experience of sailing for an extended period. Two weeks after arriving home MacArthur added a competitive element to her preparations by setting off on a single-handed transatlantic race from Plymouth to the USA. MacArthur was terribly nervous:

'When I got into the single-handed transatlantic race, sure I'd sailed the boat halfway round the world, but I was nervous as hell about the fact I was about to race against pretty much every other skipper who would be competing in the Vendeé Globe. Virtually all the other boats doing the Vendeé were using the transatlantic as a qualifier. So I spent the whole race feeling nervous; it was probably one of the races I enjoyed least because I was so nervous. I was so wound up and I wanted to do my absolute best. It was the first time Kingfisher *had ever raced against any of the other boats. We won that race. I got some confidence from that and it helped me enormously to cross the start of the Vendeé knowing that I'd beaten a lot of the other boats. But I had already crossed the Atlantic about five times and I was acutely aware that the Vendeé was a different kettle of fish. So I was a little more confident than I would have been otherwise, but by no means complacent.'*

NO NERVES – THAT'S FINE TOO

Some elite sportspeople claim to not feel nervous before big sporting occasions. Former England international footballer Jack Charlton recalls that he didn't get nervous before the 1966 World Cup final.

'I was nervous before the semi-final – very nervous – but I felt OK before the final. At that stage you've achieved something – you've got to the final. OK, we went on to win it, which was lovely. We wouldn't have been remembered as much if we'd lost and finished second. But when I was a player you got bonuses if you got to the Cup Final – you didn't get a bonus for winning.'

Former badminton champion Gill Clark didn't suffer badly from nerves, though she appreciates that other people often did.

'A lot of athletes talk about fear of failure and that's why they get nervous. They're so uptight, worrying about whether they'll perform.

'But I couldn't wait to get out there on the court. I knew I was ready and I had prepared properly. I couldn't wait to get out there and prove to myself and everybody else that I was better than that other person. I never had to calm myself down, because I never went over the top, but I certainly never had to psyche myself up either.'

THE VALUE OF NERVES

Sportspeople who do suffer from nerves shouldn't think they are unlucky. Former national athletics coach Frank Dick says there's nothing wrong with nerves. Athletes need the adrenalin that comes with them to make them sharp. Without that, he says, it's like trying to drive with low octane in your tank. There's nothing wrong with the sharpness that comes with being afraid. 'You need those bottom clenching moments!'

Round-the-world yachtswoman Ellen MacArthur always gets nervous before a race, but she doesn't see that as a bad thing. She says that the moment you stop feeling nervous is the moment you should stop racing. She believes that when you are racing across an ocean you have to have massive respect for your environment. Every time she sails out of a port she feel a sense of nervousness about whether everything will be OK, but she feels that keeps her on her toes.

MacArthur has no magic secret for mastering her nerves.

'The best thing is just to get out there and cross the start line. You concentrate on everything you have to do rather than worrying about saying goodbye to everyone and getting emotional about the fact you're not going to see everyone for two weeks or three months. You have to try and shut that out.'

Nerves shouldn't be seen as something to be avoided or driven totally away. Renzie Hanham from Gazing Principle says that nerves shouldn't be something that people feel they need to over-come. They are simply the body's natural response and trying to stop them is counterproductive. What matters is that the nervous feelings don't become overwhelming or divert the individual from their task. Former 400m champion Roger Black agrees. He believes you want the nerves to be there, but just need to make sure you don't let them overtake you.

Former Australian rugby fly-half, Michael Lynagh, certainly believes that trying to bury nerves can have disastrous results. He recalls the 1995 World Cup, when there were some new guys on the team. Australia was due to play South Africa at home. It was South Africa's first match and there was a huge build-up to it. During the run up Lynagh told the new guys that if they wanted to have a chat, go for a meal or any other help, he was there. They all claimed to be fine. However, when a couple of them got out on the field, they just 'disintegrated completely', Lynagh says. They weren't functioning properly or responding to calls as they should do. Lynagh found this an interesting experience, because these were the guys who had been trying to suppress their nervousness before the game.

For Lynagh, his pre-match nerves would ease once he was on the pitch.

> 'In big matches, I would go out and think, "Thank goodness – this is where we are supposed to be". The last game I played at Twickenham in particular was an extraordinarily nerve-racking game for me. It was a Cup Final and my last game. I'd said I was leaving, so I was particularly nervous beforehand. But I remember smiling, and breathing out. Usually, two or three minutes into a game, the nerves go. When I got onto the pitch – they were gone. On the pitch I am very comfortable, knowing I have done whatever I could to make it work.'

Sprinter Mark Richardson sees nerves before a race as a natural and helpful thing. Though he suffers from nerves he believes that all athletes do and he doesn't see that as a problem. In fact, it's a great thing to have nerves, he says.

'You need those nerves to get the adrenalin and to get the most out of yourself. To keep a lid on it I use a technique called centring. I just concentrate on my breathing and do something that calms me down. I think music can affect your moods, so if I feel that I'm almost too hyper pre-race, I listen to some relaxing music – music that's just going to bring me down a peg or two. And vice versa, if I don't feel the competitive juices are flowing strongly enough before a race, I'll listen to something that's going to pump me up a bit. The choices tend to be between hip hop and R&B.'

Richardson also draws on positive thinking when competing. He remembers a positive time in the past and then tries to get back into that state, thus generating the same positive outlook. His aim is to achieve a relaxed state that allows for peak performance, one where he has a heightened sense of awareness and arousal.

ACCEPTANCE OF NERVES

England rugby fly-half Jonny Wilkinson also admits to getting incredibly nervous before any game he plays, whether international or club games. This is because, whether the team wins or loses, he still has his own goals to complete. He has to satisfy himself and his team-mates and fulfil his ambition inside that particular game. A lot of his nerves come from knowing deep down that he will be kicking in the match environment. He knows it will be tough and there will be a lot of pressure. On the other hand, he also sees this as being just his job. He says that ever since he came into rugby he has thought of himself as a kicker – that's his job.

When it comes to dealing with pre-match nerves, Wilkinson just accepts they will be there.

'I can't get rid of them. It's the way I will always be. I want to know that everything is going to turn out fine, but no one can tell you that. The reason I go out and work is to ensure that whatever happens, I have a better chance than everyone else of doing well for the team.

'I have tried recently to understand that I can't control these nerves, and I shouldn't give in to them so badly. So before an international game, when in the hotel, I will try to get away from it for an hour. I might read a paper and try to find a story to take my mind off it. I might watch some TV to stop me thinking about things. When we are going to a game on the coach, travelling for maybe an hour, I will look out of the window and think about people walking to the game. I keep my mind occupied, rather than thinking about the coming match, which I did for the first four or five years.'

Wilkinson is also making a conscious effort to remind himself that playing rugby is fun, not just a pressurized situation where he is constantly trying to do his best and meet his own high expectations.

'After a game I will sit in the changing room when the pressure is off and think, "Yeah, I enjoyed that and it feels fantastic". I feel proud and satisfied and that I can walk out with my shoulders back and my head up. Now I am trying to have that feeling more when I am out in the middle of a game, to think to myself that this is fun and it's what I want to do. I know that, but I don't necessarily realize it until it's all finished. It's a hard game and people take a lot of knocks, but when I am out there now I am trying to think that it's what I love doing; I'm only going to be doing it for a while, so I want to enjoy it.'

Golfing champion Nick Faldo isn't immune to nerves. He learnt how to deal with them during the course of his playing career.

'When you get nervous you tighten up. That's totally natural. It's your body's defences helping you – because you're in a nervous situation, it'll tighten up and won't move. As a golfer, you need to know that that's natural. You just need to turn a bit more, or your arms have got to keep moving, or that you've got to keep the tempo going. I learnt these things over time.'

Nerves are also part and parcel of racing for Olympic rower Matthew Pinsent, who describes himself as 'bubbling with nerves' in the last few minutes before a race starts. Pinsent describes what it feels like just before the starting gun.

> 'There are the two little voices in your head. One of them is telling you you're brave and the other one's telling you you're going to lose. I don't think that changes. I think it's quite universal. In some ways it's reassuring because it's the same again and again, almost irrespective of the quality of the race. At the Olympics it's extreme and it's stressful but one of the ways of dealing with it is to say, "Okay, this is good, this is what I need, this is part of the experience." You don't want to do it every day, but it's part of your body's preparation – the fact that you go through this horrendous state of nervous anxiety for hours and hours before the race. I've never necessarily been a big fan of trying to control the nerves; it's just part of it.'

As part of a rowing crew, Pinsent thinks it can be helpful to share your feelings with your team-mates.

> 'We have little conversations with each other about how we're feeling. It's definitely OK to say you're feeling nervous, or that you're not, or that you were good an hour ago but now you're struggling. It's nobody's fault if you're not nervous and it's nobody's fault if you are struggling with the nerves; it just helps to say it to someone else.'

Pinsent believes there is little you can do to relieve the nerves until you get into the warm-up stage in the last three quarters of an hour or so before the race. At that point you can finally start moving and going through a warm-up routine, but before that you've just got to sit there.

> 'You've just got to wait it out. You just try and concentrate on very simple things. The closer the race gets you try not to deal with everything at once. You certainly blank things out. People talk about

controlling the controllables. You rule out stuff you can't control,
whether that's the weather or to a certain extent the opposition,
the crowd, or the status of the event. If you're nervous those things
become very important. But you have to say, "Okay, it's just a
rowing race. We can win this and the way we're going to win this is
by doing these two or three things very well."'

Once a race is underway, holding your nerve is just as important as it
is before the start. Matthew Pinsent knows that if another boat gets
a lead early on, it's vital not to panic and overreact.

'You need to have rehearsed enough or be experienced enough to
know that panicking doesn't work. You're probably telling yourself
that they've worked harder than you to get out into the lead and
that they are just as tired as you are. It's a matter of making them
pay for that effort. You also need good leadership and communi-
cation within the crew to make sure that panic doesn't set in and
that you don't chase the race. You have to row your own race to a
certain extent. It's no good beating off that boat's challenge and
doing something different to get back level with them, and then
finding that they weren't judging the race right anyway.

'Of course it depends where in the race it's happening and which
crew it is. In a six-boat final there are going to be two crews who
are thinking that they are fifth and sixth quickest and out of the
medals; their only tactic is just to go for it and get out in front. Every
now and then they may make the favourites panic, in which case
the tactic has worked. So you have to be aware that may be going
on in the race.'

Adrian Moorhouse says that he certainly felt a heightened adrenalin
surge during the build-up to the Olympic final in Seoul in 1988. However, he tried to manage his nervous energy so that it was there for
the race, rather than wasting it beforehand. This ability to manage
the energy takes advanced practice, so that the mental inner chatter
can be steered in a positive direction. Negative thoughts may come
in, but they only last a split second.

Moorhouse recalls the last half hour before the race, where he simply tried to put the final in perspective.

> *'I was in a room with seven guys, just looking at them and thinking human things: "It's not the end of the world; this is just seven guys; they've all got families; they all want to have a bit of a race." I reminded myself of the big things in the world that were going on. I reminded myself of people I'd lost who were close to me, or who were ill, and thinking, "Why am I getting worried?"'*

Like many of our other sporting champions, sprinter John Regis definitely suffered from nerves before a big race, though the reason for them changed over time.

> *'Initially I was afraid to win because then people would expect me to win the next race. A lot of athletes can't handle that. They cloud it by saying it's something else, but it is that fear to win. Eventually you get over that and then the pressure would be being afraid to lose, because when you step up there everybody is gunning for you. Then you put pressure on yourself because of who you think you are and how you perform and your standing as you see it within the sport. So I did get a lot of nerves.'*

PHYSICAL RELEASE

Former Davis Cup tennis captain David Lloyd accepts that everybody gets nervous before an important sporting competition. In his career he developed a physical way of dealing with his pre-match nervous energy.

> *'I never controlled my nerves. I would go out on the practice court and play full out for half an hour. That meant I went on the match court slightly tired and warm as hell. Just by being slightly tired I found it took a bit of the edge off. So I played a set or a set and a half before going on court and that helped me.'*

Michael Lynagh, former Australian rugby captain, also used physical activity as a way of coping with his nerves before a game.

> *'I always tried to do something physical on the morning of a match, maybe just going for a walk. Before a game in Scotland once I played ping-pong for a good hour. That was great fun and just released some nervous energy.*
>
> *'One of the things Dad taught me at an early age was that when people get nervous they get very closed – they don't talk and don't want to mix. So I used to go after breakfast and make a point of sitting in the public areas of the hotel – not right by the door, but in public and I would read papers. People would come and say hello.'*

Lynagh recalls the morning of the World Cup final in 1991.

> *'I found that if you sat in the hotel you just got more and more tense. The hotel was on the outskirts of London and it was a bit misty. I went out to have a kick in the grounds. Everybody else was locked up in their rooms and trying to save energy. Nobody would come out with me, so I took my boots and a couple of balls and rather than running to get the balls after I kicked them, I found a little hill. I kicked the balls up hill and then they rolled back down to me.'*

When driving to a match on the bus Lynagh was usually fairly relaxed, but if he began feeling particularly nervous he would close his eyes and run through his mental rehearsal routine – which would sometimes put him to sleep. Then, when the team reached the ground, Lynagh would definitely start getting nervous, but he accepted the feeling was there was a reason. He would always acknowledge how he was feeling. He often made a point telling the younger guys that he was feeling a bit nervous that day and asking the how they felt. Sharing feelings in this was helpful, he found, and much better than trying to bury the nerves.

In the next chapter we look at how champions can use routines to help them manage their nervous energy, before and during competition.

Chapter 15

THE ROCK OF ROUTINE

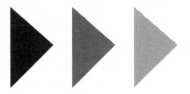

WHEN TRYING TO PUT IN A PEAK PERFORMANCE, sporting champions make effective use of routines. These can be used to help them cope with highly pressured moments, as noted in Chapter 11, or to generally keep nerves at a positive level. They also provide a familiar build-up to the start of a match or a contest. They provide a rock of support in moments of pressure.

PRE-MATCH ROUTINES

Sports psychologist John Syer works with athletes to assist them in identifying routines that support their build-up to performing and help them to create the right mental state. He questions athletes to help them become more aware of what they do in their routine.

In this way the athlete may identify something important that they weren't aware of. It may be something they want to continue doing or to change.

Syer doesn't think there is one right way to prepare, whether a week before, three days before, the day before or on the day. There is no routine that works for everybody, though there probably is for the individual, he says.

> *'My prime concern is to help my clients to become aware of what they are currently doing because, until they know what they are doing, they can't change anyway. If you help me to become aware of what I'm doing, I might be appalled but I'm also deeply interested because suddenly I have all sorts of new options.'*

Sports psychologist Professor Graham Jones has also worked with sporting top performers to help them with their build-up routines. He has helped them to recognize what works and what doesn't work, by asking them to think about past good performances and identifying common things that they did. The sportspeople can also think about past performances that were not so good and again identify any common actions or factors in the build-up. Professor Jones says that the athletes can come up with absolutely anything – what they had for breakfast or what time they went to bed the night before. Once the athlete has identified the things they associate with successful performances, they can try to recreate or do those things next time they compete. If they do so, they should feel better about the competition and their potential to do well.

Some routines are akin to superstitions. For example, tennis genius Bjorn Borg never shaved during the Wimbledon championship. Professor Jones says:

> *'At some stage he associated not shaving with performing well. It's important for most performers to have things that they associate with success, and that they try to replicate every time they compete. You try to get people into routines, and they might begin days before they perform well. As you get closer you can use triggers or breath-*

ing techniques, centring techniques and so on. It has to be specific to the individual's needs.'

The important thing is to identify the factors that really make a difference in terms of supporting a performance and not to get distracted by irrelevancies. Sometimes people can read too much into a certain routine, and the influence it has over the final result. England football coach Sven-Göran Eriksson says:

'When I was a player in the second division, for one period we played better football away than we did at home. So the manager called us in two hours earlier than normal before our next home game, put us on a bus and took us for an hour's ride. It didn't work.'

That unnecessary trip was abandoned before the next home match.

In his football playing days, former England Under-21 coach David Platt found it difficult waiting for a match to start.

'People prepare in different ways before a game. I was quieter. The hour before the game dragged on for me. I'd go in the dressing room 75 minutes before the game and it dragged on. I was relaxed. I wasn't boisterous or bouncing around. By the time I'd read the programme and had a massage I had half an hour to kill. I'd think, "What am I going to do now?" I just wanted to play.'

Platt doesn't like the teams he coaches now to be disturbed before a match.

'I don't like people coming into my dressing room who aren't involved in that particular game. I have thrown photographers out. You can disturb people. I think players are very focused in that hour between two o'clock and three o'clock. They are focused within routines. Some people will laugh and joke, but that is their routine. At Nottingham Forest we had a couple of players who put

earphones on and just sat there. People have different ways of get-
ting themselves ready for a game.'

While some people will use a routine to keep themselves sufficiently
calm, others may need to increase their excitement levels. Sports
psychologist John Syer says:

'When I was at Tottenham in the early 1980s, Ray Clemence was
goalkeeper. He was probably the oldest and most experienced
player in the team. On the day of a league match, he would to start
warming up way before anybody else. (The peak of this warm-up
was dancing from foot to foot, dressed only in his underpants,
repeating the mantra "One for all and all for one" over and over
again!) He needed this routine and a long build-up to reach an
optimal level of excitement. On the other hand, when he was
injured, Tony Parkes chose to find a quiet place in the shower room
where he could calm down until some 20 minutes before the game.
This was his way of reaching an optimum level of excitement.'

England rugby captain Lawrence Dallaglio follows a particular routine in match days to get himself in the right state to play at the right
time.

'I'm quite an early riser and I want to make sure I eat a nice break-
fast. You've got to try and build things up to a crescendo so that at
2 or 3 o'clock, whenever they kick off, you are absolutely ready. You
need the ability to be able to walk into a room at eight in the morn-
ing very focused inside but also very relaxed on the outside. That
shows you have composure and you can deal with pressure. It's
crucial to be able to keep things under control because it is going
to be hectic out there on the pitch. That has an effect on your peers
too. So it's important to be relaxed in the morning, but knowing
that today is a different day because it's game day. I am genuinely
excited on match day. I get excited because that's what you are
there for – that's the fun bit. You've done all the training, you have

got the confidence and you're the best person for the job. You're the best person there, and now it's time to demonstrate it.'

Dallaglio developed his pre-match routine over time, as he discovered what worked for him.

'You pick things up and leave other things behind and you develop a framework over a period of time. All sportsmen have rituals. And when you become successful there are certain preparations you tend to stick to, which become your own personal blueprint for success. The older you get and the more experienced you become, you add and subtract from the blueprint. Within a team sport that blueprint has to be flexible to incorporate other people's blueprints as well; what works for me might not necessarily work for the guy I am playing with. You have to respect that.'

NEED FOR FLEXIBILITY

Even when a sportsperson has developed a routine that suits them, they have to be able to adapt it to circumstances on the day. For example, after breakfast on match day England rugby captain Lawrence Dallaglio likes to relax and do his own thing, given the limitations imposed by the timetable for the team, such as the time for setting off for the ground.

'You can't always control things, but you have your own framework that you mix with what is required for the team. And you have to have a preparation routine that can adapt to kick-off being delayed, for example. Anything can happen to throw you out of your normal routine. It happens more often when you play away from home because you are less in control.'

Javelin champion Steve Backley believes that having a routine provides him with a sense of reassurance during his final preparations before a championship javelin competition starts. The problem is, the circumstances of each competition are always different.

'You need certainty, so I have a routine. The problem is that at most championships the routine is broken much more than it would be at any other competition. In a normal competition you warm up an hour before – jog, stretch and do some drills, go out into the field, put your boots on, mark your run up and do some half throws. But in the major championships it's different. In one, the final started at 6.35pm, check-in was 6.20pm. The warm-up facilities are a five minute bus ride down the road. So you go through the normal jog, stretch, drills, ankle and knee movements – all the basic physical patterns. You get up to a level of readiness and then you get on the bus. You've done your normal routine but then you've got to wait before the start of the competition, and that's a chance for things to get to a fantastic level or fall away.'

Breaststroke champion Adrian Moorhouse, found himself using up lots of emotional energy before the Olympic final in Seoul in 1988. Unusually, the final was the day after the heats, rather than on the same day – a change in routine he didn't like.

'I'd never before gone to sleep between the heat and the final and that challenged me. I couldn't stop my visualization tape, which was a problem. The next morning I got up at five and went through my race day routine. I remember wanting it to be over because it was mine to win. I felt that I wanted to get it out of my system. I couldn't wait to do it and was using up too much emotional energy straining at the leash.

'So I did a lot of relaxation, minimizing what it meant – the Olympic factor. I just focused on the process. I thought about how I would step on the block, what I would do if there was a false start, how I would dive. I just concentrated on all the processes and got away from the Olympic aspect.'

Olympic multiple gold medal-winning rower Matthew Pinsent understands that it can prove a weakness to be too dependent on a routine. Pinsent says of his crew:

'We definitely have a routine in terms of how we warm up and when we warm up, but beyond that I try not to have too fixed an idea of what's going to happen, just because I want to be as flexible and adaptable as possible. I'm certainly not superstitious. If anything, I'm superstitious about not being superstitious. You do all this training and then suddenly get upset at the last minute because you put your socks on the wrong way round ...

'Sometimes you're not given the same build-up to each race. Maybe something unforeseen happens, or the weather may change and the timing for the transport changes, so your routine might be knocked slightly. You have to sort out exactly what the ingredients of success are and I don't think it's about having a certain breathing routine 90 minutes beforehand and so on. You can't rely on those things. Gold medals are won in large amount in the training you do, not in the last minute. Okay, the last minute things are important, but only in their generality. Eventually you've got to arrive on the start line ready to race and pretty much warmed up. How you do that is up to you. I could change my routine, change my ideas, but that wouldn't make any difference. I'd hope I'd still win.'

Routines can also be limiting if they clash with someone else's. Sports psychologist John Syer recalls just such a problem. Some years ago he worked with a football player who had a routine that required him to be the last player out of the dressing room. Towards the end of his career he changed clubs and unfortunately someone there had the same routine. Clearly it wasn't possible for both players to be last out. The result? A problem.

Syer suggests that, in such situations, athletes need only to identify the feeling their routine evokes. Once they can name that feeling they can think of alternative methods of evoking it. If the football player realizes that leaving the dressing room last makes him feel calm or in control or strong, he may consider what sort of conversation, music, object, sentence or physical movement gives him the same feeling and build attention to this into his old routine. This is the kind of 'anchor' and 'trigger' approach considered in Chapter 10.

FAMILIARITY

Routines are valuable partly because they are familiar to the individual concerned. They increase the sense of security they feel in a potentially stressful time. Similarly, having a sense of familiarity about your surroundings, however you achieve it, can be a major help.

The value of familiarity is that it increases the sportsperson's sense of comfort. Most footballers would rather play at home, for example, because it's their patch. The advantage that familiarity with the home ground gives a team is undeniable. David Platt Platt, former England football captain and Under-21 England coach, says:

> *'You can't beat playing at home. Home advantage is the familiarity. The pitch might be exactly the same size at Villa Park as it is at Manchester United, but the advertising boards are different, the stands are different. At home the advertising boards give you an awareness of where you are on the pitch.'*

Sports psychologist Professor Graham Jones agrees that familiarity is what home advantage is about. If you're playing in a familiar environment, you know the level at which you can control the environment, Professor Jones says. You don't have to worry about certain aspects of it. In contrast, when you are playing away from home, you don't know what to expect. That is why coaches talk about 'silencing the crowd' early on, because they know they need to get some control over the environment. Professor Jones recalls the Six Nations match between Wales and Italy in 2001.

> *'On paper Wales should beat Italy every time, but the Italians haven't been part of the Six Nations for very long and they always raise their game. So we talked about killing the Italians off early on so they couldn't come back. In the first 20 minutes Wales took a significant lead, which the Italians couldn't claw back. It's about suppressing the crowd and controlling the environment. Knowing you've got control over things is so important.'*

Professor Jones stresses the importance of creating a conducive environment – one that allows people to focus on what they need to do, which is to perform, and not to have to worry about anything else. What matters is controlling the controllables, controlling the environment to enable people to perform at their maximum level.

Some sportspeople will make an extra effort to familiarize themselves with the environment in which they will be competing. Professor Jones believes this pays off and he encourages it:

> *'A young ice skater performing in a major championship for the first time could actually skate out into the middle of the ice in the empty stadium. I would just get her to stand there and close her eyes and imagine the noise, the music and imagine doing the routine. It's also important to get to know every nook and cranny – don't think you can do too much of that either.'*

Michael Lynagh, former Australian rugby captain, made a special effort to go and practise kicking in the ground where he was shortly due to play. When playing professionally he developed a regular routine for kicking practice before a match.

> *'I found it really helped me to go down the afternoon before and kick in the conditions at the ground at the same time that we would be playing. It just made sense. I'd have three kicks from in front of the goal posts about 20 yards out, then three kicks from the junction of the 22 and the 15 yard lines on both sides. Then I'd have three more about 40 yards out. Then I would turn around and do the same thing at the other end. If you are familiar with the territory, it just makes you feel a little bit more comfortable.'*

PLAYING AWAY

Familiarity with the home ground may help players feel more comfortable, but they also need to be able to feel secure away from home. England rugby head coach Clive Woodward says his squad feels very comfortable at Twickenham and he believes it is a difficult place for opposition teams to play in. However, the England team slogan now is 'Any team, anywhere, any time'.

> *'We feel we can play against anybody anywhere in the world. We've won big games away from home and we've lost a couple of big games. We look forward to playing those away games. If you want to be the best team in the world, you've got to get a win away from home. There's no point being able just to win at Twickenham.'*

Playing away from home does, however, make it harder to stick to a familiar routine before a match. Lawrence Dallaglio has certainly found playing away from home a greater challenge.

> *'Playing at home is the easy bit really. You've got all your friends and family, all your support systems. Playing away from home you are taken out of that support system and you are challenged – it's you against the rest of the country you are playing in. With the Lions tour to South Africa, you know that the minute you leave the shore, while you will have a few supporters out there, it's basically you against that country and you've got to pull together as a team. The sign of a good player is someone who can cope with playing away from home and playing in a game when things aren't always going your way.'*

There are things that can be done to make the team feel more secure away from home, Dallaglio feels. Taking your own medical team and any particular equipment you definitely need is a good start, because you can't rely on other people to provide what you are used to.

In the next chapter we consider another way that sporting champions rely on themselves – by keeping their inner voice positive.

Chapter 16

POSITIVE TALK

WHEN IT COMES TO DELIVERING A PEAK PERFORMANCE, sporting champions have to remain positive about themselves and their ability to win. Their inner voice needs to be feeding them positive thoughts about what they are about to do.

Roger Black, former 400m champion, was certainly familiar with his inner voice. He says:

'We all have a voice in our head and it speaks loudest to you when you walk into a stadium on your own. We don't listen to that voice most of the time – we shut it out. But there are certain moments in our lives when that voice will demand to be heard. One of those is when as a sportsperson you stand on the line. That voice calls to

you and you have to listen. If that voice is a friend, you're OK. If it is an enemy …'

POSITIVE SPIN

Champions have the ability to keep their inner voice positive. They see their environment and what happens to them in a positive light. They interpret the world in a way that supports them and encourages them to strive for success.

Performance expert and sports psychologist Professor Graham Jones has noted the ability of elite performers to put a positive spin on situations. He says that self-esteem is a big factor in helping them maintain that positive outlook, but it can be easily knocked. However, the world's best have complete control of how they feel about themselves and they don't take things personally. They take negative feedback as a way to improve. In effect they can control how they think. Professor Jones says:

'I used to work with an England batsman who was well known for scratching around a bit early in his innings. The opposition knew they had to get him out early because once he was set, they were in trouble. But he would play and miss a lot early on in the innings. This batsman would attribute it to the pitches and so on, when in fact he was playing abysmally. But he was maintaining his self-belief. He would think: "It's not anything to do with me. This ball is swinging around and moving all over the place."

'When he was eventually out he would reappraise and think there was perhaps something going on that wasn't right and he should get in the nets and sort it out. Elite people have that kind of control over what they're thinking. It's called self-serving bias. It's when you're saying, "It's nothing to do with me. There's nothing wrong with me." But once you get off the ground you get straight in the nets and work on what was going wrong.'

Putting a positive spin on a situation is a way of 'reframing' it to find the silver lining in the cloud. Renzie Hanham from Gazing Performance

Limited recalls an experience with a Seido karate world champion where he was able to turn a bad situation into a positive one.

'This guy was in line to win the middleweight championship, but then he tore his hamstring. That's a devastating thing to happen because it means you can't use your legs. But I told him about a judo champion who won his title with a broken leg. It was a lie.

'Then I reframed the situation by telling the injured karate competitor that he was actually making mistakes when he was kicking and so he should be using his hands. He went on to win the championship.'

Part of the technique of staying positive depends on the language that sportspeople use to themselves and when talking in a team situation. Sports psychologist Steve Sylvester considers the problem of a team on a losing streak that develops a negative outlook:

'Something has got lost – the shared meaning of what they are doing. I would want to interview everybody in the staff, from the management right the way through to the cleaners, to see if anything particular has changed. I would want to see what type of language is being used, compared to the start of the season because language is very important in programming how we see outcomes. If you say things like "We're on a bad run", you will be – because that's what you're saying to yourself.'

Similarly, if a team playing away from home interprets the roars of the crowd as support for the opposition and therefore hostile, they can feel vulnerable. They can start to doubt themselves. However, teams can learn to interpret the crowd noise positively, Sylvester says. A team can imagine they are playing at home every time they play. They can imagine all the negative roars are actually positive ones. Simply changing the interpretation of the sound can make the environment feel far less hostile.

NLP trainer Graham Shaw also believes that negative thoughts can be converted into positive ones. He recalls a Danish professional triathlete called Morten Fenger who was explaining what it was like to complete a triathlon – and how much it hurt. But Fenger was able to see this pain positively, Shaw says. Fenger would tell himself that if he could feel that he was hurting so much, that meant he was alive – and wasn't it wonderful to be alive! In this way Fenger was able to use the pain he was feeling to get himself into a positive state again.

Of course, there are times when a little negative voice can prove productive. Shaw recalls his own experience of running the 10km road race in the World Masters Championships in Italy when he was 49 years old. When he arrived at the start of the race he felt positive because he had spent so much time visualizing and preparing for this moment. Then during the race he used a little bit of a negative prompt. Shaw knew from experience that the toughest part of the race for him was the stretch between 5km and 8km. That's when he began to hurt and started to wilt.

> *'I used some self-talk, which was this: "You haven't spent £400 and flown all this way to be sitting in the bar afterwards with the athletes, having got a bad time, regretting for the other four days you are out here that you didn't make it hurt and put the effort in here." I made a picture. I said to myself: "You've got all the rest of the week to sit and put your feet up, so get in there now and damn well just do it."*
>
> *'A lot of people get motivated by the "away from" impulse – a negative image – and that's how I boosted myself during that race. Sometimes people need negative images to give themselves a thump. For me it was a massive "away from" that made me put up with the pain. I could go through the pain because I couldn't face the thought of sitting there talking to other people about having achieved a terrible time.'*

The negative prompt worked well. Shaw beat his 'acceptable' target time by 15 seconds.

CONFIDENCE TECHNIQUES

Simply standing in a confident manner and presenting yourself positively has an impact on how you feel. As NLP trainer Graham Shaw says, there are techniques that can be used for keeping the inner voice positive. One very simple technique uses the relationship between physiology and mental state. For example, if you sit with your shoulders slumped and head down, you are more likely to feel fed up or miserable. If you sit up, with your shoulders back a little, you tend to feel more positive. If you get people to stand in a more confident manner, they start to feel more confident.

Modern pentathlete Dr Stephanie Cook used to act confidently, even when she was feeling under pressure. She particularly worked on improving her confidence in fencing, which she found to be one of the more difficult events.

'If I lost a few hits in a row, my self-confidence would diminish and that would result in me fencing more defensively and consequently not so well. I worked on a way of dealing with defeat, so that I still walked on with my head up, looking as confident as ever to my opponents. By continuing to act confidently, this kept my determination and confidence strong.'

In addition to physical or physiological techniques, another method for cutting down negative internal dialogue – or any internal dialogue – is to divert attention to the outside world. NLP trainer Graham Shaw says:

'You could get a conference presenter to look at a dot on the wall, standing upright and feeling good. While they look at the dot, get them to notice that they can see the corners of the room – that's their peripheral vision. They can bring their vision down to notice everybody in the room. As a conference presenter, their attention is now out on the group. They have a heightened awareness of what's happening out there, which they need as a presenter to give themselves feedback. What they don't want is voices in their head

*saying, "How am I going to do this?" So in this way they have cut
down their internal dialogue.'*

Sometimes a champion might want to keep their attention focused
within, rather than on the external world. Former sprinter John
Regis says that any small negative thought could become 'the size
of an avalanche' once you were in the arena before a race. Regis
would try to avoid negative thoughts occurring and keep his thinking
positive before a race by not letting himself worry about what other
people were doing, or how fast they seemed to be running when
warming up.

> *'I used to look at people running, but when you look at people run-
> ning, everyone looks really quick. So I stopped doing that. I would
> sit looking at the floor, so I couldn't see what people were doing
> and I kept all my energies within me. They couldn't affect me and
> I could focus more on what I needed to do.'*

Former badminton champion Gill Clark used to keep up her positive
attitude by developing an attacking game strategy.

> *'You study the opponent, and you know tactically what they're
> good at.*
>
> *'Every coach would tell you not to serve to your opponent's
> strengths. But, because I'm a bit of a funny one, I think, "Right,
> she's left-handed and she always likes to play this brush return;
> she's going to play it now on my backhand side. So, the first serve
> I'm going to do, I'm going to play to her strength."*
>
> *'That way your opponent is going to think, "Heck, she's returned
> my best shot, I'd better not play my best shot any more." So I've got
> the mental edge right at the start of the match, because now she
> is afraid to play her best shot. So we can take her best shot out of
> the game.'*

Clark also drew confidence from knowing that she had considered
her tactics thoroughly. If she was playing a singles match, the night

before she would go over how she wanted to play and how she was going to try and impose dominance from the start. If her opponent was likely to play a certain way, Clark would think what she was going to do to counteract it. Similarly, the evening before a doubles match she would sit down with her doubles partner and talk about their opponents, what tactics they were going to try and use, what they would do if the opposition used tactics that were exposing their own weaknesses. Having done this, Clark could go to bed knowing that she had planned for whatever her opponents threw at her the next day.

Similarly, former Davis Cup tennis captain David Lloyd would develop a thorough game plan for each match he played.

'I used to write down, as honestly as I could, my strengths and weaknesses on one side of the page. Then I would watch all my opponents and I would put down all their strengths and weaknesses, as fairly as I could. I would examine the games and the tactics of the way we all played. So when I went on court for a match I knew all about our strengths and weaknesses and had a game plan.'

STAY IN THE NOW

When golfing champion Nick Faldo won the British Open at Muirfield in 1992 he started out feeling extremely positive, but then things began to slip. Somehow he managed not to dwell on what had gone before but kept concentrating on what he needed to do now to take the championship. At the time he was world number two, had just won a tournament in Ireland and he was feeling confident. Faldo recalls the event vividly:

'I'm playing great and I'm hot favourite to win. I thought, "Yes, this is my week to win again". I opened with 66, 64 and had a four shot lead. Then on the Sunday all of a sudden I got reeled in. I started making some mistakes. I bogeyed the eleventh. I three putted the thirteenth. After that I said to Fanny [Sunesson – caddy], "You

know, I'm alright. You know I'm alright." Then on the fourteenth I hit straight into the bunker. I kept saying, "I don't know what's going on but I'm alright." Then I looked at the leaderboard and I was two back.

'But one of the tricks I was working on that week was to forget everything. I suddenly said to myself, "OK, forget everything that's happened over the whole week, good or bad. Just forget it. It's all gone. You've got four holes to play; you better play the best four holes of your life."

'I'm now walking off the fourteenth green to tee off on the fifteenth. I hit the famous five iron, a little half shot which finished three foot from the hole. On the seventeenth I hit an absolutely perfect drive with a four iron. The best you could do was to get 20 foot left of the hole and I hit it right there and two putted for a birdie.

'Now I'm tired and then I heard an almighty groan from the eighteenth and I just sensed that John Cook had taken five. You've got a hundred yard walk to the eighteenth. Every step I said "You've got four to win, four to win." And then I hit two perfect shots. The second, with a three iron, I hit one of my greatest, best shots, straight at the pin. Then I made a two putt and I won.'

Former England footballer Alan Shearer had a great ability not to dwell on missed shots. He would remain positive and concentrate on the present moment of the game, a skill that impresses former England captain David Platt. Platt says:

'When Alan misses a chance he just "blows" it away. He breathes and it is gone. He sniffs up his nose and that is his way of saying it's gone. He just moves on from there thinking he'll get another chance, he'll get another goal. That's the mental strength of the man and that's why he is one of the leading goal scorers every year.'

In some sports, if things aren't quite working as smoothly as they might, a champion is able to adjust accordingly to keep in the game until things start to 'click' again. Champions know what they have to do to stay in with a chance of winning. Former Davis Cup tennis captain David Lloyd says that great players win even when they are not at their best. They have to – otherwise they are out of the tournament. Lloyd says:

> *'You've got to learn to know your own body and your own mind. You've got to learn to know when things aren't quite right, so you can go into a slightly different gear to minimize the problem, and you do it automatically. You may have a slight injury and you've got to somehow get through it so you're still alive the next day. It's a survival technique.*
>
> *'Rod Laver used to tell me that when he wasn't playing well he didn't hit any softer, but he would hit down the middle of the court to cut the angle out. Then as soon as he got that line right, he moved it sideways.'*

PSYCHING OUT

Part of the process of staying positive involves not getting distracted by any psyching out games that the opposition try to use.

Sally Gunnell recalls waiting in the call room after warming up before the 1992 Olympic 400m hurdles final. She kept her cool and exuded confidence, regardless of what was happening around her. Gunnell says:

> *'All the finalists are in there psyching each other out. I remember Sandra Farmer-Patrick strutting her stuff, moaning about this and that and giving me daggers. I was thinking, "Right, I'm in charge here." I would give off an aura. I don't know how I did it, but I was just lying there with my legs up on the wall, saying I was conserving energy. Everyone else would be charging around. But I was thinking: "I've warmed up, I've done everything I can do. There's nothing else that could get me prepared. I am in total control." This is the message I was giving out to everybody.'*

When it comes to psyching out others, the greatest champions don't tend to do it as a result of some strategy; they just behave with instinctive confidence that can have a negative impact on other competitors with perhaps lesser self-belief.

Former national athletics coach Frank Dick thinks what matters is simply to be totally competitive – something the athlete has practised through visualization or mental rehearsal beforehand.

> *'We practise being totally competitive because when you go out to compete, it's not just a physical thing; it's everything about you. Daley Thompson would chat to people and I'm not sure he ever thought of it as consciously psyching somebody out. If you start getting involved in the notion that that's what you have got to do, you know you're a loser. You're dealing with the tricks of the trade before you've delivered the trade. You do these things instinctively – it's part of the competition, part of the drive.'*

Former sprinter John Regis says that many athletes tried to psyche him out before a race, but it never worked. He felt that if they were spending that much time trying to psyche him out, then they couldn't be that confident with their own ability. Regis recalls:

> *'A lot of athletes would walk in front of me and then look me in the eye. In the 100m in a way you could accept it, because everybody's in a line. But if I'm in lane five and the guy in lane two comes and walks right in front of me I think, "What the hell are you doing?"*
>
> *'A lot of athletes, when they can see you sitting down waiting and psyching yourself up, they will come and stand next to you and try to deny you your ability to focus. A lot of these kinds of games are played.*
>
> *'Some athletes will take their tops off and show their physique to get the crowd going. I did that a couple of times in my early days. It's a lot of fun actually.'*

When on the blocks, waiting for the starting gun, some runners would try to trigger a false start from the runners next to them. Regis guarded against this by closing his eyes in the seconds before the gun went off.

'Guys move their little fingers and if you catch that with your eye, you wonder what's going on. You think, "Fire the gun". You think you've missed the start. I closed my eyes so when the gunfire did come, I knew exactly what I was doing.'

Athletics coach Ron Roddan, who worked with 100m champion Linford Christie, knows that a lot of psyching out goes on in the final run-up to a race. About 20 minutes before a race the athletes leave their coaches in the warm-up area and go into the control room. Roddan says:

'In that room a lot of things happen. A lot of mind games go on. Linford told me that some people came out shaking. Some people have such a strong aura that it puts other people off. Another coach told his athletes to stay away from Linford in the control room because he had that effect just by being there.'

Christie clearly had a natural ability to put weaker opponents off by his sense of self-belief. Sometimes, however, he would proactively try to make a point to his rivals. After Christie won 100m gold in the Barcelona Olympics in 1992 some American athletes started saying he wouldn't have won if Carl Lewis, the world record holder, had been competing. Christie was not amused.

By the time of the World Championships at Stuttgart the following year, 1993, Andre Cason was number one and Lewis still held the world record. Christie was up against them both and determined to prove a point. Roddan recalls Christie's attitude to those World Championships.

'Linford said, "Let's go to the warm-up". Cason was there doing starts and long runs. Carl Lewis was there. Linford took his top

off and started warming up in Cason's lane. He made Cason run round him. Straight away, Cason had lost the race. I had never seen Linford do that before. He then walked back to me and said, "It's time. Let's go." He didn't like the Americans because of their attitudes; they said he wouldn't have won the Olympics and he wanted to prove a point. And he did it in the best way possible.'

Christie won the 100m final in 9.87 seconds, pushing Cason into second place (a time of 9.92 seconds). Lewis was fourth in a time of 10.02 seconds. Christie was, understandably, delighted.

When champions such as Christie deliver such top performances they sometimes describe themselves as having been 'in the zone'. In the next chapter we look at what elite sportspeople mean by this, and whether they can enter the state at will.

Chapter 17

INTO THE ZONE

CHAMPION ATHLETES OFTEN REFER to the almost mythical desired state of being 'in the zone'. But what exactly do they mean by that?

THE ZONE EXPLAINED

Former sprinter Mark Richardson talks about being in the zone when in the winter of 1996, after suffering from food poisoning, he forced his way into the 4×400m relay team. Running the last leg in 43.60 seconds, he recorded the fastest relay split in the final of all the competitors and the fastest relay split ever run by a British athlete. So what is it like to be 'in the zone'? Richardson describes it thus:

'It's a very strange feeling. It's as if time slows down and you see everything so clearly. You just know that everything about your technique is spot on. It just feels so effortless; it's almost as if you're floating across the track. Every muscle, every fibre, every sinew is working in complete harmony and the end product is that you run fantastically well.'

Champion hurdler Sally Gunnell says she only entered the zone twice – once when winning Olympic gold in Barcelona in 1992, and then when winning the world championships a year later.

'What I call being in the zone is when the gun goes and I don't remember any of the race. It's dreamlike. My mind just switches off. You go into automatic pilot. I don't remember what happened down the back straight; I don't remember going over the eighth hurdle or even crossing the line.'

Sports psychologist Steve Sylvester says that such a lack of memory is quite common amongst sportspeople who manage to get into the zone. Sometimes they can't remember what they actually did, because they've tuned in to it and done it without thought. This is a characteristic of being totally connected to your performance – so much so that you can't remember the detail of it, because you're flowing, you're not processing, Sylvester says. If you're not processing on a conscious level, it's harder to remember what you actually did.

Former sprinter John Regis describes what being in the zone felt like to him:

'It was the belief and knowledge that you were going to run a very good race. It didn't always necessarily mean you were going to win, but it meant that the consistency of the performance was going to be at the highest level.'

When in the zone, time seemed to go into slow motion. Regis says:

'It felt as though I was running the replay, when it's slowed down. It didn't feel like 19 seconds. It's like you are going through a time warp, going back in time and seeing everything that's going on. It feels like slow motion. It's a strange feeling.

'A gun could be fired next to me and I wouldn't hear it – you're so in tune with what you need to be doing. I can feel everybody's strength, everybody's power, if they are able to turn it on or not. At the same time I'm doing what I have to do. When you get that feeling, you are totally in control.'

GETTING INTO THE ZONE

The big question, of course, is how do you get into the zone? Former sprinter Mark Richardson's experience was that mainly it 'just happens'. He says you can use visualization to try and help you get in the zone in the race, but in reality it's just something you fall into. Richardson says when it clicks in, it's the most natural place in the world to be.

Similarly, champion hurdler Sally Gunnell never had a method for deliberately getting into the zone. She says:

'I don't think it's something you can put yourself into; it just happens. There are lots of feelings that go with it: confidence and belief, things like that. It just happened twice for me – in the 1992 Olympics and the 1993 World Championships. The other years when I won titles, such as the Europeans in 1994, I wasn't in the zone. In the Europeans I can remember bits and pieces of the race, being in the back straight, coming off the eighth hurdle. I wasn't in the zone.'

For former sprinter John Regis, there was nothing special he did or could do to put himself in the zone. It related to the number of races he had run in the season. By about the sixth or seventh race he began to feel he could access the desired state, and then he was able to stay there until the end of the season.

Regis found that as each competition went by he would perform well in different stages of the race, sometimes early on, sometimes the middle or perhaps the end. He says:

> *'It took about six races to put it all together. Once I saw that picture it was done – locked in. I didn't have to worry about it.'*

Sports psychologist and performance expert Professor Graham Jones acknowledges that there is no straightforward way to get yourself into the zone at will. If it was easy, every sportsperson would be in the zone all the time. His recommendation is to recognize what you associate with good performances and what you associate with bad performances and then get rid of all the bad performance associations; you work with everything you've done that's associated with good performances. You need to replicate those factors to give yourself the best chance to let a good performance happen. Professor Jones says:

> *'You want people to be relaxed mentally and to feel in control and you don't want them to worry about the process. You want them to know what the process is, and just do it.*
>
> *'People will know very early on whether they're in the zone or not, but there's no answer to how you get someone there. You just know what makes you perform well and you give yourself the best possible opportunity – then you just hope.'*

However, sports psychologist Steve Sylvester believes it is possible to enter the zone at will. He says you can tune into it whenever and wherever you want to. It's just a question of realizing that you can. Sylvester says:

> *'A lot of people say it just happens – they're triggered and then they're in the zone. But I have the view we can help people with the process of tuning in. I call it "readiness to perform".*
>
> *'I'm working on the concept that you have complete choice about how you tune in to your performance. If you're not tuned in,*

what pay-off is there? One of my views is that you choose your own performance. So if you do well, you're in the zone.'

THE SUPERSTATE

Javelin champion Steve Backley has been in the zone on several occasions. One such time was during the 2002 European Championships in Munich, where he took the gold medal. Backley says of his win:

'It was a very conscious, controlled performance. That's what being in the zone means for me. It's accessing something above and beyond normal successful behaviour.'

Backley believes that in competition, success goes to the individual most able to manage his or her mood or state. As he says, when you've got 12 or 15 healthy guys, all capable of delivering a high level of performance, you have to access the states that optimize performance to win the gold medal. That's the skill.

Backley believes that this ability to access the required state is what makes the difference between great athletes and the real champions – whom he calls 'warriors'.

For Backley, the perfect state is what he calls a 'superstate'. He recalls his first experience of entering a 'superstate'. The year was 1990 and he had just won his first European gold medal. Immediately afterwards he went to compete in Budapest and though tired, he realized he dearly wanted to win the competition. He promised himself he would do his best and then rest afterwards.

'I'd had a bit of an unbeaten streak at this time. I came into the first round and threw about 82m, which ordinarily would have been enough to win. Then this big Russian guy stepped up and did 82.90 to go ahead. I'd already taken my boots off and I totally lost focus. I was out of the zone.

'When the Russian went ahead of me I just saw red, metaphorically speaking. I put my boots back on and as I was doing that there

seemed to be a subliminal tape in my conscious mind that was dealing with all the peripheral stuff. It was like I was just watching what was going on. From that moment for the next minute and a half I was in this superstate. I put my boots back on, walked out to the javelin and went through the normal procedure, but it was all as if I was two or three feet behind and looking down on myself. I don't remember running in.

'The result was 85.90m – a British record.

'I came away a bit spooked, but it made me ask questions. What happened there?'

Backley believes the superstate is the result of extreme anxiety or pressure to achieve – the result of a flight or fight situation, coupled with the belief that you can come out on top. It isn't just athletes who experience it, Backley believes, but ordinary people in a traumatic situation, perhaps caught up in some major disaster.

Having experienced the superstate in Budapest, Backley wanted to be able to achieve it again.

'I was thinking that if I can get there again by choice, I can do whatever I want. That for me is the Holy Grail. I have a better understanding of it now and an ability to access it. I have used it since but it isn't easy. You need a certain set of circumstances. You need to be healthy and to have great, stable preparation. I can't turn it on immediately, from one second to the next. In a major championship I will gather this state over about three or four weeks.'

Backley also believes that the superstate is accessed out of adversity, not out of success or pleasure. An athlete who has just put in a poor performance and so increased pressure on himself is more likely to access it than one on a roll of top performances.

The process that Backley has developed to try and access the superstate during competition centres around self-analysis. He asks himself questions about his performance and technique and answers them in ways that reinforce the desired result. For example, when throwing the javelin Backley needs to keep his left shoulder in a certain position, across his body. So he asks himself, 'Why am I doing this?' The real reason in terms of technique is to stop himself spinning out of line, but he might give himself another reason, that he is slightly embarrassed coming in to the throw. He says: 'I answer myself with a very rational answer that will reinforce why I am putting my left side away.'

It is essential, however, to avoid derogatory questions that can reinforce a negative reaction. Asking, 'Why didn't I train right?' is not helpful. Asking 'What do I need for 85 on my next throw?' is more positive. Backley says: 'Then you're off to a positive start because you are looking at a positive outcome.' For Backley, as a competition approaches, the result of continued questioning can be to push his mind into overdrive. He can also start feeling tired. This isn't bad news, though. He knows then that the superstate is about to come out. He says:

> 'It's almost a bit of Star Wars stuff – it's the force. It's because you are becoming a warrior and it's an amazing thing.'

When competing in the 2000 Olympics, Backley could sense the superstate coming on.

> 'I had a growing sense that I was going to do something. What really set me off was when I got my key and went to my room. There was my bag on the bed. I was on the top floor and I went to the window and opened the curtains. I looked straight through the window of the house opposite, which was directly lined up with the house opposite it, and it framed the Olympic flag on the staging. It was about half a mile away. Talk about the hairs standing up on the back of your neck. There was the Olympic flag right smack bang at my bedroom window. I thought a superstate was coming on.'

In the Olympics Backley performed well, beating the previous Olympic record, before being pushed into silver.

Backley accessed his winning state again in the European Championships in Munich in August 2002, where he took gold – for the fourth time in a row. The achievement came hard on the heels of a gold medal in the Commonwealth Games in Manchester in July. Backley says that his preparation for Munich began before the Commonwealth competition had actually finished. In fact, it started as soon as the first round was completed. Having thrown 86.81m, Backley was way ahead of the rest of the field and knew that he had won.

'In the next round I was thinking, "You've got Munich next week. You've got a qualification requirement of 83m. What is the best way for you to qualify?" It was like I was asking myself a series of questions.'

Backley began forming a plan for how he would achieve the required qualification throw. He then used the second round in the Manchester Commonwealth Games to practise his qualification throw for Munich. Then he stopped throwing altogether.

'I had already won, and I'd practised my qualification throw. I asked myself, "Is there anything more to be gained from this competition? No. Is there anything to lose? Yes, you could get hurt. So stop."'

Backley says he 'turned his back' on the rest of the competition in Manchester and has hardly any memories of it. His preparations for the European Championships then continued.

'I practised the qualifying throw and had a conversation going on in my mind. The fact that I'd won the last three was in the back of my mind, but I didn't focus on it like that. It was more in terms of "This is mine, you can't have it. This is meant to be. This is my baby. I haven't lost one of these." I was developing a kind of love affair with the event. "If you're going to try and take this off me, you will lose. There's no way I'm going to let you take this easily." It's a feeling of really going to war.'

When the European Championships in Munich got underway, Backley achieved the required qualification distance and then began gearing up for the final, gradually developing his superstate.

Believing that sleep is vital for storing up energy and supporting the superstate, Backley slept during the day of the final. He admits he may have slept too much, because he felt a bit groggy during his warm up and wasn't throwing as well as he would like. He still felt somewhat sleepy during the first round, but put in a reasonable throw of 88.29m and took second place.

> 'I knew there was more to come. The first throw was good, but it wasn't as fast as I could have done. It was quite a controlled throw – I didn't lash through it. The second throw was my worst on the day and slightly tailed. That made me focus on alignment and being faster on the runway, so I had a plan. If you have a plan, belief and want it enough, it's going to happen.'

The third throw went further, but it was in the fifth round that Backley brought everything together, throwing a mighty 88.54m to take the lead and win gold.

Even when top sportspeople don't feel they have entered that wonderful state of being 'in the zone', they still need to remain highly focused during competitions. We examine how champions create and maintain such focus in the next chapter.

Chapter 18

FOCUS AND REFOCUS

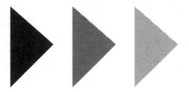

It is generally accepted that sport's greatest champions have a supreme ability to maintain their focus during competition.

But what is 'focus'? What does it mean when sportspeople say they need to maintain their focus? Former national athletics coach Frank Dick relates this anecdote by way of explanation:

> *'When Babe Ruth was in his last season in baseball he was in a batting slump. He wasn't playing well and the team was in danger of going out of the World Series. Ruth was two strikes down and he was given a bit of verbal by some guy behind him. Ruth replied by telling the guy to watch the green out there, because that was where the ball was going. Well, with a bit of licence, that's where the ball went. Ruth got a home run.*

'Ruth was asked later about what he was thinking when he was standing on the plate. Was he thinking, this is my last chance, with two strikes down? Was he thinking about the guy giving him a hard time? Was he thinking that if this went wrong, he'd be out?

'Ruth said he wasn't thinking of any of these things – "I was think about hitting the ball".

'That's what focus is.'

VITAL FOCUS

Javelin champion Steve Backley appreciates the importance of generating and maintaining his focus before a competition begins. He likens the period after the warm-up, when waiting for competition to begin, to a scene from *Star Wars – Episode I: The Phantom Menace*, where Darth Maul is battling against Jedi Master, Qui-Gon Jinn, played by Liam Neeson. The two are separated mid battle by a force field for a few minutes. Qui-Gon spends the time in meditation while Darth Maul paces like a caged tiger. Backley says:

'There's a fantastic scene where the guy with the red and black face [Darth Maul] and Liam [Qui-Gon] are in a full-on battle. Then the security bars go up and the bad guy is strutting up and down and giving up energy. Liam sits on the floor, shuts his eyes and waits. That is a nice fictitious example of the real thing in athletics where you've had the warm-up and then it's a matter of waiting and some guys are strutting up and down. It's a matter of retaining focus and how you do that is a personal thing. I go back to some of the more simple stretching routines. I have an ongoing dialogue about how I can access more potential, how I can be better. I'll go through an ankle drill exercise. I'll go through the motions of a throw, very slowly and controlled. After you go through the bag room and they check your bag, I go out and stretch. I have a real focus on feeling the stretch, feeling it going through the shoulder, across the body, getting really in touch with the feelings and rhythms but without expending energy.'

During the competition, retaining focus remains key. Backley says:

'Your focus determines your reality. It sounds so obvious, but it's easy to forget. In a relatively simple event – throwing something down a field – remembering a simple phrase like that keeps you in the present.'

Ron Dennis, boss of the McLaren racing team, believes that top drivers need focus if they are to be successful. Focus in the motorsport sense is reflected in total dedication, he says. Drivers can't be weak in any area. It's a tremendously physical sport, and they have to understand the psychological side as well. They have to be able to withstand high cockpit temperatures and dehydration. They have to be able to maintain extreme concentration for prolonged periods. As Dennis says, Formula One racing is not a 'burst' sport like the 100m is for sprinters; it requires sustained concentration throughout a lengthy race.

Dennis believes that McLaren driver David Coulthard has the capability of winning a world championship, because he has the discipline and focus to succeed. Dennis says:

'Michael Schumacher once commented that he felt confident following David because he was making no mistakes and driving so perfectly. Coulthard has the focus to win races.'

At the beginning of his career, golfing champion Nick Faldo was totally focused on his golf, almost selfishly so. All he thought about was golf. As his career developed and he became managed by IMG, Faldo enjoyed not having to worry about simple tasks such as paying bills. That left him free to focus his mind totally on his golf.

'They mothered me; they did everything. You went and played golf and just handed your problems to someone else. A sportsman has to have a clear head.'

Faldo didn't always find it easy to keep his concentration steady during golf competitions. In particular, when Faldo was going through divorce, he found off-course distractions multiplying around him. He says:

> *'At such times your mind is more cluttered and it takes a very strong mind to stay focused. To win Augusta when I was just start- ing to go through divorce and I had the media all over me … One of the qualities I saw then in myself was a determination not to give in just because hell's flying around. But you can only take a cer- tain amount of that. You need an awful lot of physical and mental strength to get through it.'*

Faldo remembers being totally engrossed in his shots when he won the British Open in Muirfield in 1992. During the last day he saw his lead demolished and then taken away from him, before he came back to seize the title on the eighteenth. Once he had won, he relaxed.

> *'If you watch, my shoulders physically drop. The adrenalin just goes wallop. I tried to stay in the same adrenalin mode off the golf course for those four days. I tried to stay in the same mental state.'*

Faldo had spent the week totally involved in his golf and his attempt to win the British Open crown. He explains what that level of involve- ment and focus is like:

> *'You need someone around you who understands you and that you are quiet in the morning. You are not talking, you're thinking and you don't want them asking if you're alright. You want to be left alone because your build-up and preparation is very impor- tant. The minute you get out of bed you're thinking about the day, replaying shots and situations.*
>
> *'At the beginning of the week I visualized coming up to the eight- eenth hole with a three iron into a right-to-left wind and I'd hit my fade shot in there. And then on the last day, I was coming to the*

eighteenth with a three iron and a right-to-left wind. How wacky is that? But the visualization is all part of your preparation.'

When on the fairway, Faldo's concentration was totally focused on his shots.

'You have to look at that pin and know exactly what you have to do. You can't think of the crowd or anything else. I have my swing thoughts and keys that I've worked on, that I have proved stand me in good stead.'

Each individual needs to find the thoughts and keys that work for him when developing a focusing technique, Faldo believes. He recalls meeting with Dr Dick Coop, who worked with American players, who asked Faldo the following question: 'If you have to spend a dollar on your shot, how would you spend it? Would you spend 25 cents at the pin, 25 in the air and 50 cents at the ball?' Faldo says that trying to answer that question gave him an insight into the kind of person he was.

'Some guys spend a dollar on the pin; they just look at the pin and think "I'm going to hit at that". They don't think of anything else. I probably need at least 50 cents back at the ball. I focus on my target, but I know that what I do here will get the ball to there.

'So we're all different. That's really important. When I work with kids now I help them to find out who they are. Once that's in you, I don't think you can change it much. Some people are target oriented and some people need to know how the pedals turn before they get there.'

TASK AND PROCESS FOCUS

Sports psychologist Ian Lynagh highlights the importance for athletes of being able to maintain concentration and keep their attention focused on what they are doing. He explains that concentration relates to the broad class of being able to stay involved mentally with what you are doing. Attentional focusing is the narrow subset of that – your attention is focused on the exact little thing you need to focus on: someone is hitting a tennis ball at you at 150 miles an hour and you have to be able to see it clearly and hit it back.

What is important, Lynagh says, is task focusing – the ability to stay focusing on what you are doing and not get distracted by the score or other people or heckling. This is a difficult thing to do. It is hard to stay focused on the simplicity of swinging a golf club – even though you might be swinging it for £500,000 at that moment.

Howard Wilkinson, former Football Association technical director, agrees. He believes that aspiring champions need to learn to concentrate on the process of their particular sport – their performance – rather than on the outcome.

> *'There's still too much emphasis on outcome. More people can become winners if they can focus on process. It's hellish difficult, because winning – getting the gold medal or crossing the line first – is a fantastic motivator.'*

Wilkinson believes that coaches and others working with sportspeople can reinforce the process aspect.

> *'If you're the influencing force on someone, the biggest gift you can bring is to give them the comfort, stability and consistent rationale of process and performance. Then the emotional peaks and troughs tend not to be so bad.'*

Olympic rower Matthew Pinsent experiences a high sense of focus when rowing during a race, although the object of his focus can change. He pays no attention to his environment or any potential distractions.

> *'You're focusing predominantly on the techniques and the tactics of the race. Sometimes you're much more internal, focusing on technique and what you're doing to try to make the boat go*

quicker; and other times you're wrapped up in what the opposition are doing. But beyond those things you never think about the big race, the crowd or anything else.'

Sprinter Mark Richardson explains how he concentrates on his technique when running the 400m. He segments the race into three parts.

'I aim to get out well and hard because that sets me up. I need to take speed into the back straight and the back straight is all about relaxation, just being aware of yourself. And for me it's a matter of focusing on my technique, making sure my hips are tall and that I'm running efficiently. Then around the top turn is the business end of the race. That's when you start to make your move before, in the last 100m, you just bring it home.'

Dr Stephanie Cook, Olympic gold medallist in modern pentathlon, had to maintain her focus over an extended competition involving five different disciplines: shooting, fencing, swimming, riding and running. In order to be successful in each separate event she had to develop the ability to direct her attention to the task in hand, and not let herself be deflected by thinking about her performance in preceding segments of the competition. Dr Cook says:

'In modern pentathlon, how you approach it mentally is crucial because you're not just preparing yourself for one event. The mental preparation you need for the shooting is very different from what you need for the running. Added to that, on the day of the competition, you have to deal with what's happened during the day as you go into each event. You are competing over the whole day. You might have had a good event and a very bad event and that's obviously going to affect your general mental approach. That's why you have to train mentally to be able to put whatever has happened aside and focus purely on what you're doing. You have to focus on the process, not the result. If you focus on the process, the results take care of themselves.'

She admits it is hard to put a poor performance in an event out of your mind. However that is what the top sportspeople have to do if their performances in the next event aren't to be adversely affected. Dr Cook says:

'It's obviously very difficult to completely forget about it and move on, but in effect that's what you have to do. It's a case of staying in the moment and not being affected by what has happened before or what might happen after. You have to stay in the moment and deal with the process that you are going through for each event. Take each event as it comes. Take each fencing hit as it comes. With the shooting event, as you start getting near the end of the competition, it's tempting to start thinking about your final score. It's very dangerous to start doing that. You've got to clear your mind and view each shot as its own entity.'

Sports psychologist Professor Graham Jones agrees that focusing is about keeping concentration on the present moment, and not getting distracted by past events. He says:

'It's about getting people to recognize what's happened is history. There's not a single thing they can do about it and so there's no point in worrying about it. Similarly, looking into the future is a distraction. Some golfers after 7 holes who are five under start thinking about being ten under after 18. That's as bad as being three over and thinking they're going to shoot an 81, because they're not focused on what they have to do right here and now. It's about control – what are they controlling here and now, because they need to focus on it.'

Michael Lynagh, brilliant former Australian rugby fly-half, also believes it is vital to stay focused on the immediate task at hand. He wouldn't dwell on missed kicks when he needed to be focused on the game.

'I used to put kicking in a separate box to actual play. A rugby goal kicker has to play his game regardless of how his kicking is performing. If you miss a few kicks at goal it's wrong to try and make up for it in general play. You go out and play your game. Quite regularly you see a goal kicker who misses a kick and then immediately in the next couple of plays tries to make up for it by forcing his hand; often it can lead to a downward spiral. It doesn't help his team, his performance or his goal kicking. Once you are playing, goal kicking is irrelevant until you have to goal kick. You need to be really clear what your task at hand is.

'With the kicking, you try to learn what went wrong, why you missed the last one. But you don't focus on it during play. I can remember times when I have kicked terribly, yet scored two tries and the team has won. In my mind it doesn't matter how we do it, as long as the goal is achieved in the end.'

Lynagh stresses the importance of focusing solely on the particular play at that time.

'One play you might be defending, and the next attacking. You focus on the immediate task. Now that's not an easy thing to do, particularly in rugby, when somebody has just belted you and is trying to put you off your game. How you deal with that is very important. You can lose your head and chase that person, but if you do, he's succeeded in spoiling your concentration on your task.'

Lynagh focused on the process, not the outcome. He says that if you concentrate on the process, the outcome will happen.

'Don't worry about the scoreboard in a rugby match. Concentrate on each play. At the end of the day the scoreboard will look after itself. If you have played well, it will be OK. If you start concentrating on the scoreboard, protecting a lead, then your individual skills are going to fail.'

FOCUS UNDER PRESSURE

Michael Lynagh famously maintained his focus during the 1991
World Cup quarter final against Ireland at Lansdowne Road. Australia was expected to win, but just before fulltime, Ireland stole the
lead. Lynagh recalls the closing minutes of the match:

> *'With four minutes to go, Gordon Hamilton scored a try in the left-
> hand corner which put Ireland one point ahead. The conversion
> was kicked by Ralph Keynes, so they were three points ahead. I
> was acting captain that day and I knew I had to find out how long
> there was to go. The referee said there was four minutes. So I had
> to come up with some sort of plan for how we were going to escape
> from this. The first thing I said when I got back to the group was,
> "We have enough time. There are four minutes to go". That was
> immediately a positive message to the guys. Then I said, "We will
> kick off long, Ireland will kick out. We will have our line out on the
> 22. Forwards, I want you to win that ball and leave the rest up to us
> at the back" – me, basically. The last thought I left them with was,
> "If you have the ball in your hands and you are in any doubt about
> what to do, hold onto it and run towards the opposition goal line."
> It was very simple stuff.'*

The move went as planned, with the Australians winning a 22 yard
line out and eventually David Campese getting the ball. When he
was tackled he held onto the ball and started pulling towards the
Irish goal line. Lynagh was pleased. When the scrum was given, it was
his turn to get the ball. His team-mate Timmy Horan suggested they
go for a field goal, but Lynagh rejected the idea.

> *'During the week we had found there was a chink in the Irish
> defensive armour in the back and we had worked on a move
> accordingly ad nauseam during the week. We had done it four or
> five times during the game. We had scored once and every time we
> made a break. So I thought, this is the time when that planning and
> preparation comes off.*

'So I called the move. Timmy was saying, "Field goal, field goal," but I said, "No, we are doing this move".

'So we got the ball from the scrum. I passed it to Timmy Horan at inside centre, we missed out Jason Little and passed to Marty Roebuck, who came out wide. Then Jason would loop round Marty, pickup the ball and give it to Campo. Campo got the ball with space. With ten yards to go and one man to beat, you are expected to score nine times out of ten. Campo got pulled down just short. I was jogging on the spot just there and picked up the ball and doodled it over – and that was it! We had won the match.

'For me it was my favourite moment in rugby, not because I had scored the try, but because I had guided the team. I had brought fifteen different individuals with different skills and back-grounds together at that moment, with mayhem breaking loose in Lansdowne Road. I said what we were going to do. We had planned for it during the week, we had done our preparation and we got those individuals to concentrate on their jobs and do it. That's why it's my favourite moment.'

How did Lynagh manage to keep his concentration and focus during those vital moments, when he was deciding what to do?

'You have the ability to narrow things down and focus only on the things that matter. There's a lot of irrelevant information that comes from the outside and in an emotionally charged situation like the Ireland game, some people don't have the ability to block it out. I say "block it out" but it doesn't even enter because it's irrelevant. That includes the crowd, the score, what the opposition is doing. Whatever is happening around you is irrelevant to your job.'

In the Ireland match, Lynagh had two choices – kick for goal to get a tie, or take the more challenging route of going for a match-winning try. Lynagh opted for the try.

'I felt that was our best chance for winning the game. I was pre-pared to take responsibility for that. I was very clear what I needed to do. We were very clear what we each needed to do in the team. The repercussions, had we not scored, didn't enter my mind at the time. But I guess, had we not scored, I would still feel it was the right decision.'

In all sports, top athletes need to keep a cool-headed focus when it counts. Modern pentathlon becomes particularly exciting when the last event arrives – the 3000m run. Competitors are given staggered starts based on their total scores so far. The person with the most points starts running before the person in second, and so on. This means that whoever wins the race has won the competition.

When Dr Stephanie Cook stepped up to the line for the race in the Sydney Olympics, she was 49 seconds behind the leader. She knew that the more people she overtook, the higher she would finish. However, she also knew that she had to run according to her own plan, and not let herself get distracted by other runners. Dr Cook says:

'I had a reputation for being a good runner. I'd always said, going into Sydney, that if I was within a minute of the leaders going into the run that I stood a good chance of running myself into a medal position.

'You have to make sure you don't get too excited about trying to beat people, and therefore lose all sense of being able to pace the race. You don't want to set off too hard in the attempt to overtake people and then burn out before you reach the end. It's a question of pacing the race completely right.

'In Sydney I knew that I had to run my own race. If you see people in front of you it gives you an added incentive to push that bit harder and overtake them, but you can't let yourself do that too early. You've got to stay in control.'

In Sydney Dr Cook managed to do this perfectly – achieving even splits throughout the race and coming home in first position to take gold.

What about when players appear to explode during a competition – shouting or storming about. Does that mean they have lost their focus? Not necessarily.

Former Davis Cup tennis captain David Lloyd accepts that it is good practice to focus on one point at a time and throw missed points out of your mind. However, he found that getting worked up could help him maintain his focus and drive.

> *'It's not good dwelling on a missed point. But I actually needed something to happen on the court. I needed to be very cross. I played better when I was cross. I needed something to excite me. I needed to think the world was against me. I liked that. It made me think "I'll do something".'*

Lloyd believes all tennis players became cross, they just didn't all show it in the same way.

> *'I'm sure Borg felt cross inside. He was just able to keep it in. I'm sure every single tennis player feels the same thing inside. It's just the way you show it. There is no way that Chris Evert didn't think, "What a f**king awful line call that was". But she didn't say it. McEnroe said it.'*

Lloyd believes a good coach needs to assess early on what approach works best for a player. If a player needs to show emotion, they should.

> *'As long as you keep it within the bounds of not cheating or being sent off, you've got to let the player do it because that's what makes that person better than the other person. You mustn't take that away.*
>
> *'The game of tennis is instant, it's quick, it happens on the spot and you can't take that flair away from a person. You've got to let kids play their way.'*

FOCUSING TIPS

Gazing Performance Limited, an organization specialising in mental conditioning and improving human performance, believes that controlling attention under pressure is the most important key to success. Gazing's Renzie Hanham says that one of the major keys to success lies in the deliberate focus of attention. In a stressful situation people can have negative thoughts and start acting them out. People give things labels, make judgements and then have an emotional response to them. For example, Hanham says, imagine you are competing in a multi-sport event. You are currently running up hill and the world champion runs past you. You think to yourself, 'It's the world champion!' You look at their legs and see how strong they are. You start thinking of articles you've read about them recently, how fit they're looking. You have an emotional response and start to do worse in running up the hill. You do worse because your attention is no longer on the task and your thoughts become diverted away from the task and onto such things as 'I'm not good enough … I knew I should have trained more', and so on.

This kind of emotional response leads sportspeople into what could be called a 'negative content loop'. Their perception of what is happening triggers an emotional response that distracts their attention away from where it ought to be – on the process of what they are doing – in the above athlete's case, on the process of running up the hill. The automatic emotional response results in a poorer performance. Instead, athletes need to remain focused on the process of what they are doing, but this requires training.

The first step is to understand that such emotional responses are occurring and having an effect. Then people can start to practise observing their responses, without hooking into their emotions, Hanham says. In this way athletes can learn to separate their emotions from events and retain greater control over their attention, so remaining focused on the process.

NLP trainer Graham Shaw considers how a sportsperson can stay focused during a race or an event. He stresses the importance of awareness.

'When you are running in a road race, for example, you can be lazy; you might see something you hadn't noticed before and think, "That's interesting". But that's not going to be any good to you in the race. You need to get in the habit of asking yourself things like, "How am I running? What am I doing now?" That way you'll automatically improve. The key thing is staying in the "now".'

But what about runners who go into an almost catatonic, trance-like state? That can happen when people become engrossed in the rhythm of their actions and are sustaining the action over a certain period of time. Shaw says:

'You will often go into that catatonic state when running or swimming or doing something like that. It connects with being in the flow zone. Yes, you can go into a trance, you can get into the flow, but if you're not periodically checking how you're doing, you almost become bereft of choice. It's different from beginning to analyse everything to the nth degree. It can be helpful to periodically check out how you're doing and make any adjustments.'

However, Shaw warns against over-analysis. This could, for example, ruin a tennis backhand or a golf swing that is working perfectly. Shaw says.

'Feel is fundamental. You could really help to screw up somebody's golf by over-analysing. Golfers who hit a really good shot say it just feels right. So you don't want to over-analyse, but you want awareness so you know when you're in the flow and when you're not.'

Former sprinter John Regis believes he suffered from over-focusing during the Barcelona Olympics in 1992:

'I was probably in the best shape of my life. In the first round I ran 20.4 seconds. Then in the second round I ran 20.2 and it was comfortable. I knew there was a monster in the tank. In the semi-final

I equalled the British record. On each of these I'd been rehearsing the races the day beforehand.

'Then in the final, for some reason I'm on the blocks and suddenly my mind starts going through what I'm going to do in the race.'

Regis heard the starter say 'set', but he was still thinking about how he would run the race. Then suddenly the gun went off and he panicked.

'I just take off and I'm running like a headless chicken. For the first time since 1989 I panicked. I'm down in the race and I've got to really run. I ran the turn of my life. I ran it way too hard and then came into the home straight with nothing in the tank. I finished sixth in the Olympic final. There's no word to describe how bad I felt. Everything building up to that had been perfect. But I made the classic mistake of over-focusing.

'I haven't the foggiest idea why that happened. For this race I just decided to rerun everything in my mind. Something triggered in my mind to make sure I'd got it right. But I was absolutely gutted.'

Sports psychologist Professor Graham Jones explains that it is vital not just to focus, but to focus on the right things. Readjustment may be called for. Awareness is key. You have to be aware of when you're focusing on the wrong thing. Then you need to refocus. Professor Jones gets performers to ask themselves questions periodically, such as 'Am I focused? Am I focused on the right things?' If they are not, they need to focus on something else.

Well-established routines can help sportspeople to maintain focus during a competition or match. Sports psychologist Ian Lynagh says that a tennis player will learn to play totally focused on one point at a time as though it's a whole athletic event in itself. To do so they will have developed segmented routines, which they will use as build-ups to particular points. For example, Lynagh says, they will have a pre-service routine – bouncing the ball a certain number of times, taking a deep breath and focusing on the spot in the court that they want to hit. They will try to do that routine every time. If they are receiving, they will have a routine for that.

The routines are usually repetitive, Lynagh says, and they help players focus on what they are doing. When people are under pressure they feel more secure if they have a little strategy to think about and carry out. It helps you to get your mind off the fact that this is match point for the Wimbledon championship. The routine helps you focus on the immediate task, rather than thinking about the significance of the point or anything else that could prove distracting.

PRACTICE MAKES PERFECT

During his career, golfer Nick Faldo spent some time working with a psychologist. As a result, he learnt to stop thinking about the shots he played as simply good or bad. Instead he graded them from one to ten, with ten being the best. The psychologist would then ask Faldo what a ten shot would be. Faldo says:

> 'Being realistic, I'd say that a ten might end up three feet from the pole. He would say, "OK, do a 10 for me." You'd stand there and think, "Do a 10". You'd hear a shot and it would go, plonk, three foot from the pin. I'd think, "Wow!" I've hit some amazing shots in my career as a result of that. That was also my first teaching about being totally focused on your target.'

Linford Christie also improved his focus over time. When Christie was running the 100m at the peak of his career he always looked as if he was staring down a long tunnel. However, developing that kind of tunnel focus took him several years. Then it just clicked, says Christie's long-time coach, Ron Roddan. The strength of his focus could even put other athletes off. Christie's competitors would be jumping around, but he would just stand there. His focus was plain to see.

Champion National Hunt jockey Richard Dunwoody found that his mental preparation and ability to focus at will improved over the course of his career.

'When I started I was mentally unprepared for a lot of rides. But as I was doing it day in, day out, that mental preparation became stronger. I found it was easier to switch on and off towards the end of my career. You'd go into the weighing room and be larking around one minute, and then as soon as you were out in the paddock, that was it – you were totally focused on the race. You were down at the start and your mind was on your opponents, the way your horse should be ridden.'

Champion 400m runner Roger Black learnt during the course of his career to focus on the things that he could control and not worry about the rest. He sees this as being proactive, rather than reactive.

'Most people in sport are reactive – they react to things going on around them. All the champions I've met are proactive. They don't waste any time worrying or focusing on anything they cannot directly control. The most obvious things to worry about are your opponents. But the reality of a race like the 400m, where you are in separate lanes, is that you cannot directly affect how your opponents run. You can influence them just by being there, but you can't really do anything to put them off. There is no point focusing on them.

'For example, if you were running against someone like Michael Johnson who half-way round the track suddenly puts in a kick, then you have a choice – you either react and run with him and come last, or you don't focus on him and you do your own race.

'That ability to focus on the things you can control and have influence over, and not worry about things you can't control, is very important. Prior to the Atlanta Olympics the papers always talked about how hot and humid it was going to be. All athletes were talking about the weather. I didn't worry about it. I knew it was going to be hot. I knew I would have to drink fluid and I knew that was about as much as I could do. In reality, I was lucky and the four days I ran it rained. It wasn't hotter than anywhere else I had run. If I'd wasted my energy worrying about the weather it

would have been a total waste of time. So it's about controlling your thoughts.'

Modern pentathlete Dr Stephanie Cook worked hard to develop her focusing ability. She practiced mental exercises designed to improve her concentration. She could do these exercises in a variety of situations, not necessarily when actually training. One exercise involved spotting red cars when driving.

'You start out making a really conscious effort to look out for them, and then after a while you just start seeing the red cars without concentrating on the task so much. You can translate that exercise into certain fencing moves.

'In another exercise we had a piece of paper with a lot of numbers written at random in a grid. You had to find each number in turn and cross it off. You had a time limit and you couldn't cross a number off until you had found the one before it.

'These exercises were important because when competing you have to concentrate for an extended period. In pentathlon you also need to be able to broaden your focus and then bring it back to a very narrow focus for different events. You need to be able to change your range of focus and your concentration span, depending on which event you are doing. It's important to be flexible in that way in pentathlon because all the events are so diverse.'

Sprinter John Regis learnt during his career that he didn't need to maintain a constantly high level of focus at all times. He realized that if he allowed himself to enjoy and absorb the atmosphere around him before a race, that actually released some of the pressure he was feeling. Regis recalls an early learning experience.

'In the Olympics in 1988 in Seoul I was very stiff. I wasn't looking at the crowd. I thought the crowd could take me out of my game. And then I got knocked out in the semi-final.

'I thought, "Why was that?" because on the circuit I'm relaxed, I have fun. I thought "OK, when I need to focus, I focus". I learnt

that. So when going out into a big area and people are cheering for you and the announcer says "In lane five, John Regis from Great Britain" and reads a list of your achievements, I would wave to the crowd. Applause actually helped to calm me down. I would lose myself in the crowd, waiting to see people I know. Then when the starter said "Gentlemen …", I cut everything else out. I was in the zone and ready to rock 'n' roll.'

Analysis IV

PEAK PERFORMANCE

CHAMPIONS TRAIN HARD IN ORDER TO DELIVER an unbeatable performance when it counts – on the day of competition. In Part IV we looked at how elite sportspeople manage to produce their best efforts when it really counts.

CHAPTER 14

In Chapter 14: Nerve Control, we touched on the subject of nerves – a topic with which virtually every sporting champion is familiar.

We found that even the best sportspeople suffered from nerves as competition time approached. Olympic hurdler Sally Gunnell found it hard to sleep the night before a major competition, but when she finally stood on the starting line, the foundations of self-belief that she had laid down through thorough training and preparation gave her the confidence she needed to overcome her anxieties.

Nerves shouldn't necessarily be seen as a bad thing, however. They do have value. They create adrenalin that can lift a performance.

So how did our sporting champions handle their nerves? For many, the first step was simply to accept that they would be there. England rugby fly-half Jonny Wilkinson admits to getting incredibly nervous before international and club games. He accepts this. He reads a newspaper or watches a little TV on the day of a game to keep his mind occupied. Olympic rower Matthew Pinsent says he is 'bubbling' with nerves before a race. He describes the two voices in his head – one positive and one negative. He doesn't fight these voices, but accepts that the nerves are part of the experience – part of the body's preparation for competing under stress.

Such acceptance is an appropriate response. Renzie Hanham from mental conditioning specialists Gazing Performance says that top performers accept that they need a certain level of nerves to perform at their best. People who start thinking they are too nervous risk diverting their attention away from the processes they should be concentrating on. Top performers are able to keep their attention on what they are doing, rather than being diverted into worrying about their nerves.

Trying to ignore nerves can be unwise, as Michael Lynagh pointed out. Some young team members playing for Australia in the 1995 World Cup tried to suppress their pre-match nerves; as a result, they didn't perform well on the field.

Being active proved helpful to some athletes in managing their pre-competition anxiety. Before a match Davis Cup tennis captain David Lloyd would hit balls on the practice court long enough to take the edge off his nerves. Former Australian rugby fly-half Michael Lynagh liked to go for a walk or kick a ball about outside his hotel in the hours before a game.

There are always exceptions in any group, and some of our interviewees did claim to have been nerve-free when competing. Jack Charlton said he wasn't nervous before the 1966 World Cup final. Similarly, England rugby head coach Clive Woodward felt excitement rather than nerves in his playing days when a big match approached. Even without nerves, they were able to perform at the high level they required to succeed.

Applications

- Accept that you will feel nervous in certain situations. Understand that those nerves help to sharpen your performance and therefore are to be welcomed.
- Don't try to just suppress your nerves. It won't work.
- Think about situations where you handled your nerves effectively in the past. Did you do anything in particular that you could repeat in future? This could be doing something physical to let off steam or keeping your mind busy by reading a gripping book. Try to identify what works for you.

CHAPTER 15

If champions experience nerves before competition, the comfort of routine can help to keep them focused on the task in hand. In Chapter 15: The Rock of Routine, we looked at how members of the sporting elite develop and use routines to support their performance.

Successful routines are those that help to create the right mental state before a competition. Part of the value in a routine lies in the emotions with which it is associated.

Routines can develop accidentally, or deliberately with the help of sports psychologists. The aim is to identify actions that have a positive impact on the individual, arousing them to the appropriate level or generating positive mental thoughts. Once the individual knows what it is they do that has a positive impact, they can repeat that every time before competing.

The key is to identify what really works and to focus on actions that are within the individual's control, and not dependent on others. If your routine involves always wearing a pair of 'lucky' socks, then you make yourself vulnerable should you lose them. If your routine requires you to be last out on the pitch, you could have a problem if someone else in your team wants to do that too.

Renzie Hanham from mental conditioning specialists Gazing Performance encourages little rituals that people can use to control their attention – as long as they are repeatable and dependent entirely on themselves. The person must be able to control the ritual.

Champions have to be flexible enough to cope if their routine is interrupted or upset. England rugby regular Lawrence Dallaglio accepts that his routine on the day of a match has to fit around the team schedule and has to adapt to unforeseen circumstances, such as the start being delayed. Olympic rower Mathew Pinsent certainly has a warm-up routine, but beyond that tries to be as flexible as possible.

Where routines can be helpful is in creating a sense of reassuring familiarity, even if you are competing away from home or in a strange environment. Some footballers prefer playing at home, for example, because they feel they benefit from home advantage. This is partly why successful rugby kickers like former Australian rugby captain and renowned fly-half Michael Lynagh would go and kick in an unfamiliar ground the day before he was due to play there. He established a firm routine for kicking practice that helped to familiarize him with the new environment.

Applications

- Are there certain things you have done in stressful situations that have helped to keep you focused on the task in hand and not become too nervous or worked up? If so, these could become handy routines to use in similar situations. Is there a certain song you like to listen to? Are there certain images you like to picture? Do you pack your bag in a certain order to reassure yourself you haven't forgotten anything? Check that these actions and activities are within your own control and readily repeatable.
- If you have a routine you already use, think about whether it meets the repeatability and controllability criteria. If your routine

is dependent on someone else or can't be repeated easily, try to find a new one.

- Look out for routines that other people use effectively. Could you learn from that routine, perhaps adapting it to meet your own needs?

CHAPTER 16

In the heat of competition, sporting champions manage to remain positive about their ability to win. In Chapter 16: Positive Talk, we looked at how they did this.

Even when in stressful competitive situations, members of the sporting elite can interpret the world and what happens to them in supportive, positive ways. Even if something happens that objectively seems bad, they can turn it around into a positive opportunity.

The ability to do this depends on the language that people use when thinking or speaking to themselves. For example, a triathlete could interpret the pain he felt in competition as a wonderful indicator that he was alive.

Some techniques for keeping a positive outlook are extremely simple. Just standing in a confident way will make you feel more confident. Modern pentathlete Dr Stephanie Cook appreciated this; she focused on keeping her body language positive and walking tall even when her fencing wasn't going as well as she would like. Champions also accept that sometimes their performance can slip, but if they just hang in there and stay in the competition, they give themselves a chance of coming back.

Just thinking about what you need to do at any one moment is also a good technique for warding off negative thoughts and staying in a positive space. Similarly, focusing your attention within yourself, and not watching what others are doing, can also support positive feelings. Former sprinter John Regis made a point of not watching others warming up because in the past he found it made him worry about how good his rivals looked. Olympic hurdler Sally Gunnell maintained a strong sense of calm and focus when she was waiting in the call room before racing. She sensed she gave off such a strong aura that it put her competitors off.

Champions can try to psyche each other out, unconsciously or consciously. Linford Christie, 100m champion, seemed to put other people off just by being in close proximity to them; his sense of belief was almost tangible. However, he could also deliberately psyche rivals out if he was so minded – warming up in someone else's lane.

Ceri Evans from mental conditioning specialists Gazing Performance accepts that in competition, athletes or players often try to put each other off by disturbing their focus. Such tricks are designed to divert the other people away from focusing on their own processes. If you find yourself on the receiving end, it is important to continue to place your attention on the things that you can control or influence.

Renzie Hanham from Gazing Performance explains that diverting from process can be harmful to performance because it is often accompanied by an internal dialogue which has to do with whether you can perform or not. One part of you says 'you can' and one part says 'you can't'. Inevitably this impacts negatively on the quality of your processes because your attention is divided. The physical results of this internal dilemma are feelings of heaviness, lethargy and a drop-off in co-ordination. The psychological results are doubt and uncertainty, which lead to poor decision-making. Because we are not sure we can trust ourselves, our thinking is inaccurate. We lose our confidence.

Conversely, Hanham explains, when we are totally in process and on task there is only the thought 'I do'. There is only certainty, an inner stillness and a conviction that you are in the right place at the right time. You are, as some people call it, 'in the zone' – a state we considered further in Chapter 17.

Applications

- Make use of simple physical techniques – such as standing confidently – that can encourage you to think positively.
- Pay attention to the language you use when talking to yourself mentally. Do you tend to use a critical internal voice? If so, try to

speak to yourself in more encouraging tones, which emphasize the positive aspects of situations or events.

- If you know you will face a situation that tends to put you in a negative frame of mind, think in advance about how you can describe it to yourself differently. For example, you may be feeling anxious about going through an assessment process for a new job. You are worried that the assessment exercises will highlight your weaknesses in report writing. Instead, think about how you will be able to show your strengths in team-building and communication. Focus on how the experience should generate valuable feedback to help you develop your skills. It is a great opportunity to learn about yourself. Do you feel more excited about the experience now?
- Get into the habit of asking yourself what process you should be focusing on right now. This helps to stop you getting diverted by emotional responses to events.
- If someone else is trying to put you off, don't pay attention to them. Remind yourself that it is what you are doing that counts.

CHAPTER 17

When sportspeople deliver their best performances, they often talk about having been 'in the zone'. In Chapter 17: Into the Zone, we looked at what the sporting elite means by this and how they try to get into that state when they need it.

When sportspeople get into the zone, what they do feels effortless. Former sprinter Mark Richardson describes the sensation of time slowing down and being able to see everything clearly. Olympic hurdler Sally Gunnell says she felt she went into automatic pilot, so much so that she couldn't remember what happened in the race once it was over. This is not unusual. Athletes can become so in tune with what they are doing that they have no recollection of what they actually did or how they did it.

Renzie Hanham from mental conditioning specialists Gazing Performance stresses that for all of us, 'there is only now'. In real terms as we experience life, there is only one point in time available to us

– the present moment. Whether we are reflecting on the past or planning for the future, we can only do this 'now'. This is an important point, Hanham says, because much of our attention is unconsciously diverted by things past and future. When we are under pressure we start to identify with past or future events as if they were happening in the present moment. This distorts our perception and filters the way that we respond to events. Clear thinking becomes lost as we revert to familiar patterns of behaviour – what we are comfortable with.

When athletes speak of being 'in the zone', they are operating in the 'now'. There is just no room for doubt because doubt is of the future. Being in the zone happens when you are totally on task and in process. There is no room for diversions. That doesn't mean you are blank – far from it. You are still receiving information and that information is being digested accurately and efficiently and adds to the quality of your process.

Hanham suggests that it is useful to practise staying present when reflecting on the past or planning for the future. One way of achieving this is by staying aware of your body, i.e. your breathing. This simple technique stops you from identifying so strongly with your thoughts that you start responding as if the thoughts were real, as opposed to just thoughts. The prime issue here is control of attention and being deliberate about where you place your attention.

Getting into the zone is no easy matter. Most interviewees admitted they had no guaranteed method for doing so. The state might be associated with certain emotions, such as confidence and belief, but there were no guarantees that these would lead them into the zone.

For javelin champion Steve Backley, the zone was like entering a 'superstate' – an experience he first enjoyed in 1990 when he came from behind to win an international competition, achieving a new British record in the process. In the experience, Backley felt dissociated – it was as if he was watching himself making the throw from two or three feet away, rather than actually doing it himself.

From that time Backley worked hard to try to recreate the superstate at will, doing so by asking himself questions about his performance – a form of self-analysis. He developed theories about it, such as that lots of sleep was required in advance of competition. He also noted that the superstate seemed to be created out of adversity, as a result of extreme anxiety or pressure.

While athletes may strive to achieve such a superstate or enter the zone, they need to guard against becoming obsessive about it. Ceri Evans from Gazing Performance says that concentrating too hard on trying to get back into the zone, or indeed whether they are in the zone or out of it, can be a diversion that actually impedes performance. If they focus on how to get back into the zone, they can be diverted from focusing on the process of what they are doing. The important thing is to continue to focus purely on effective process. Whether someone is in or out of the 'zone' is an outcome of this heightened concentration. For most athletes, it occurs infrequently during their careers. It may be more helpful not to see it as an 'all or none' phenomenon. In this way, the athlete can concentrate on just improving their focus of attention, something they do have control over, rather than whether they are in the zone or not, which may or may not occur. Concerning oneself with things that have happened in the past and potential negative outcomes in the future weakens the connection or engagement with the present, and makes entering the 'zone' more unlikely.

Applications

- Being 'in the zone' can be useful for anyone who wants to be totally engaged in what they are doing.
- Think about occasions in the past when you felt 'in the zone' or 'in the now'. Was there anything particular that you did to achieve that? Is there anything you could try to repeat in future?
- Don't get too hung up on the outcome – the zone – at the expense of the processes involved in what you are doing. You want to keep your attention focused on the processes that you are completing now.

CHAPTER 18

In Chapter 18: Focus and Refocus, we looked at how sporting champions manage to retain their focus during competition.

Focus is all about keeping your mind and your attention on the task in hand – not what is going on around you. This isn't easy. Even sporting legends such as Nick Faldo could struggle to remain totally concentrated on their sport when their personal lives hit problems. However, at its best, Faldo's focus was impressive. From the moment he woke on the day of play he was preparing himself internally and thinking about the day ahead.

During competition, the key is to retain focused on the task or the process involved at any particular time. During a race Olympic rower Matthew Pinsent, for example, would never let his focus stray to thinking about the crowd or the importance of the occasion. He mainly focused on the technique of rowing. Modern pentathlete Dr Stephanie Cook didn't let herself get distracted when running in her last event at the Sydney Olympics. She stuck to her race plan, regardless of those around her.

Being focused involves staying in the present moment, and not letting past events distract you. This means poor previous performances, shots and missed kicks must all be set aside. Nor is it wise to start thinking about the future, and what may happen later in a match or game.

The sporting champions we interviewed understood the importance of being able to segment their performances, depending on what they were doing. Former Australian rugby fly-half Michael Lynagh would concentrate on kicking when he was kicking, then focus on the rest of the game during open play. If he was performing badly in one area of his game, he didn't let himself dwell on it when performing in another area. Nor would he think about the scoreboard, but simply about each play as it happened. His ability to retain strong focus, even when under extreme pressure, enabled him to snatch wins in the closing minutes of games.

However, some champions also described occasions when they felt they had 'over-focused'. At the last minute they began thinking in too great detail about what they were about to do. There is a balance to be struck between thinking about each element of a tennis shot or a golf swing and focusing on the familiar feel of what you do. This can actually destroy performance by disrupting the flow.

Ceri Evans from mental conditioning specialists Gazing Performance says that despite being a remarkably complex organ, one of the main constraints on brain functioning is that humans have a limited ability to focus on more than one thing at a time, particularly under conditions of pressure. With a golf swing, for example, professional golfers will actually focus on very few things. They won't think about every element involved in the swing because this would be likely to cause mechanical breakdown, or paralysis by analysis. They need first to have over-learned the skill. This means that the basic mechanics are firmly enough established that they don't need to think consciously about every element of the swing as they do it. They may then focus on the feel of the swing, rather than multiple technical elements.

Practice is important when working to develop good focus. The champions we interviewed learnt over time what preparations and techniques helped to maintain their focus. Dr Stephanie Cook completed mental exercises designed to improve her concentration and focus.

Experience also taught the athletes the importance of not getting distracted by things beyond their control. Champion 400m runner Roger Black learnt that worrying about the weather during the Atlanta Olympics would only be a waste of energy.

Maintaining strong focus is a skill. Champions need to learn that emotional responses to events around them distract them from what they are doing. Ceri Evans from Gazing Performance says that some champions learn not to attach emotive labels to people or circumstances. Instead they observe calmly. In this way they can keep their attention on the process of what they are doing. This detached viewpoint can help to retain focus, without unhelpful emotions generated by labelling and judging getting in the way.

Applications

- If you want to develop a greater sense of focus, develop the habit of asking yourself periodically what you are focusing on. If you are not focusing on the process of what you are currently doing, gently bring your attention back to the process.
- Understand that past and future events are not relevant to what you are doing right now. If you find yourself dwelling on a mistake you made last time you were in your current position, bring your mind back to the process of what you are doing now.
- If you find you need to focus on several different things at different times, be clear about what is most important now. Segment what you do into separate chunks of activity. Whichever activity you are doing now, make that the focus of your attention.
- Don't waste time focusing your attention on things you cannot control.
- Practise observing events without becoming emotionally involved. Focus your attention on what is happening, rather than on attaching emotive and emotional descriptors.
- If you want to improve your concentration, play games that can help to train your mind appropriately.

Part V
TEAM SPIRIT

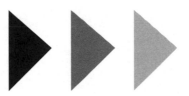

Chapter 19

THE RIGHT COMBINATION

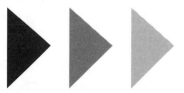

IN MANY SPORTS NO ONE INDIVIDUAL can ensure a win. It is the team effort that counts. Putting together the right combination of individuals is therefore critical for the overall success of the team – and everyone in it.

TEAM SELECTION

When choosing players for the team, England manager Sven-Göran Eriksson aims to try and create an overall positive chemistry. He says:

'It can happen that you don't select players who you know may not fit in with the group, even if they are very good players. You put in

players who you know will give you something, even if they are sitting on the bench. They create a good atmosphere, are positive and support the eleven who are playing. That's extremely important, especially when you are competing away in a World Cup.'

Jack Charlton was selected to play for England relatively late in the day. He believes that Alf Ramsay, despite selecting him, didn't like him. However, Charlton was included in the team because he fitted the desired pattern of play. Charlton recalls:

'I was 28 coming up 29 when I got my first cap. I asked Alf, "Why me?" He said, "Well Jack, I have a pattern of play in my mind – the way I want the team to play. So I always pick appropriate players to make the pattern work. I don't necessarily always pick the best players, Jack."'

Charlton absorbed this information and used it himself when he was a manager. He understood that as a national team manager he had to start with a desired way or pattern of playing. Then he had to select the players who would be able to make that pattern work. He couldn't just pick people for the team because they had talent.

HIGH MAINTENANCE PLAYERS

Within any team there may be so-called 'prima donnas' – potentially hot-headed and explosive on and off the field, but with the kind of talent that can turn a game around. Howard Wilkinson, former Football Association technical director, prefers the term 'high maintenance' for such players. Wilkinson explains that the decision as to whether to include them in a team comes down to a cost-benefit analysis. The analysis recognizes that such players bring huge value to a squad, but at a cost. The question is, which outweighs the other?

The impact on other players needs to be taken into account, as Wilkinson knows:

'Don't underestimate the other players. A player delegation of three, including the captain, once came to me when we were doing well as a team. They came to see me because they felt I was being hard on a particular player. The issues were to do with sharing the load, respecting each other and being honest. The delegation said they understood why I was being hard, but on behalf of the team they wanted to tell me they were prepared to put up with this player, because he scored. They knew that when he got the ball, if he got a chance, he'd get a goal. So they were prepared to put up with him. They said that it might be unfair, but if they were prepared to put up with it, then I had no need to waste time highlighting it any more. I should just mention it, but move on.'

Wilkinson accepted the players' request, but stressed he wasn't copping out or compromising on the values that the team had all agreed to. It was simply a matter that the team had taken a vote and decided to take this action from a cost-benefit viewpoint. It was a professional decision.

Wilkinson believes that even players with reputations for being difficult can be influenced for the better if they buy in to the team goals. This involves clearly explaining what the team is striving for, and the steps required along the way. In addition, getting players' agreement to a set of agreed rules – both written and unwritten – is the key to avoiding dramas on and off the pitch. Wilkinson says:

'Vinnie Jones was an angel on the pitch in his two years with me compared with his previous record. I think he was booked once and not sent off. And off the pitch we never had a front page scandal. Most of it was low-key or never got anywhere because we had this book of rules, some of which were written, but most of which were unwritten.'

David Campese was a key member of the Australian rugby team, even though he had certain challenging characteristics. Former Australian captain Michael Lynagh says Campese was always a welcome member of the team:

'Campo always put the team first. Yes, he did have some individual traits, but none of us wanted to change them too much. Some of his comments would hurt, and they would be directed at some of the players in the team, but he would be brought into line. I remember sitting in Sydney at work and I picked up the Sydney Herald; *there was Campo in the paper saying, "Lynagh is hopeless – I don't get enough ball". I rang him up and asked why he said such things. But he didn't mean it; he just said it. He didn't mean to hurt people.*

'He was actually one of the guys who was very keen on discipline. He came into the team in 1982 as an 18-year-old; I joined him one year later as a 19-year-old. He was really the superstar from day one; everybody wanted to talk to him. He was a Tiger Woods of Australian rugby, a Jonny Wilkinson of Australian rugby. The older guys protected him and kept him in check and made sure that he was schooled in the traditions of Australian rugby. He was one of the proudest guys in regard to the old school tradition, all the way through until he finished. He would be the one who would be chipping the young guys coming in saying, "You can't do that; this is the way we do it."'

THE CAPTAIN

Selecting the captain is particularly important in putting together the right combination of players in a successful team. England manager Sven-Göran Eriksson is impressed by David Beckham's qualities as captain. He appreciates the fact that Beckham doesn't shout, but just by his behaviour on and off the pitch, the other players follow him, listen to him and respect him.

In the match between England and Greece in 2001, Beckham took the extra time free kick which assured England's qualification for the 2002 World Cup. This is just one example of the mental strength that Beckham has shown on many occasions. Eriksson says:

'Even his World Cup penalty against Argentina wasn't easy. Any player could easily see the goal as being very small and the goal-

keeper as very big, because all the nation is watching and this is an opportunity to score.'

Michael Lynagh was captain of Australia from 1992 to 1995. He recalls his experiences of having that role, and the differences between himself and his predecessor, Nick Farr-Jones. Lynagh says:

'I enjoyed the responsibility. I had been captain of school teams in both cricket and rugby and various teams in Queensland. My one problem was that I am a fairly quiet and reserved person. As captain you do have to make an effort to be heard and have points of view and talk to people. Nick Farr-Jones was very good at that; he was a very outgoing and personable person and that is why I thought we made such a good team when he was captain and I was vice captain. I looked after everything behind him on the pitch and he looked after everything in front of him. Off the pitch we were very good friends but had very different personalities. In a way we complimented one another very well.

'When Nick retired and I took over, I had to reinvent myself a little bit. But if I stood in the dressing room and started thumping the table and swearing at the forwards and saying "Come on, you have got to do this and that", they wouldn't have taken me seriously because they knew that wasn't me. Part of captaincy is delegating to people who are in a position to do that, and that is what I did. I got people within the team who were experienced as my deputies. They weren't necessarily vice captains but they were leaders of men within that team and within groups of that team. That is how I overcame my shyness in terms of being a captain. I could look after the backs, because I had done that for many years. With the forwards, I got key people within the forwards to look after them – to stir them up and do what forwards do.

'So I delegated, but I also became more assertive in terms of team meetings. Before I was captain I was quite happy to listen and work things out later, but now I had to lead meetings and that was quite a change of direction for me.'

Despite his enjoyment of the captain's role, Lynagh tried not to forget that the success of the team was more important than his own personal glory. Lynagh says:

'The team has always been very important to me. My personal goal was always to try and get the team to play better. I was disappointed when I missed out on being captain on a few occasions, but at the end of the day if I was in the team – terrific.

'At Saracens there was an occasion when someone was dropped as captain and he moped around and didn't perform. I hadn't agreed with the decision to drop him as captain, but when I saw his reaction I knew it was the right decision. I thought he was the wrong person to be captain because he was putting himself before the team. He wasn't the right person to lead because he thought about himself before the team.'

TEAM SPIRIT

Team spirit comes from a general recognition amongst all team members that the good of the team comes before the needs of the individual. Roger Black recalls how the British 4 × 400m relay team beat the Americans in the 1991 World Championships.

'On paper, we were not capable of winning the gold medal, but we had a shared belief – that the greater good of the team was more important than any individual ego. That is the secret of teamwork. The 1991 British 4×400 team was myself – an individual silver medallist in the 400m, Derek Redmond, who was the British 400m record holder and who was coming back from an injury, John Regis, a 200m runner, and Kriss Akabusi, the bronze medallist in the 400m hurdles.

'We won the 1991 gold because of something that happened the night before the race. Choosing the running order wasn't difficult. You would generally put the best athlete on the last leg and an OK athlete on the first leg and the other two in the middle.'

The original chosen running order was therefore Redmond first, Akabusi second, Regis third and Black fourth. However, the night before the race Black and Akabusi decided they needed to change the order. Black says:

'We had chosen the right team, but the right team for second place. Sometimes in sport you have to dare to win. You have to take an opportunity. We knew we weren't doing that. We had to become proactive as a team and make the Americans react to us, which they would never do with this order. They would go from the front and be in the lead. Off they would go and win. We had to change that. We had to make the Americans think before they even walked into the stadium.'

The team decided they needed to surprise the Americans by putting Black on the first leg, followed by Redmond and Regis, with Akabusi on the last leg. Black says:

'We knew that was our only chance. It was a risk – a big risk. We called an emergency meeting with the team management and said we wanted to change the running order. I will never forget their faces. It took about half an hour of intelligent discussion. One of the team managers said something, which I think is a great example of good management, which was, "In the end you are the four guys who have to run. We will be sitting in the stands watching you. If you really believe in each other as a team, you must do this." So we shaped our destiny.'

Black recalls the impact that the new, unexpected order had on the Americans. When the British team went and sat on the benches before the race in their revised order, the US team members were extremely surprised. Black says:

'Before you go out into the stadium you have to sit in the order you are going to run in; and when I went and sat on the first bench, we "had" the Americans. All they had been thinking about was how

fast they were going to run, and they had been arguing about who was going to run the last leg.'

The Americans were shocked because the fastest runner always ran the last leg and never the first. There were various reasons, as Black explains:

'When you are the fastest runner in the team and you are the world's silver medallist, you don't expect to run the first leg. It had never been done for three reasons. Firstly, because you look rubbish because you run in lanes; secondly, you get the slowest time of the team. Thirdly, if the team happens to win you don't get your picture in the paper. The guy on the last leg gets all the glory.'

However, the four British athletes decided to put their egos aside. Black says:

'I was very happy to do that. We all were. The Americans weren't. When we walked out into the stadium the four of us didn't have to talk to each other at all; we had the Americans beat because they were going, "Wow, what's he doing first? What's going to happen?" They were being reactive and we were being proactive.

'That night when I stood behind the line to run that first leg, I wasn't running for myself, I wasn't running for Great Britain. I was actually running for John Regis, Derek Redmond and Kriss Akabussi. That to me was a moment of absolute perfection of teamwork. It was truly amazing because what was interesting was that Kriss Akabussi didn't choose to run the last leg because he wanted personal glory; he did what I think many people wouldn't have done. He put himself under a lot of pressure. Of course, he got all the credit and all the glory, but you put your ego to one side for the greater good of the team.

'That to me was such a wonderful moment because individual success is great but you can't really share it with anybody. When

the four of us get together we still reminisce. We have got that bond for the rest of our lives.'

The Australian 1991 World Cup rugby team was an impressive one, former captain Michael Lynagh believes, because of the players within it and the strong team ethos. The team included an older, experienced core of people who were probably at the peak of their powers. Then there was also a young group, whose talents were enormous and who were very easy to mould into a team. Lynagh recalls:

'We all got on very well. There was a good vibe in the team. We enjoyed each other's company away from rugby. Our wives were friendly with one another. But we were winning, so there weren't many problems to have to deal with.

'There were certain values in the team, certain standards that were set, ways you were expected to behave. It was very much a self-governed operation, but there were rules.

'Discipline came from within the team. If somebody was out of line it wouldn't be the manager or coach who came down on them; one of the guys in the team would quietly have a word.'

Sports psychologist and performance expert Professor Graham Jones knows that team selection is crucial for the formation of a strong team with a positive team spirit. He firmly believes that you can't have eleven stars in the same team. Some teams fall down because they try and create that. They have too many people competing for the same roles, the same adoration. Balance is crucial, Professor Jones says. You need some stars in the team, but you need other people who are just as important. Internally everyone knows that and everyone has to buy into these values.

SUPPORT TEAMS

In motorsport, the team around the driver is vital for success. Ron Dennis, boss of the McLaren racing team, knows the importance of getting the mix right. Some teams give guidance and support, he says, and some don't. The environment in McLaren helps to support the driver, and the team includes people who are experts in a range of different areas. They can give advice, for example, on issues not directly associated with the motor racing itself, such as how to handle adverse publicity.

McLaren driver David Coulthard benefited from the McLaren support after he survived a traumatic plane crash, and drove in a race just days later. Dennis says:

> *'I have tremendous admiration for him, but also personal pride in how we reacted and shielded him from the media to enable him to collect his thoughts. I was proud of the role of the team, and my contribution to it.'*

Even in normal circumstances, the team needs to work in a unified, focused way to deliver success on the track. As Dennis says:

> *'You constantly have to define the goal, and the role that everyone has to play to achieve it. It's like a chain. You have to make sure that everyone understands they have a role to play, and that they can make a difference. It's like in football where there are also so many people behind the scenes. Everyone has to be of a mindset where they know they can make a difference, including the guy checking the studs to make sure that none are loose.*
>
> *'These cars are complex animals. You get a great sense of achievement from getting them off the line and surviving the first lap. The driver is an ingredient – an important one – but an ingredient in the makeup. No driver has won a Grand Prix from sitting at the start line in his underpants.'*

That said, the driver is a central element. On race day, the driver takes centre stage. Dennis says:

> *'The driver is one element of the team and he becomes the focus of everyone's efforts at a Grand Prix. There are various points where you feel yourself thinking, "Now it's over to him".'*

Once teams are selected, their members still need to function well together to achieve consistent winning performances. In the next chapter we look at how top sportspeople work together to achieve a great team performance at the right time.

Chapter 20

TEAM BUILD-UP

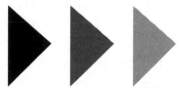

BUILDING A STRONG TEAM TAKES TIME and commitment from all those involved – team members, managers, coaches and support staff.

TEAM VALUES

Sports psychologist and performance expert Professor Graham Jones knows that team members need to buy into a common set of values if the team is to become strong and successful. Those values are important in terms of the way the team does things, and the things that are acceptable. Professor Jones has worked with teams on developing team charters and has encouraged them to police themselves. He feels it is important to empower the team to determine what happens if someone contravenes the charter. That empowerment encourages the development of a strong team spirit. Professor Jones says:

> 'You recognize and accept that you are all part of the same team. You develop a common vision, so that you are all working towards the same thing. You accept that people are different. There may be different levels of skill, but everyone has something to contribute to the team.'

In addition to team values, strong teams require a culture where it is OK to make mistakes, says Renzie Hanham from Gazing Performance, specialists in performance improvement. Strong teams have a culture of looking after people and keeping them safe and secure. Trust is very important. In dysfunctional teams, if someone makes a mistake, they pay for it. Team members identify themselves as being challenged all the time and that becomes counter-productive. They see a criticism as a threat. Hanham adds that team spirit arises out of good or useful shared experiences, such as enjoyment or good performances. People that are winning are generally happy.

NLP trainer Graham Shaw believes that developing a supportive culture is important in terms of training players not to panic in tough match moments. Teams can learn how to cope when things go wrong in competition. He recalls the England–Brazil match in the 2002 World Cup.

> 'When Brazil scored, while it was a terrible time to let a goal in, I think the match was totally lost then. I don't think it was down to David Seaman. As a team, one of the things that's important is what happens when things begin to go wrong. If we let a goal in, what are the things we are going to say to each other and do and how are we going to hold our heads?
>
> 'It's interesting that when Arsene Wenger is interviewed after a match he focuses on talking about the performance. He doesn't get too carried away if he's won. If he's lost 1–0, he knows that from time to time you perform well but let a goal in and lose. He knows, however, that over time if they perform well they'll win.

'How many times have Manchester United scored a goal near the end of a match? How do they do that? They don't do that by panicking. What they do is say, "We know that most of the time, if we continue to play in this way, we'll score".'

Shaw says that a team can prepare in advance for adverse situations. Team members can be encouraged to think in advance about how they will react should the opposition score. In effect, they need to learn to keep their heads up, to avoid wasting time on blaming someone and to get straight on with the match.

Howard Wilkinson, former Football Association technical director, believes in the importance of getting every player to buy into the team's objectives and the process for achieving them.

'Get their agreement, get them to buy into it, and then use that as the reference point. Show them you're prepared to take the giant step; show them you're prepared to be innovative; show them that the goal can be achieved. But take the fear out of it by showing them how you're going to get there, by breaking it down into things to concentrate on in the short-term, and what you can affect in the long-term, and why and how.'

Wilkinson doesn't believe there are any tricks or gimmicks that can really create team spirit.

'I've tried them, and they weren't for me. I've always thought it is more about having agreed objectives with everybody buying into them. It's about having an identifiable coat of arms or trademark for the way we do things here; making certain values important and emphasizing them all the time: respect, trust, being fair, sharing, doing your best.'

Players joining the squad from elsewhere need to buy into the team values quickly. Wilkinson likens membership of the team to being like mountain climbers roped together. A football game is just another milestone to reach on a mountain climb. Everyone in the team is roped together and there are certain ways of doing things in order to get to the top safely and in the most enjoyable way. If you can explain this to players, they will accept that they need to behave appropriately as a team.

TEAM COMMUNICATION

Sports psychiatrist John Syer believes that effective communication is vital for developing team spirit. Syer and his colleagues employ a model derived from Gestalt Therapy to define a team building approach. Syer says:

> *'Initially team members must become aware of themselves. If I don't know what I'm doing when I'm with my team, I'm not going to perform very well. I also need to be aware of other team members: what impact I have on them, how they are different to myself and how they are different to each other. Then I come to appreciate those differences – not necessarily to like them – but to appreciate that this player needs to do this in order to perform well and I must find a way to allow him to do this.*
>
> *'The heart of the process is giving descriptive feedback to each other about what they see happening, what they see each other doing, what they see happening as a result and how they feel. It's not what they think, but how they feel – expressed in one word – that counts. We call this descriptive feedback, whereas the normal type of feedback is evaluative and is concerned to congratulate or criticize.*
>
> *'When we're working with a team, we focus on what people are doing and help members to report their experiences. By making feedback descriptive, comments between team members arouse interest rather than defensiveness.'*

Syer suggests that team members communicate how their performance is helped or hindered by the performance of other team members. This kind of information is rarely given. Yet Syer says that if you always give descriptive feedback and appreciation, then you get all the things that the team needs: contact, communication, respect, trust, team spirit.

The exact team-building exercises that Syer would go through with a particular team would depend on the particular circumstances. However, the exercise itself is not important. What is important, Syer says, is that you facilitate people talking to each other in a way they understand. He says:

'We have to speak to make contact. The skills of communication are central to this. But exactly what I do depends on the particular team. In fact I always start by meeting each member of the team individually. That's because everyone's experience of what is going on at a given moment is slightly different. We notice different things. With a team, it's important that people have the chance to express their own reality.'

Round-the-world yachtsman Sir Chay Blyth also emphasizes the importance of effective communication when building team strength. He says you have to be able to communicate in such a manner that people will believe you. It's not about presentation skills, but about conveying enthusiasm. You've got to inject them with enthusiasm.

Blyth refers to Richard Branson to illustrate his point.

'Richard does a lot of inspiring, but he's not a very good speaker. So how does he do it? First of all, he's got a charismatic presence. He also allows the individual to think that, whatever they're saying, it's the most important thing ever. When he's talking to them, who-ever it may be, they believe that what they say to Richard is really, really important to him and that he really listens to him. That's an amazing quality.'

Team communication was an important element of the build-up to one of Blyth's team sailing challenges. To encourage team spirit, Blyth took his group of sailors to Scotland.

'I took them up to a small cottage in Scotland for three weeks. I'd written a training programme and for three weeks there were 25 of us in a cottage with only two bedrooms upstairs and a sitting room. We lay on army camp beds. We simulated conditions on a boat so they had to make their beds up and keep the place clean and tidy. We went for a run every morning. We had discipline. We had discussions chaired by one of the guys. We'd break into watches. We did various activities so we had to work as a team.'

TEAM BUILD-UP

Lawrence Dallagio, England rugby captain, knows that his success as an England player depends on the achievements of other team members. He says:

'We have an expression in rugby that you have to look after your own back yard. If everyone in the team does that, and everyone is pulling in the right direction, then you get the result you want. Ultimately, because it's a technical game, you are relying on other people's performances for you to succeed.'

The difficult part, however, is to try and ensure that everyone performs well at the same time. As Dallaglio says, in a team game you have to get all the components to be at the right level at the same time. If an individual is mentally stronger than his opponent and he's physically better, then he's going to win. But in a team game, if three or four players turn up and play well but the others don't, it's very difficult. The mechanics of team sport involve trying to get the best out of everyone at the same time. If you do that, you get a perfect performance.

Dallaglio recognizes that achieving peak performance during the 80 minutes of the game requires a gradual building up of intensity in terms of mental preparation. But players need to remember to switch off too. Dallaglio says:

'When you are practising you should be mentally thinking about the game as well, but there is a temptation in rugby not to get too focused too early, because it's no good training brilliantly and then not playing well. You have to have the ability to be able to switch off a bit once you have finished a training session and be able to relax. Then you go back to the training, and then relax again, and then go back to it and get yourself ready for the game day.

'I actually find it easy to be able to switch off, even though you still have the knowledge that you are only, say, 48 hours away from battle.'

In the week before a game, preparations include analysing the opposition.

'You look at what you are going to do, and you look at what the opposition are going to do and how you are going to stop that. There is part of the week where you have to pay respect to the opposition, analyse their weaknesses and strengths and work out strategies to counteract them. You have to work out technically how you as an individual, and as a team, are going to overcome the opposition's strengths – your game plan. There's a fair bit of mental work that goes into that. The closer I get to a game, the more I start to think about the team I'm playing against. I start to picture the opposition. I start to visualize them. I put myself in the game environment and atmosphere, so that you're not there for the first time when the whistle blows; you've already been there and you know what to expect.'

Individuals playing sport as part of a team need to be sensitive to the needs of the team when preparing to compete. As Dallagio knows, they can't just expect to follow a routine that works for them. Individual routines have got to be flexible. Individual performers can have much more influence over what happens, but as a team player, Dallaglio says, sometimes you've got to give a little bit for the sake of the team. That may mean making adjustments in terms of your own preparation.

When building up for a match, Dallaglio believes that sometimes a poorer performance in practice can result in a better showing on the pitch in the real game.

> *'Clearly, the better you can practise, the better you are going to play. But you sometimes find that when you practise poorly, you end up playing much better because you have an edge – you are worried about how you play and it can focus your mind. Then sometimes when you practise really well you go out there and for some reason it doesn't seem to go too right; maybe mentally you are relaxed a bit. If you talk to any sportsman they might outwardly project the fact that everything is brilliant, because that is the way we are, but in fact they have got a bit of doubt and a bit of nerve and that can often inspire the performance. If you play well, you'd like to replicate that every week, but it doesn't work like that. You just have to try and work out what you do and the best formula for yourself. Closer to the game it becomes much more of a mental process.'*

Ron Dennis, boss of the McLaren racing team, understands the challenges involved in keeping a team motivated. He believes it is easier to motivate people when things are not going so well than it is when they are enjoying a period of success. In fact, he says, motivating people who are successful is the most difficult thing to have to do.

Dennis likens a team to a flywheel, fuelled by the energy that comes from the desire to win.

> *'It slowly gets up speed and reaches the speed needed for success. And you start to succeed. Then suddenly something happens – perhaps the technical or team manager retires or you lose one of your drivers – but you still win. What happens though is that there is a dropping down of energy input into the flywheel. When you start to fail it's after a sustained period of lack of effort. And it takes time to build the whole thing back up again.'*

In other words, the biggest enemy of continuous success is continuous success.

EXTENDED TOURNAMENTS

During competitions such as the football World Cup, players have to be able to handle living together away from home for extended periods. It is important to create a harmonious team spirit, as England manager Sven-Göran Eriksson knows.

> *'That's very important and very difficult. It depends on the results you are achieving; the best medicine for having a good ambience is winning football games. You can never beat that. But when you are together for such a long time it's important that you are not only practising, eating and sleeping; you have to do other things too. You can go and play golf, or out fishing. Sometimes we go to dinner in other restaurants. You have to create events, otherwise it will be very boring.'*

After the 2002 World Cup Eriksson asked his players for feedback on certain aspects of the team organization, to see whether there was anything that could be done differently next time to help them. For example, Eriksson wondered whether the team would rather move around different locations, rather than always travelling to and from the same base camp for matches which resulted in some long journeys. The feedback was that players liked to stay in the base camp, because that became their home from home. Having such a base gave players a sense of familiarity with their surroundings and added security.

Security and confidence are also boosted when schedules run to time. Eriksson explains:

> *'In a football team, it's important to know exactly when you will be leaving your hotel and arriving at the stadium. You want to arrive there exactly at the right time – not two hours before, not one hour before, but one hour twenty minutes before. Sometimes things happen – there's traffic or the police escorting the bus are too slow. But it's important to arrive at the right time, because if you have too much time, you don't know what to do with it. If you*

have too little, then you are rushing too much. I actually think it's better to have less time than more time, because you don't know what to do in the dressing room if you have too much time; you lose concentration.'

When involved in Davis Cup tennis, team captain David Lloyd worked hard to create a great team spirit. He says:

'We played golf, we made sure the players had videos in their rooms. We were a real team. We used to have a dinner the Thursday night before the doubles. The youngest person always made a speech on the day of the dinner and the older ones always helped him.

'As soon as I was captain I introduced the old-fashioned way of bringing in a bag boy – basically a young, fit player who learns the ropes and does things like clean the boys' shoes. It let him get to know what playing Davis Cup was like. It let him feel the entertainment, the electricity. That young kid was the one who did the speech. I'm not saying he liked to do it, but we all helped him out.'

Lloyd arranged for the team members to wear smart suits and shoes – creating the sense that they were a top team – the Davis Cup team of Great Britain. Lloyd felt it was important that the players felt well looked after. He made sure they stayed in the best hotels and that all room expenses apart from private phone calls were paid for.

Jack Charlton recalls how Don Revie, Leeds' manager, worked hard to make sure his squad was well looked after. This was particularly important when players were playing perhaps three games a week and spending regular periods away from home. Charlton says:

'Revie kept us away from home. We stayed at Blackpool and went to the pictures, we played bowls. We travelled from ground to ground and back to Blackpool or somewhere we stayed around Leeds. On a Friday night we'd always be in some hotel. The nearer the end of the season got, the more time we spent away from home.

But you had freedom, you got massaged, you got rests, you got ready for the next time and you had a positive attitude. That was Don Revie's influence. A lot of it rubbed off on us.'

Howard Wilkinson, former Football Association technical manager, knows that mental fitness is important for coping well with protracted tournaments. Wilkinson says:

'A big part of tournament football is about R&R – mentally and physically. It's very important. In the last World Cup, England were away for six weeks. If they had gone to the finals they would probably have been away for seven and a half weeks. That's very unusual for football.

'And with international tournament football, you're in a hotel and because of the high profile, you're unlikely to go exploring the streets.'

So apart from coping with the physical challenges of playing in a different climate or adjusting to a new time zone, top players also need to be able to cope with boredom. They need to be able to handle going from a very active state into a very low gear. It is great, he says, if people are happy reading a book and can sleep easily, that's smashing, but some people find the periods of inactivity hard.

STRATEGIC PLANNING

Strategic planning in a team situation so that everyone knows what they need to do is essential for sporting success. Former Ireland manager Jack Charlton stresses the importance of having a preagreed pattern of play. He says everyone thinks that if you've got eleven of the best players in the world, you would automatically beat everybody. Unfortunately, that's not the case. The team members have to work together, Charlton says. They have got to fit into some sort of pattern, because without that they have nothing – no intent, and no knowledge of where to play the ball.

As Charlton explained in the previous chapter, he selected players who suited the pattern of play he wanted to develop. That pattern of play could vary, however.

'With the Irish team I designed a game I called "putting them under pressure". FIFA decided they would call it "pressing". You played the ball behind people, but instead of just letting two forwards chase, everybody followed the ball and pushed in. We didn't let people out of their half. We had great success with that game once the players understood what was necessary.'

Charlton also believes it is better to give players one simple instruction, rather than a choice of options. It is better to tell a player to knock the ball behind the fullback every time he gets it than suggest a choice of actions.

'The more you complicate the methods of playing, the more difficult they are to get through to the players and the longer it takes them to accept what you say. Normally by that time you will have got the sack!'

The limited time that a national side has for training together makes simplicity even more important, Charlton feels. A national football manager only gets to work with the squad about once every couple of months. Therefore the method of play the manager gives them has to be very simple and easy for them to understand, because afterwards they will then go back to their clubs and play a totally different type of game. If the pattern of play is simple, Charlton says, and each player has been told individually what is expected of them, they will remember quickly when they come back together again as a national team.

One of Charlton's great strategic successes in terms of developing a new pattern of play came at Middlesborough, the first club he managed after leaving Leeds United in 1973. When Charlton arrived the side had a problem getting caught offside when attacking. Charlton devised a solution whereby a midfield runner, Alan Foggon, would hold himself deep onside and then chase after balls played forward behind the defence. The key for the move to work, however, was that the two forwards had to run back faster than the defence who were trying to use the offside rule. Charlton says:

> 'They had to remember to get out quicker than the defenders and not turn and chase a ball when they were offside. Now you think it's easy to tell people something and get them to do it. It's not easy. It took six months before I could get the two forward players both feeding off to an onside position instead of staying in an offside position. It took six months to get it through to them. But when they grabbed it, we murdered the division.
>
> 'Foggy did it remarkably well. The moment he had got through, everybody turned round and raced back. The number of times that Foggy used to stand on the ball or slide along the ground on his face and put the ball over the bar – but it didn't matter. We won the Second Division Championship by 15 or 20 points. We got promoted into the First Division in my first year through a method and way of playing.'

Charlton admits to having run-ins with some of his players who found it hard to adjust to the desired game plan. Charlton says:

> 'I am a teacup thrower. Players affect you in different ways some-times, I react to them not as a manager, but as another player. I tell them I am in charge and they do what I want them to do. If they don't want to do what I want, then they can walk out the door. National football was like that all the time. I even had run-ins with Liam Brady, who was a great player. He found it very difficult to adapt to the way I wanted the Irish to play because he wanted to play from the back and I wanted him to play off the front two. I won!'

Charlton claims the game that gave him greatest satisfaction was when Ireland, which he was managing, played Brazil in Dublin. Part of his satisfaction came from the fact that Liam Brady performed his role perfectly. Charlton says:

'I had been trying to get through to Liam how I wanted him to play. I told him I didn't want him playing off the back four, but off the front two, so he was playing in midfield and getting close to people up front.

'Liam that day was brilliant. We beat Brazil 1–0 and Liam scored the winning goal. Liam looked as though he was going to cross the ball to the far post. Everybody reacted and the goalkeeper went across to the far post. Then Liam struck the ball straight in the bottom corner on the other side of the goal. It was because he was in a position that the opposition didn't like and I felt that I had been responsible in some way for getting Liam into that position. With Arsenal, Liam would take the ball off the back four and play it through midfield. I didn't want him doing that. I wanted him taking it off the front two and then playing from there.

'With these things, the player doesn't need to agree with you and more often than not they don't. That's why you see managers standing on the touchline yelling at people. They're not doing what you've been telling them to do and working with them on. That's why you see managers running down the touchline and pointing. You're trying to get messages onto the field. Whether they get the message is debatable, but at least they know you're looking at them and pointing.'

Charlton also appreciates the value of attention to detail when preparing for matches, a lesson he learnt when playing for Leeds United. Leeds' manager Don Revie put huge effort into his briefings, seemingly knowing about all the players in every opposition team. Charlton says:

'After lunch we would sit down with Don for half or three quarters of an hour while Don went through his notes. He itemized every player – how they played, where they played the ball, whether they were good, whether they were quick. He knew every player in the Football League better than they knew themselves. It was called attention to detail. We knew where they would cause us problems. After the first six months we would fall asleep and he would start

yelling at us. He would yell, "We've spent bloody hours chasing round all over this country to get information to give to you that will win you the game tomorrow if you listen. Don't you fall asleep on me!"'

Team briefings aren't only important during team practice. They come into their own in the closing stages before a competition, and particularly just before a match. In the next chapter we look at how team captains, coaches and managers brief their teams just before, and during, competitive games.

Chapter 21

TEAM TALKS

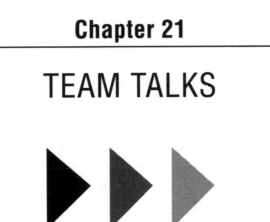

WHAT HAPPENS IN THE LAST MINUTES before a team goes out to compete? In this chapter we consider the most successful changing-room routines for encouraging a top class performance.

THE CAPTAIN'S ROLE

The captain plays an important role in helping to create a positive team state before a competition. Michael Lynagh, former Australia rugby captain, was generally pretty quiet before matches.

'When I was captain I would walk around in the dressing room and talk a bit, see that everybody was alright. I would get people

together to ensure everybody was ready. Even when I wasn't cap-
tain, as a leader in the team, that was still my role.

'When I was captain sometimes some of the forwards needed a
firm voice. If I started banging the table they would realize some-
thing was up. I was never really loud. I used to get other people to
do that for me. I made sure the vice captain and so on knew what
they were doing.'

Lynagh didn't find he needed to spend much time on motivating the
Australian team.

'When you are dealing with guys who are fairly elite sportsmen you
don't really need to motivate them. They were very self-motivated.
Before a game it was more about pointing the herd in the right
direction and bringing all that individual motivation together. I
used to do that in a different way to Nick Farr-Jones, who was
captain before me. Nick was quite an orator; he would stand up
and away he would go.

'In contrast, I would go and spend time with individual people
within the team. I would make the effort to go and have breakfast
with somebody and then have lunch with somebody else and go
and have a cup of coffee in the afternoon with somebody else. That
took me out of my comfort zone. I used to have guys who I was
comfortable with and would spend a lot of time with. But instead
of playing golf in the afternoon with my regular mates I would
make an effort to go and talk to people like Garrick [Morgan],
which was great fun. I would have to do that, to see how they were
feeling and if they were happy. That was important to me because
if you are not happy, your motivation wanes.

'The guys could see that I was doing this, and that I was trying,
and they reacted accordingly. So there was good feedback for me.
That is how I ran the team.'

David Lloyd, former Davis Cup tennis captain, believes that individual team members need to be treated differently, according to
their own personalities and styles of play. The key to a good Davis

Cup captain, he says, is to get inside the players' minds because they are all very different. Lloyd says:

> *'People used to ask me why I didn't talk to Tim Henman on court, but there isn't any reason to talk to Tim on court. He doesn't want to be spoken to. If you speak to him he gets pissed off and doesn't play. With Greg Rusedski, you can't get him hyped up. Some people you have to rev up, and some people you've got to keep in low gear.*
>
> *'With Tim, you don't really have to do anything. He goes into a slight trance and then you just leave him. You know he's going to get out there and win. If he's got a problem, he'll ask you.'*

PRE-MATCH TALKS

On match day, coaches and managers have a last chance to inspire their teams to deliver a great performance. So what do top managers and coaches actually say and do?

When trying to give his players the final push towards a great performance, England coach Sven-Göran Eriksson talks to them for five or ten minutes before leaving the hotel. At that stage he focuses on repeating his analysis of the opposition – areas where they have strengths and that the team should look out for, and areas of potential weakness that they can attack.

> *'I talk about our way to play, but it's just for five or ten minutes, and it's more or less a repetition of what we've done during practice. With the national team, when you have them together for two or three days, what you do is try to organize them. There's not a lot of technical work because we don't have time to do that. So the pre-match talk is repetition of what they should already know from practice. Then we go to the stadium, and just before the game starts I say a few words – just what's important. That depends on how I see the players looking. Are they concentrating? Are they white in the face? Are they nervous? So it depends.'*

Eriksson believes it important to try to give his players courage, particularly the younger ones, and to remind them they can beat anyone. Why can't we beat Germany?

Howard Wilkinson, former Football Association technical director, has developed and adapted his approach to the pre-match talk during his career. As a young manager he felt he had to be like Winston Churchill inspiring his men. He would try to cover every point that had been addressed in training the week before, plus a whole lot more information.

> *'As I got older I got to the point where on match days, unless I could absolutely not avoid it, I would cover nothing technical other than a few big reminders about the game plan, or process. I might react to a mood in the team, but that's all.'*

England rugby head coach Clive Woodward doesn't go in for rousing team talks before a match.

> *'I'm not big on that at all. I don't think you need a team talk to motivate them. In my playing days the team talk was tribal – about having pride in England. Now before we go out, the England team is very calm and focused. And when they go out onto the pitch there's often ten minutes to go before the start of the game. You don't go blasting out of the changing room. When they go out they're just thinking about the game. We have complete silence for a minute beforehand to think things through. So it's very cool, very calm, just reinforcing one or two key messages. It's all performance based. It's not about winning or about having pride in England. We know all that. We have to keep our thoughts clearly on the first kick off, our first moves, the first tackle, the first offence. You just want to visualize the start of the game.'*

Jack Charlton, former Leeds regular, recalls manager Don Revie's team build up before a match at Leeds United.

'We all went on the field and warmed up and did some exercises together. We'd run up and down and the crowd would watch. Most clubs do this now, but Leeds United started it. Then we went up the tunnel back to our seats. I've always been a believer that when you come back into the dressing room after you've done your warm-up you should sit there and think about the game, and think about what you've been working on during the week. The manager might remind you a bit, but you don't jump up and down or stretch or do anything but sit down and think about how you will play the game. Think about the things that will affect you in the game and what you need to remember.

'The coach, like myself, might remind you what's necessary. I used to say, "Just sit down, and close your eyes and rest, relax". They're going back onto that field and going to have to run around for another hour and a half. So there's no good in running around and jumping in the dressing room. Sit down, relax and think about the game. When you go out you'll have enough time to loosen up.

'So this is what we repeated pretty much before every game. You'd have ten minutes to sit, relax and get your mind on the game, to think about what we'd been working on and what was expected.'

HALF-TIME TALKS

At half-time, managers and coaches get another chance to motivate their players. They have a chance to make tactical adjustments, to point out areas of weakness that need attention and simply to encourage a great effort in the second half.

Just as England rugby head coach Clive Woodward tried to encourage a sense of cool, calm focus before the start of a match, so coolness and calm is the order of the day at half-time too. Woodward says:

'At half-time we have three minutes of silence while the players take on food and put on clean kit. We then split forwards and backs and have three minutes, hopefully being cool and calm, just

getting the right points across. We then come together for literally a minute and on a board will be three or four points for the team. We just go through those and then we hand over to Johnson, the captain. It's very tempting to walk in and scream and shout, but that's not what it's about.'

England football coach Sven-Göran Eriksson may look calm on the outside, but he admits that he gets upset and disappointed when his team is behind or underperforming. However, at half-time he focuses on what he needs to do to encourage a better result, rather than just venting his own feelings.

'In half-time, if we are behind, you have to be positive. You have to give the players the right advice about what to do in the second half. At half-time I first give the players a few minutes before I start talking, so that they are calm. Then it's important at half-time that you don't talk about everything that happened in the first half, because they can't take it all in. You have to concentrate on two or three important things, which will help to change the performance in the second half. You can't give them ten or fifteen details, because they can't take in that much information.'

Former Ireland manager Jack Charlton agrees that half-time talks require great control from managers if things aren't going well. Charlton says:

'At half-time, on the odd occasion that things aren't going exactly as you want them to, you've really got to bag your tongue before you go into the dressing room; the last thing the players want you to do is to stand there yelling at them at half-time, because nothing will get through to them. You are there to watch the game, see what's happening and explain to the players what's happening and to point out to them what their responsibilities are. If they're not doing their jobs you talk to them, you instruct them. You don't yell at them because no good manager ever got through to anybody by yelling at them. You've got to control that in yourself.'

Charlton did sometimes lose his temper, however. He recalls a match between Ireland and Liechtenstein that Ireland needed to win in order to qualify for the 1996 European championship.

'At half-time we could have been winning 5–0, but they were not interested in playing us at all. They just stopped us from scoring and they were doing well at it. At half-time I went into the players and told them we weren't getting at them quick enough; we weren't getting enough people up forward. I was yelling my head off. Andy Townsend [Ireland midfielder] said to me, "Hey boss, it's not like you. Stop what you're doing." I said, "Andy, you're dead right pal." But this was a one-off game that we had to win. But we drew and it cost us qualification into the European championships.

'I was upset over the game, but I didn't shout at full-time. It was over then; it was too late. I shouted at half-time – and that did no good whatsoever. The players needed from me to know about how to do what they needed in order to get back into the game, to get a goal back that they needed – that would win them the game. They wanted me to be positive, not negative, which is the way all coaches should be – positive, not negative.'

Charlton says that players have to be given direction and an understanding of what is expected of them. At half-time he was not afraid to pick out people who weren't doing what they ought to have been.

'You don't watch a game in the first half and then go into the players at half-time and start yelling at them all. You yell at two or three, because it is usually two or three who are causing the problems. They are not going into the areas you want them to go, or not playing the ball where you want, so you single people out. I have never been afraid of that, though some managers are. They try and treat the whole team as a unit, but you can't. There are bits of the unit that make it work better than others. People who aren't doing what you want them to have to be pointed out. You have got to tell them why the game is not going well and why you are substituting a guy. Someone might think he's playing great, but I might

not think he's crossing the ball enough. I never treated a team as a whole and never blamed the team. By half-time you usually know what you have got to put right. It's then up to the players to listen and remember. What I am saying to them will put the job right in the second half.'

Former England Under-21 football coach David Platt has honed his half-time talk techniques over his career.

'I made the mistake early on of going in and talking when the physios were still looking at injuries and giving people ice and talking to players. If you do that, you don't get the focus.

'Now I usually give the physios a minute or two to look at players. Then I make sure everybody is in and ask if everybody is alright. Then I hit the four serious points that come from the first half. Then I can go round the room on an individual basis to raise other points which revolve around an individual or a group of two or three together. But I don't want to lose the effect of the four salient points.'

Platt says he does sometimes get angry, but he accepts that can be problematic. You can sometimes say things you don't want to say.

'It's important then to have staff around you within the dressing room at half-time. They recognize when maybe you have gone a bit too far. The worst thing that can happen is if you give people a rollicking at half-time and then your staff pick up on the same thread and do the same. You only have fifteen minutes to lift them up to go out for the second half. Conversely, you can come in after a bad half and say, "Never mind. These things happen."'

Platt actually finds it harder to brief the team at half-time when things are going well.

'Those 15 minutes take a long time to pass when you have done well. If you are not doing well there can be more to say. When you

have done well you don't change too many things round and you find that you have maybe five or six minutes to kill. Sometimes you can sense a relaxation in the players too.'

The team talk at half-time won't necessarily change the course of a match, but it could do. Delivering a clear-headed, incisive and simple briefing can help to put players back on track to victory – or help them to maintain or even extend a winning lead. Learning to give such team talks is therefore an invaluable skill that any coach or manager can develop.

Analysis V

TEAM SPIRIT

IN PART V WE LOOKED AT THE GROUP EFFORTS that achieve success in the sporting world, whether in team sports or in terms of the supporting personnel around a solo performer.

CHAPTER 19

In Chapter 19: The Right Combination, we looked at the importance of selecting the right individuals to create a successful team.

We found that team selectors look for some of the characteristics we identified earlier in this book as being important for personal success. For example, England football manager Sven-Göran Eriksson looks for players with positive outlooks. England rugby head coach Clive Woodward looks for people who are open to new ideas and will try new things. He likes to include players who will learn from each other and try to raise their games to meet the standard that a team-mate sets.

Some gifted sportspeople have the reputation for being 'prima donnas'. Their huge talent can be a match-winner, but their difficult temperament can also be disruptive. Should bad behaviour be tolerated? The answer has to depend on the view of the team. Most sportspeople will accept difficult personalities if they make the difference between winning and losing. However, coaches and managers can make it clear what they will accept and what they won't. Sometimes players need a firm hand.

Renzie Hanham from mental conditioning specialists Gazing Performance says that other team players are generally all right with having prima donnas or rock stars in the team – if they are genuinely superior performers. Problems can arise if someone thinks they are a superior performer when they are not.

When selecting the team captain, different managers may look for different personal characteristics and abilities. Mental strength is always needed, but captains aren't always extroverts. They do have to be respected by their team-mates, however.

Ceri Evans from Gazing Performance says that one of the roles of the captain is to influence the team members in terms of where their attention is placed in pressure situations. Sometimes that involves providing an overview for the team, and sometimes a change of attention is required.

Once the team is picked, it is important to encourage team spirit. Clive Woodward wants his men to feel elite and special and to create a culture of excellence around them. They also need to understand and accept the needs and rules of the team.

Team spirit may require you to put the needs of the group ahead of your own, as Roger Black did when deciding the order in which the British 4×400m relay team would run in the 1991 World Championships. By giving up the glory of running the last lap, Black played his part in taking the gold medal away from the American team.

When building support teams, again the creation of a positive, inclusive environment is important. Everyone in the group needs to understand the role they play and understand its importance. As Ron Dennis, boss of the McLaren racing team knows, the driver needs to perform on race day, but he wouldn't even get to the start line without an effective support team.

Applications

- When selecting teams, be clear about what qualities you most value in the team members.
- Don't automatically rule out including so-called 'prima donnas'. Such individuals can be valuable team members, if their performances justify inclusion. Teams need the best players to win.
- When appointing a team captain, there is no one type of personality that is necessarily right for the job. Captains can have different personalities – some more extrovert than others – but they must always command the respect of their team-mates.
- Be prepared to accept that the greater good of the team may mean your personal pride has to take second place.
- All team members need to understand and appreciate what other team members contribute to the team result.

CHAPTER 20

In Chapter 20: Team Build-up, we looked at how team members, managers and support staff can work together effectively to create a strong team.

We found that England rugby head coach Clive Woodward believes in a strong team code. Team members need to accept and buy into the team rules, perhaps even setting the rules themselves. Our interviews certainly showed it was important for all team members to buy into a common set of values and to follow a common vision.

Renzie Hanham from mental conditioning specialists Gazing Performance says that when there is absence of alignment within any group, there will be disharmony, disruption and the potential for diversions. In a group situation it's essential to have clarity and agreement around direction, purpose, goals, roles, responsibilities and the plan that will get you to where you want to go.

The team culture needs to be one where members feel confident and not always worried about making mistakes. The team needs to be strong enough to be able to remain focused on the task in hand, rather than pointing the finger and blaming each other.

Effective communication within the team is vital for creating the right environment. Members need to be understanding of the differences between themselves and others and able to give and accept feedback. This requires an environment of trust and mutual respect.

Ceri Evans from mental conditioning specialists Gazing Performance says that strong teams are made up of strong individuals. Everyone should be able to express themselves, so long as that self-expression supports the team structure and goals.

The challenge in team sports is to bring each individual to the peak of their own performance at the right time. This requires each team member to prepare thoroughly, not only in terms of physical training but also in thinking about how to beat the opposition – analysing their strengths and weaknesses.

Team members also need the ability to be able to move their attention between focusing on their own processes and focusing on the wider field of play – considering where the other players are and what would be an effective team move. The Gazing Performance approach talks about the 'gazing principle' – the deliberate movement of attention between an overview and the detail. As Ceri Evans from Gazing Performance explains, at times you need to focus on detail, but at other times you also need an overview to be effective. Influential players in rugby, for example, need to know where other people are. They need a sense of the wider space as well as a sense of their own position. They need to attend to their own particular tasks while also being aware of the bigger picture. It is the deliberate movement between the overview and the detail that's critical. The same applies in business, Evans says. Effectiveness can be improved by having an awareness of the overall framework one is working within, and the specific task or process at hand. For example, a sales-person trying to make a sale will be helped by placing their attention on the specifics of the selling process. However, they may also be assisted by maintaining an overview of the whole process, and where the current interaction sits within the larger scheme of things. This involves an interplay between guiding principles and practical detail. Both are needed; one without the other is less effective.

During extended competitions, it is important that team members can relax sufficiently. They need to be able to cope with boredom, too. When staying away from home, creating a sense of familiarity around the team camp is also important. It is crucial that coaches and managers ensure the team feels well-cared for and comfortable.

Effective teams understand their strategic play, and how to work with each other to maximum effect. Sometimes learning new patterns of play can be difficult. Jack Charlton, when manager at Middles-brough, found it took time and constant repetition of instructions to get his players to act as he wanted in the heat of a game.

Applications

- If you are a team coach or manager, you need to provide clear direction to your team members.
- Team spirit requires everyone to accept the team's values and rules. Encourage team members to play a part in setting team rules to encourage compliance with them. Peer pressure is an important element in encouraging positive behaviour.
- Encourage a supportive team culture where members feel confident about taking decisions under pressure. Coaches and managers can help to do this by developing an atmosphere that avoids apportioning blame.
- Think about how team members communicate with each other. Encourage the sharing of ideas and thoughts about how to improve team performance, but without direct criticism of indi-vidual players. You want to try to develop an atmosphere of trust and mutual support.

- Encourage team members to practise moving the focus of their attention from their own performance and processes to that of the team. Encouraging this movement between the narrow and the wide focus helps individuals to understand how their role impacts on others, and how to perform it most effectively.
- Think about how you can help your team relax but remain focused on the task in hand during extended competitive situations.
- Allow time for repetitive drilling of new team manoeuvres or procedures to give team members the chance to learn them properly.

CHAPTER 21

The final moments before competition begins are important for team success. In Chapter 21: Team Talks, we looked at how captains, coaches and managers can try to send out their teams in the best possible frame of mind.

The captain's role is important, but one that varies depending on the individual involved. Former Australian rugby captain Michael Lynagh would walk around the dressing room talking quietly to team members. He didn't find he needed to give big motivational talks. Captains with different personalities, however, can say some inspirational words to the whole team if they like. The right approach depends on the personalities involved.

Coaches and managers will have briefed their players thoroughly by the morning of competition. They make sure they don't overload their players with extra information or new instructions late in the pre-match preparation. England football manager Sven-Göran Eriksson speaks to the team for just five or ten minutes before they leave their hotel on the way to a game. He briefly repeats his analysis of the opposition and its strengths and weaknesses. Just before the game starts he again says just a few words, chosen in response to the mood he sees in his players. Above all, he aims to give them courage.

England rugby head coach Clive Woodward also tries to keep things simple on the day of a game. He gives players a small number of key points for them to concentrate on. Again like Eriksson, he doesn't go in for rousing team talks before a match. He knows his players are already motivated to do their best.

At half-time again the top coaches and managers understand the importance of not overloading their team players with too much information. Woodward hones in on just a few points to remember when play recommences. Top coaches and managers also realize that players need time to refresh themselves, change their kit or see to any niggling potential injuries.

Ceri Evans from mental conditioning specialists Gazing Performance says that if you want to change the way things are going, you need to influence the attention of the individual or the whole team as a group. There is a danger in overloading them with information. If people are performing under pressure, you need to give them simple, clear messages. It is not possible for people to effectively place their attention on multiple things at the same time. If it is felt to be necessary to give more than two or three pieces of information or direction, it is more practical to give specific advice to sections of the team. You can link a phase of play to a certain thing they should think about. Keep it to a few messages, otherwise the players get overloaded.

Managers believe it is important that they try to retain a cool head. Shouting at players, even if their play has been frustrating, is not considered generally the most effective way to improve the second-half performance. This isn't easy, as Jack Charlton sometimes found when managing Ireland's national football squad. However, when he did let off steam, he found it didn't help the players, or the result, at all.

The one time shouting can be helpful is if a player has got stuck in some unhelpful state. Renzie Hanham from Gazing Performance, says shouting can be used to break that state. If someone is in a state of inertia, numbness or indifference, shouting can disturb it and start getting them back to focusing on some meaningful processes.

As ever, coaches and managers have to use their experience and judgement to determine the appropriate response in the circumstances they currently face.

Applications

- If you are a captain, remain true to your own personality. Introverts do not need to give rousing speeches before a match if this is not natural to their temperament. Quiet, personal encouragement to individual team members can be as effective.
- Coaches or managers should not overload team members with information at the last minute. If you are coaching or managing a team, try to keep final briefings highly focused. Give people a few key points to concentrate on.
- In the middle of a match, competition or any other extended event, coaches can help to put teams back on track. Again success lies in not overwhelming team members with detail. Focus on what individuals or sections in the team need to do to raise their performance.
- Coaches and team managers should try not to lose their cool in the heat of the moment. Shouting at teams and individuals will not usually generate improved performance. It is far better to speak calmly and maintain your own focus on the task in hand – briefing the team effectively.

Chapter 22

MIND GAMES – A FOOTNOTE

DURING THE RESEARCH FOR THIS BOOK we interviewed sporting champions, coaches, sports psychologists and performance experts. In conclusion, we offer the comments of three experts on our findings. Firstly, Professor Graham Jones from Lane4, a specialist human performance consultancy, offers an overview of the key results from our interviews. This is followed by a commentary from Renzie Hanham and Ceri Evans of Gazing Performance, specialists in performance improvement and mental conditioning.

PROFESSOR GRAHAM JONES, LANE4

- The interviews conducted for *Mind Games* show that elite performers don't perceive themselves as making sacrifices, only choices – this is a very important distinction.
- The performers talk about the close support of significant others (family etc.) in providing them with a balanced perspective on life. Social support is crucial in the early stages of their sporting experience/development. But these family supporters are not pushy! I have come across numerous young performers whose 'pushy' parents have been an obstacle to their development.
- As all the scientific literature strongly indicates, belief and confidence are an important part of these performers' psychological make-up. Quality training and 'hard work' are important sources of this belief.
- There is no room for negativity in the minds of these performers. And when negative thoughts do creep in, they're very good at reappraising and changing them to positive ones.
- 'Loving the big occasions' comes through as significant. Some performers crumble under the pressure of the big events – these athletes love the pressure.
- In focusing on performance, it's important to focus on all aspects, including the processes. To focus merely on winning – without focusing on how – would be entirely inappropriate.
- Fear of failure comes through as prominent in some of these performers' success. This somewhat contradicts my own experience of elite performers, in which they are driven more by the satisfaction of success.
- Goals come across as crucial to the performers' success. Goals are important because they not only provide the 'plan', but are also an important source of confidence, motivation, control, focus etc.
- Success isn't the only driver – internal motivation in the form of personal pride and satisfaction is crucial. This links into the notion of 'proving others wrong'. For me, this does not drive the most elite performers.

- The performers place a lot of emphasis on role models who have inspired them. They provide the standards and persona they are trying to emulate.
- Visualization is something they all do. Visualization, imagery and mental rehearsal are different techniques that they all use. These help them deal with pressure, rehearse skills, build confidence, consider 'what ifs', and build familiarity in preparation for competition.
- The best performers plan for every scenario meticulously.
- Simulating the pressure of competition in training is something they all do.
- Learning from mistakes and seeing them as part of the development process is also important.
- The comments on coaching relationships show that top performers don't necessarily have to get on with their coaches, but they do have to have mutual respect as well as trust and belief in one another. Having a shared vision and challenging one another comes through as a significant characteristic of successful coaching relationships.
- Most elite performers don't try to psyche out the opposition – they don't need to! Furthermore, to try would only take up some of their own valuable energy and attention.
- Being able to switch off is crucial.
- Being 'in the zone' is something everyone aims for but it's difficult to achieve consistently.

RENZIE HANHAM AND CERI EVANS, GAZING PERFORMANCE

The mental processes involved in superior performance present us with a puzzle.

On one hand, most people in the field accept that the mental aspects of performance are important, if not crucial, in achieving the highest level in sports.

On the other hand, there is much less clarity about what this involves exactly.

Part of the answer to this puzzle probably lies with the relative intangibility of mental processes: they are much less concrete and explicit than the technical or physical aspects of sports performance. Consequently, some even regard psychological approaches as having a mysterious, elusive or even shadowy quality. *Mind Games* represents a detailed attempt to address this paradox by making the mental processes more explicit and accessible via first hand accounts from a series of top sports performers.

Obviously sports stars are not equipped with special brain anatomy that makes them different from the rest of us. This implies that it is the way that they *use* their brains that counts. However, we are all capable in some contexts of exhibiting the mental processes that are commonly held as important for top sports performance, such as high levels of concentration and motivation. This leads to the conclusion that the mental processes characteristic of the leading sports performers are not necessarily *different* to those used by lesser performers, they are just more highly developed. Crucially, top performers do it when it really counts, when they are under pressure. Put this ability together with the right genetics and technical ability, and they become the complete package. The implication of this line of reasoning is that there are important mental skills underpinning sporting success that can be potentially developed, given the right conditioning process.

Mind Games gives us valuable insights into the personal preferences for these mental drills across the sporting domain. The accounts emphasize that effective mental skills take significant periods of time to refine and hone. In truth, many of the high performers gave accounts that indicated their mental skills were quite rudimentary and crude during the earlier parts of their sporting careers.

With such a rich resource as *Mind Games*, one of the challenges is to translate the wealth of information into something that is accessible and practical for athletes and players of lesser experience or ability. Where do we start?

Mind Games reinforces our view that the ***prime issue*** for athletes and players in the pressure of real-time competition is their *control over where they place their attention*.

Imagine a rugby player who drops a pass during an important match. The player then has a choice. They can place their attention on what the other players, coaches, or even the watching crowd think about their mistake. Alternatively, the player can place their attention on making sure they are in correct field position, focusing on their specific role in the next pattern of play, or perhaps they might go through a mental ritual designed to redirect their attention onto some other useful processes.

Although it is posed here as a choice, maintaining or redirecting attention onto useful processes is not straightforward. It can be very difficult to achieve, especially under pressure. It takes repetition and high quality rehearsal under conditions of simulated pressure for individuals to master their control of attention in various sporting contexts. In fact, as the personal accounts in *Mind Games* indicate, the mental side of high performance is as much about avoiding diversions as it is about attending to the quality of useful processes. Even athletes and players of the highest quality can perform suboptimally if their attention becomes diverted from the task at hand.

The control of attention becomes a game in itself: the job of the player or athlete is to retain their focus of attention on useful processes and not to have this focus disturbed by the opposition. It is the opposition's job to try to upset this focus of attention.

Several coaches and athletes in *Mind Games* talk about the distinction between focusing on outcomes, such as winning or losing or playing well or badly, and focusing on the processes that lead to those outcomes, such as the feel of the ball when they kick it, or the rhythm of their swing in golf. Although focusing on outcomes can be important in terms of motivation and perseverance, the most important aspect during actual sports performance is focusing attention on some aspect of the process that will contribute to successful outcomes. After all, the outcome is the end result of processes done well.

Many people can achieve control of attention in normal conditions, but being clear-headed and accurate in stressful environments is essential to superior performance. The ability to think clearly under pressure is how we would define mental strength. Several athletes in *Mind Games* expressed a similar view.

Much can also be learned from the accounts of athletes about when things have gone wrong. Sometimes the diversion for an individual is so preoccupying (e.g., 'that prop just hit me, I *have* to get him back') that our attention gets stuck, going round and round as if in a *loop*. Negative perceptions about a situation drive negative emotional responses. These negative emotions can lead to unhelpful behaviours, which reinforce negative perceptions, and a downward spiral is formed. Some of the athletes and players described experiences that we would categorize in this way.

One of the comforting things to appreciate is that we all have our attention diverted from time to time, and we all get in loops. It is just that top performers have conditioned themselves so that, even under pressure, this happens less often, and when it does, they recognize it quickly and can get their attention back onto focusing on important processes

It is important to point out here that being able to function under intense pressure is a skill that is contextual. In other words, you may find yourself being able to control your attention in some situations but not others. Why is this? Partly it's to do with training and drilling ourselves to respond in a certain way in certain situations; partly it depends on the emotional significance the event holds for us; and partly it's to do with how we define ourselves as individuals. If we feel at risk and have little control in a certain situation then unless we have trained ourselves otherwise we will have a propensity to get into loops, which will drive unhelpful responses. The main issue here is to become aware of what triggers these loops and takes us off task.

Avoidance of diversions or quickly regaining control of attention when diversions do occur is half of the battle. However, elite performers described in *Mind Games* are also very specific about the precise nature of the processes on which they focus their concentration. Over many years they constantly refined their techniques and skills, conditioning themselves so that the basic skills were performed consistently and reliably, sometimes to the point that they become second nature. It was clear to everybody that David Beckham's free kick winner in injury time against Greece – to give England a chance of qualifying for the 2002 World Cup – didn't happen by chance. Mental strength is based upon, and emerges out of, the integration of refined physical practice and intense mental focus.

For this reason, preparation is clearly a fundamental requirement on the pathway to sporting success. And skill acquisition is perhaps the most important part of this process. The two central principles of skill acquisition are *repetition* (drilling the skill over and over) and *specificity* (trying to do it as accurately as possible, and in conditions that resemble the real thing as closely as possible). Both are important. Many of the athletes and players in *Mind Games* told of their commitment to this sort of process. A useful way to look at this process is as the serving of an apprenticeship or going through a rite of passage – it's important to take a longitudinal view if you want to develop higher levels of performance over time to enter the world class category. It usually doesn't happen overnight. Constant refinement over many years is almost a prerequisite for the levels of performance achieved by some of the individuals in *Mind Games*.

A distinguishing characteristic of top performers is that they develop and implement plans better than the rest of us. They pay a lot of attention to *detail*, and, critically, connect this with an *overview*. They invest the practical detail with a sense of significance and purpose concerned with what they are trying to achieve overall, and the strategy for achieving it. In this way, detail can take on special significance. They drill the movements, sometimes obsessively, imagining, knowing, or hoping, that on a special day in the future, it might make the difference between being a world champion and being second best. Plans are meticulously made so that the day-to-day grind has real meaning by being attached to goals and desires that motivate and, sometimes literally, drive athletes and players forward.

Differentiating between competence and confidence also seems to be important. Confidence needs to be based upon physical skills that have been drilled until the individual can keep a clear head under pressure and perform the necessary skills at an optimum level. Competence is based on a robust propensity to reproduce specific skills under pressure, which arises out of the conditioning process and experience. Indeed, real learning is experiential. Whatever strategies are employed need to be experienced in order for the athlete to be clear about what works for them. The strategies need to be repeatable. All too often athletes can exhibit supreme confidence without undergoing the necessary skills and physical training to underpin this confidence. Without developing competence first, confidence is like a house built on sand. It can look good but when placed in a pressure situation, it may collapse.

Underpinning all of this is what motivates or drives an individual to succeed, to push themselves to their limits. In our experience, it is useful to distinguish between people who, within a given context, are motivated either *towards* or *away* from feeling something. In simple terms, sports performers want to feel something or they don't want to feel something. It can be a combination of both. This is often described as a desire for success or a fear of failure, but on its own, this is simplistic. It is more accurate to say that they have a desire to experience *the feelings* that success brings, or a need to *avoid the feelings* triggered by failure.

Different feelings will dominate for different individuals. For instance, success might bring feelings of being respected, admired, accepted, power, competency, superiority, control, or a combination of several of these things. On the other hand, failure might bring uncomfortable feelings of shame, guilt, inferiority, inadequacy, or rejection. Just which of these aspects will be dominant will depend upon the individual, their life experiences, and, crucially, how they define themselves. If an athlete defines him or herself as the best in the world, then avoiding failure and striving to be number one will be strong drivers indeed.

The origins of these powerful feelings have long roots back to our early development, and are not readily accessible to change. This explains why many coaches feel powerless to affect the way that individuals are. Coaches are not therapists. Nevertheless, having more detailed knowledge of the nuances of the emotional drivers for each individual can pay dividends, because it has implication for motivation.

In our view, the individuals concerned have to take responsibility for connecting with what motivates them, and how they define themselves. The coach's role is to create an environment in which the individual players or athletes are allowed to tap into emotional drivers. It is true that some charismatic people seem to have an ability to talk to teams in a way that individuals of different make-ups can all identify with, but for this to have an enduring impact is uncommon. More common is the coach who feels he or she has to give a team address, which has the effect of disengaging as many players as are engaged.

However, coaches can influence the motivation of their players and athletes, if not have entire control over it. This requires detailed knowledge of the way that they define themselves (e.g. a team player, the best, a winner, a consistent performer, a skilful performer, a hard man, and so on), and the feelings that these identities engender or avoid. By appreciating these aspects of the individual's make up, the coach can know what to say, and when to say it.

Identifying emotional drivers gives both the athlete and coach an indicator of what may be motivating the athlete. For some it is moving towards an identity and the associated feelings. For others, it is moving away from an unwanted identity (second best, loser, injury prone) and the associated feelings. Neither is better than the other but knowing which is dominant is essential if you wish to reach your peak performance levels.

Mind Games will help provide inspiration for many readers. You will no doubt have identified with different individuals and different aspects of the book. If *Mind Games* encourages you to begin deliberately developing skills in the area of mental strength, then it will have provided an invaluable service. Mental strength is vital if you want to improve what you do on the sports field, on the track, or in the water, particularly if you aspire to high levels of sporting performance.

APPENDIX I

SPORTS PSYCHOLOGIST IAN LYNAGH, father of former Australian rugby captain Michael Lynagh, has developed a simple sports psychology model that strongly influenced the content of this book.

The model consists of four key elements:

- *Personal* – the personal factors that are developed in an athlete's personality that are conducive to high performance;
- *Motivational* – the development and maintenance of a drive to succeed;
- *Mental skills* – the acquisition of psychological skills to complement and support motor and technical skills; and
- *Performance* – psychological processes and strategies underpinning performance under competition pressure.

The following sections provide a greater explanation of these four key elements in Lynagh's model.

PERSONAL FACTORS

Ian Lynagh explains:

'The first part of the model focuses on the person in the round. What are the personal factors that make up someone who goes on to achieve? There is some commonality across successful athletes.'

According to Lynagh's model:

- The personal factors include a number of elements, such as the athlete's values and beliefs concerning themselves and achievement.
- Successful sportspeople also need a positive mental attitude towards themselves and the external sports world.
- Top athletes take personal responsibility for themselves. They are self-motivated and self-disciplined.
- Personal control is also an important element of the personal characteristics – including mental, emotional and behavioural aspects.
- Finally, champions need to be able to tolerate frustration. They demonstrate patience and persistence.

MOTIVATIONAL FACTORS

Ian Lynagh says:

'Mature athletes will have thought through their motivation – why they play sport. For some it will be coincidental – that they went to a school that played a lot of cricket and they get into the cricket team and were encouraged. It started out being opportunistic, but they stuck at it and developed purpose. Athletes play sport for

many different reasons, sometimes multiple reasons. It may be the challenge, the social side, the rewards and status, or that they saw it as a good career.

'The most mature reason why people do sport is because of the challenge of wanting to establish control over a task – it becomes more of an intrinsic striving, an internal challenge, than the desire for status or other extrinsic things such as prestige and rewards, getting a medal.

'Sport provides a process for learning to grow as a human being. Most sports are stupid or meaningless. But we identify a difficult challenge in the sport so that we need to train and develop skills, which involves self-discipline and self-management and taking responsibility. It's all about factors that help human beings grow to become more than we are.'

According to Lynagh's model:

- Top sportspeople have a defined sense of underlying purpose that gives meaning to what they do.
- Vision and clearly defined, graduated, step-by-step goals also mark out successful competitors.
- Desire is an important factor in success – champions have an emotional commitment to their sport that energizes their behaviour.
- Top athletes manage to achieve balance in that they can switch on and off as required.

MENTAL SKILL FACTORS

Ian Lynagh says:

'Sometimes athletes who are really good acquire mental skills naturally, and don't even know they are acquiring them. They learn to concentrate, to focus, to stay calm, how to pump up or not to get over-aroused and push too hard. They learn through experience and modelling what others do.'

According to Lynagh's model:

- Champion sportspeople can control their levels of arousal – the degree to which they get pumped up, managing their nervous systems effectively.
- Top athletes have the capacity to focus their concentration or attention.
- Top performers have the ability to control their thoughts and keep them task-related – they don't become distracted easily.
- Visual imaging and mental rehearsal is used as part of preparation for performance.
- Top athletes have a strong sense of the feel of what they do – kinesiological awareness.
- Successful sportspeople monitor themselves effectively, evaluating their performances. They also have the self-regulation or discipline to keep training.

PERFORMANCE FACTORS

Ian Lynagh says:

'Performance factors are to do with how athletes prepare for and maintain performance during competition. They have a routine that gets them physically, mentally, emotionally and tactically ready for a game. Good athletes do that almost ritualistically and good team coaches have a really set pattern for preparing the team.

'To do this, it's important that the athlete learns what their ideal performance state is. You can't prepare yourself unless you know what state you are in when you are perfectly ready. That takes a bit of trial and error.

'I have identified five essential states required within a person for them to be perfectly ready. These are the five basics for an ideal performance state. These are firstly, being mentally calm. You can't concentrate if your mind is racing. Secondly, you are task-focused – focused on the task of bowling the ball or kicking

the ball. Thirdly, you have to have the right arousal, so you are not too pumped up and not too flat. Fourth, you have to be confident and have self-belief that you can do the task. Fifth, you need to be success-oriented or have a high expectancy of success. The self-fulfilling prophecy is pretty important. If you think about losing, you are going to lose. If you are not success-oriented in life, you get what you expect. If you expect to lose you will, because you have set a goal of losing in your mind.

'I would never send an athlete or team onto a pitch without at least attempting to get them in a state where they are functioning that way – that they are calm, they know what their task is, their arousal or anxiety is under control, they have confidence in them-selves and they are out there thinking of winning, thinking and believing and expecting to succeed.'

According to Lynagh's model:

- When preparing for competition, sporting champions have established routines to ensure they are mentally, emotionally and physically ready.
- When performing, champions remain focused on the task.
- Champions control their physical and mental arousal appropriately under competitive performance situations.
- Top athletes manage their states so that they are not put off by distractions or setbacks.
- After the performance is completed, champions review how they did and learn from the experience, resetting training goals.

APPENDIX II

Professor Graham Jones from Lane4, a specialist human performance consultancy, has undertaken extensive research into the mental toughness of top sportsmen and women.

In one such research study, Professor Jones and his co-researchers, Dr Sheldon Hanton and Declan Connaughton, drew on the insights of ten international sportspeople, three women and seven men, who had all represented their country in major events such as Olympic or Commonwealth Games. They came from the sports of swimming, sprinting, artistic and rhythmic gymnastics, trampolining, middle-distance running, triathlon, golf, rugby union and netball. The sample participated in a focus group session, individual interviews and a final stage to rate the results generated.

The sportspeople were first asked to generate a definition of mental toughness. The final result was as follows:

'Mental toughness is having the natural or developed psychological edge that enables you to:
- *generally, cope better than your opponents with the many demands (competition, training, lifestyle) that sport places on a performer, and*
- *specifically, be more consistent and better than your opponents in remaining determined, focused, confident, and in control under pressure.'*

As Professor Jones and his co-researchers noted, the definition emphasizes that mental toughness is not just about dealing with competition pressures; it is also about coping with general training and lifestyle challenges and balancing the personal demands that result from competing at the top level with the maintenance of a social and private life.

Having generated the above definition, the participants then generated an exhaustive list of the fundamental prerequisite qualities and attributes of the 'ideal mentally tough performer', drawing on their own experiences and impressions gained of other top sportspeople they had met. Having identified twelve such attributes, they then ranked them in order of importance, with the following results:

1   Having an unshakable self-belief in your ability to achieve your competition goals.
2   Bouncing back from performance setbacks as a result of increased determination to succeed.
3   Having an unshakable self-belief that you possess unique qualities and abilities that make you better than your opponents.
4= Having an insatiable desire and internalized motives to succeed.

4=   Remaining fully focused on the task at hand in the face of competition-specific distractions.
6   Regaining psychological control following unexpected, uncontrollable events.
7   Pushing back the boundaries of physical and emotional pain, while still maintaining technique and effort under distress in training and competition.
8   Accepting that competition anxiety is inevitable and knowing that you can cope with it.
9=   Not being adversely affected by others' good and bad performances.
9=   Thriving on the pressure of competition.
11   Remaining fully focused in the face of personal life distractions.
12   Switching a sport focus on and off as required.

As Professor Jones and his co-researchers noted, self-belief emerges as a crucial attribute of top sportspeople. This self-belief needs to take two forms – related both to ability to achieve goals, and the belief that you are different to and better than your opponents.

The findings also show that international sportspeople need to be highly motivated, being able to use setbacks to bounce back to peak form, as well as having 'insatiable' desire to succeed.

The importance of retaining focus and control is also highlighted in several of the identified attributes: remaining fully focused on the task in hand, regaining psychological control following unexpected events, not being distracted by others' performances and remaining fully focused despite distractions in your personal life. The need to be able to switch the sports focus off as well as on also appears in the list.

As the researchers noted, the ability to cope with competition anxiety and the ability to thrive on the pressure of competition appear relatively low down in the list. While clearly important, the ability to cope with competition pressure was not considered as important as other aspects such as self-belief and motivation.

These findings were originally published in the *Journal of Applied Sport Psychology* in 2002 in an article entitled, 'What is this thing called "mental toughness"?: An investigation of elite sport performers' by Graham Jones, Sheldon Hanton and Declan Connaughton.

BIOGRAPHY – PROFESSOR GRAHAM JONES

Graham is Director of Research and Product Development at Lane4 Management Group Ltd. He has over 100 publications in the area of high-level performance, including books on stress and performance and the psychology of elite performance. He is also a former editor of the international journal, *The Sport Psychologist*. Graham is a chartered psychologist with the British Psychological Society and a registered sport psychologist with the British Olympic Association. His applied work includes consulting with numerous elite performers, including professional golfers on the European Tour, the 1996 Great Britain Olympic team, the Wales rugby union team, the British Bobsleigh Association, the Great Britain hockey team and the Royal Marines. He has also worked with many individual, world-ranked performers from a variety of different sports. Graham's experience of working with business executives spans nearly ten years, and includes working with senior executives at Ericsson, ICL, Fujitsu, Coca-Cola, Safeway, Lloyds TSB, Bourne Leisure, JP Morgan, Deutsche Bank, Roche Pharmaceuticals, Woolworths, 3M and the UK Atomic Energy Authority.

Lane4 Management Group Ltd

Operating at the leading edge of the human resources and management consultancy sector, Lane4 is fast establishing its reputation as the UK's premier performance development brand. Lane4 has a unique heritage based on elite sporting and commercial achievement combined with an unparalleled understanding of the psychology of human performance.

Lane4 was established in 1995 by Adrian Moorhouse MBE, Olympic gold medallist, leading sport psychologist Professor Graham

Jones, and experienced director Adrian Hutchinson. Lane4 derives its name from the lane in which Adrian Moorhouse swam when winning his Olympic gold medal at the Seoul Games, the lane allocated to the fastest recorded time in the heats and so most likely to produce champions.

Lane4 has established a strong track record in the corporate community for its innovative work in the field of performance development. Its consultants include Olympic champions, internationally renowned performance psychologists and leading-edge organizational development practitioners, who facilitate the application of concepts and practices into the business environment. They have co-created and implemented performance development programmes with leading companies across a range of commercial sectors.

Lane4 work with a number of clients both nationally and internationally including: Bausch & Lomb, Bourne Leisure, NHS Logistics, Immigration and Nationality Directorate of the Home Office, Coca-Cola Enterprises, Dresdner Kleinwort Wasserstein, UK Coal, UK Atomic Energy Authority and F Hoffman La Roche.

Lane4 areas of specialization, all of which are underpinned by their own research-based models, diagnostics and approaches, are:

- creating high performance environments,
- performance leadership,
- performance coaching,
- high performance teams, and
- personal performance.

APPENDIX III

GAZING PERFORMANCE LTD (GAZING) has provided training to multi-nationals, government departments, managers, teams, leaders, and individuals in sports and business in over 60 countries. They have established partnerships in several of these countries and have trained over 7000 people.

The approach used by Gazing is based on the belief that it is the mental state of the individual or team that can make a substantial difference to the quality of that performance and invariably the outcome.

We believe that the prime issue in human performance is the control of attention. In this respect, sports performance is no different from performance in other domains, such as teaching, research, or business. The common factor is that success is underpinned by clear and effective thinking in pressure situations. One major aspect of clear thinking is The Gazing Principle, which refers to the deliberate movement of the focus of attention between the immediate situation that an individual is confronted with, and an overview.

Gazing has developed an innovative approach to mental conditioning, which is based on a 'map' that visually tracks how mental processes function in pressure situations. Importantly, the map illustrates how things go wrong under pressure as well as what leads to effective performance.

In particular, the map distinguishes between attention that is focused on useful process, and attention that is focused on unhelpful diversions. This distinction is so fundamental to high performance that we have colour-coded the map, so that athletes and players locate themselves either *in the red* (the colour of *diversions*) or *in the blue* (the colour of *process*). The colours make it simpler to locate where attention is placed at any given moment, even in pressure situations. A quick mental check can clarify whether attention is in the red or the blue, and then adjustments can be made accordingly.

When attention is on process, the focus of attention is linked to the present moment. If attention is placed on diversions, attention is diverted away from the task at hand onto negative interpretations and consequences, such as what people might be thinking about them. Negative emotional responses result, which affect thinking and behaviour. Attention becomes stuck on things that have happened in the past or things that may happen in the future.

Although 'process' and 'diversions' are to some extent jargon terms, in our experience athletes and players are helped by this dichotomy. It helps with communication because it simplifies the control of attention down to a form that can be applied in stressful situations.

The map illustrates how sporting performers can become trapped in a *negative content loop*, arising in response to various triggers, such as a match being lost or an individual experiencing a slump in form. For example, an individual having a poor game can become concerned about being dropped from the team. This emotional response could lead to unhelpful behaviours, for example being unnecessarily aggressive, freezing during the next match, or becoming ambivalent. These responses can result in poor performance, which only serves to reinforce the initial concern.

Escaping such a negative content loop requires awareness, recognition, mental strength and the ability to think clearly under pressure. This can be developed by encouraging the separation of emotional responses from the real issue at hand, for instance by learning to stop applying automatic labels or judgements to events. Performers need to think more clearly, and understand that their past experiences may have created biased filters with which they view their current and future experiences. They need to ensure they have accurate information to protect themselves from defensive thinking.

The individual's particular biases or filters drive a conditioned response that can become such a part of the athlete's coping mechanism that they become almost invisible. It then becomes important for the athlete to recognize these filters and response patterns that inhibit their performance. When sportspeople respond emotionally to an event they can suffer from *issue/response/confusion*. Some emotional responses can get in the way of correct perception, clear thinking and effective action. What effective performers achieve instead is *issue/response/separation* – the ability to assess an issue or event dispassionately, without being led by an automatic emotional response. As a result they can think clearly and remain focused on what to do.

The design and organization of the map mean that it is possible to remember it and to locate oneself on it, even in one's own mind during the midst of a pressure situation.

GAZING PARTNERS

John Esposito

John is a top-level performer in both sales and sales management. He initiated the development of Gazing following a ten-year career working for a blue-chip multinational corporation. John has conducted successful training programmes in more than twenty countries, including presentations by interpreter. He has an outstanding international reputation in training. John has also achieved high standards as a sportsman. He holds a fourth degree black belt in karate, has competed at national level and was responsible for establishing a karate school in London.

Martin Fairn

After graduating with an honours degree in business studies, Martin joined Rank Xerox (UK) Ltd for a 14-year career that spanned a variety of roles, both in the UK and outside. The early part of his career included a range of sales roles from commercial sales to key account management, and then three years as a sales manager in Central London. Following that, he then took responsibility for quality and customer loyalty for the UK company, which included managing the industry-leading 'Xerox Business Excellence Programme' based on the European Quality Award. Finally he moved to Canada, where he spent his last three years with Xerox as general manager in Toronto. Martin joined Gazing as sales director; since then he has been responsible for business development and has delivered training ranging from our basic sales training to senior management effectiveness and team building. Besides a highly successful career with a blue-chip organization, he can also point to a lengthy career as a first class rugby player, in which he achieved international representation.

Renzie Hanham

Renzie Hanham works closely with Dr Ceri Evans in Gazing product development. Renzie brings a wealth of experience in the field of sports psychology to Gazing. He is a seventh degree black belt and is head instructor for Seido Karate in New Zealand, and has taught and practised martial arts for some 44 years. Renzie was employed as mental conditioning coach for the New Zealand Triathlon Academy and was at the Sydney Olympics with the New Zealand triathlon team. He has worked with world champion athletes in a variety of sports and was himself a nationally ranked judo player and a New Zealand representative in karate.

Dr Ceri Evans

Following his graduation with distinction in medicine from the University of Otago in New Zealand, Ceri was awarded a Rhodes Scholarship to study at Oxford University, where he gained a first-class honours degree in experimental psychology. Ceri is a member of the Royal College of Psychiatrists and was awarded a PhD in psychiatry from the University of London. He has played as a pro-fessional footballer in the English First Division and played 85 times for the New Zealand football team. In collaboration with Renzie Hanham, he has developed a 'map' of human performance in com-petitive situations. He has applied this knowledge as a mental trainer to a national championship-winning rugby team and in a variety of sporting settings.

INDEX

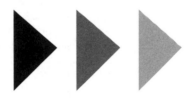